READING
MARK

• exlibris •

Bas van Iersel

Translated by
W.H. Bisscheroux

THE LITURGICAL PRESS
St. John's Abbey • Collegeville, Minnesota 56321

Copyright © T. & T. Clark Ltd, 1988

Translated from the Dutch edition
Belichting Van Het Bijbelboek: Marcus, © 1986 Katholieke Bijbelstichting,
Boxtel.

Typeset by Bookworm Typesetting, Edinburgh
Printed and bound by
Billing & Sons Ltd, Worcester

First Printed 1988

ISBN 0-8146-1820-0

Contents

1

WAYS OF READING MARK

A Book Raised to a Square

This book is somewhat unusual in several respects. Firstly because it is a commentary on another book, the gospel according to Mark – henceforth simply called Mark – and secondly because as a commentary it differs in more than one way from other commentaries. Most books we read – whether they are works of fiction or non-fiction – are books in their own right and read for their own sake. Commentaries, on the other hand, are different in that they are books about books, what might be called books raised to a square. They follow the text of the first book more or less closely, commenting on it word by word, sentence by sentence, episode by episode, part by part, and are written to help the reader better grasp and understand the first book, in our case Mark.

The writer of such a commentary is himself first of all a reader, be it a better informed and often a more experienced reader than most. He can therefore be a guide in helping other readers find their way through the book. The purpose of this commentary is the same, namely to assist the reader to understand Mark. It is, in other words, designed to be read alongside Mark and not as a substitute for Mark. Reading it without reading Mark would amount to reading a travel guide of a country one never intends to visit. Such a reader, having reached this point, had better stop reading at once, wrap the book up and give it to a friend who does intend to read it alongside Mark. Anyone who decides to continue should read the complete text of Mark before the third chapter of this book if at all possible. They should certainly read the section of Mark discussed in each chapter before reading the commentary.

Differences From Other Commentaries

But the present book is also unusual as a commentary in that it differs rather from what is generally found in current commentaries on Mark. To begin with, most of them look very learned, which they are. Footnotes, discussions with other experts, and bibliographies in one or more sections, all testify to their scholarly nature. Such commentaries are normally directed to a reading public of academic colleagues and other people familiar with this approach, so their authors need not be afraid to use technical terms and presuppose specialized knowledge and skills.

As this commentary is intended for the general reader rather than for experts, the use of technical terms has been kept to the indispensable minimum. But the fact that it lacks the usual hallmarks of learning does not imply the absence of an underlying method which, I hope, has been consistently applied, although it is not described here.

Beyond Fragments

The most important difference between this and other recent commentaries on Mark is that the present book takes its starting-point from the seemingly self-evident notion that Mark, as a book, constitutes a unified whole whose individual parts cannot be read separately without violating the book as well as the part concerned.

This starting-point is less commonsensical than it seems when seen in the light of the age-long custom of synagogue and Christian congregations alike of reading shorter or longer fragments from the scriptures at each assembly. Certainly with Mark, but also with Matthew and Luke, this is the obvious thing to do, for the book appears to have been written so that it presents a connected series of generally short or very short episodes which are easily distinguishable and even separable. This is because in content and form these pericopes or episodes are more or less self-contained. This once inspired a colleague of mine to compare the book to a string of beads.

The Origin of Mark

Biblical research during the last few decades has proceeded from the hypothesis that for the most part these episodes had originally been handed on in the community as individual miniature stories or sayings before they were put together in Mark and the other gospels. This has led to a method of inquiry which in its emphasis on the origin and development of the text distinguishes between what already existed in the tradition and the way this was subsequently collected, revised and edited by the author or rather the editor, as he is characteristically called in this type of investigation. The pre-existing material can be classified according to form, origin and function, while research into the way the editor dealt with it enables scholars to find out why and for whom he wrote his book. In this way separate layers of different origin and date are revealed in the text.

Although certain assumptions of this method have been criticized lately, there is no denying that it has greatly enriched our understanding of the processes that were at work in the making of the gospels. This is why most commentaries that do not comment upon Mark sentence by sentence, deal with the text episode by episode and analyze it in accordance with the above method. There are, however, several reasons why the same approach cannot be used in reading Mark. Firstly, it is simply impossible for anyone reading the text to be simultaneously aware of all the separate layers present in it. Secondly, the concentration on each individual unit and the close attention to detail required by this method make it very difficult not to lose track of the main argument of the book and fail to really read Mark as an integrated whole. Thirdly and most importantly, there are no indications whatever in the text itself to warrant such a kind of reading.

Mark as a Single Coherent Narrative

Leaving aside the above hypothesis about the origin and formation of the gospel, this commentary proceeds from another and more obvious fact, namely, that Mark has been transmitted as a book which forms such a unity that it can only be understood by someone who reads it in its entirety and tries to apprehend it as a meaningful whole. We should add to this the equally important consideration that the book has the character of a narrative and should be read accordingly. This is why ample use is made in the following pages of the insights of structural linguistics, especially into the nature of narrative structures and the way they function in communication.

Our starting-point implies that the writer of Mark is regarded as an author in the strictest sense and not only as a collector or editor of what had been said or written by others before him. On the other hand, if the hypothesis that most sub-stories had existed independently before they were incorporated into the book is correct, its unity cannot be expected to be greater than that of a mosaic, for it is extremely unlikely that the elements fitted so neatly into the story the author had in mind that the seams do not show. But scholars and readers who wish to explore the unity of Mark are, unlike those investigating its origin and formation history, not intent on highlighting tensions of that kind, as they tend to hinder rather than help the understanding of the book as a whole.

To say that Mark has a narrative character implies that the author assumes a specific role in his book and thereby requires his readers to adopt a role similar to his own. These two corresponding roles are called "the narrator" and "the narratee", terms specially coined to differentiate them from the roles existing between writers and readers of treatises, apostolic circular letters, poems or apocalyptic visions. In the role of narratee the reader becomes directly involved in what the narrative reveals about the various characters and their actions but only indirectly in what the narrator wants to say with his story.

The characters in Mark are chiefly Jesus, his followers, the crowd, his adversaries, those who want to be healed and, exercising power over some of them, the demons. These characters and the things happening to them exist in the world of the story which is structured by the places where the story is enacted and the time within which it unfolds. These are the elements of the story that are of great importance in the analysis of Mark, so they will be considered first in the discussion of each part.

Story and History

It does of course make a difference to the narrator as well as to his narratees what the relation is between the world of the story on the one hand and the situation and actual events of the real world on the other. In the case of science fiction things may be very far removed from reality, provided that the reader can recognize what the writer invents. In the case of a fictional story set in places and a time similar to those known by his intended readers, the writer is far less free to deal with these circumstances as he pleases than he is with the actions of his characters. In addition to this, a writer of a historical novel or play must observe definite limits when dealing with his characters. Yet such an author also usually wants to communicate more with his work than the mere narrative.

Thus, in his version of the myth of Oedipus Rex, Sophocles expresses among other things the conviction that man cannot escape his fate, however hard he tries. And in Igor Stravinsky's opera-oratorio version of the myth, composed to a text of Jean Cocteau, the same conviction is considerably reinforced through the application of new means. The only person using French in the opera is the speaker acting as narrator, while all the voice parts are in a stiff, primitive sort of Latin, written by Jean Daniélou.

Like Oedipus Rex, Mark is about a well-known historical figure. This fact, together with the use made of source materials containing pronouncements of Jesus and flashes of narrative, must have set limits to the author's freedom. But this by no means implies that he had to confine himself to an account of what had actually happened to Jesus. Unlike Sophocles, he does not write about a figure who is dead and definitely belongs to the past. Instead, he speaks about Jesus in the full conviction that he is not only a figure of the past but someone who, although he was killed, is nevertheless a living person who is still important. Precisely for this reason the author of Mark cannot content himself with an objective and matter-of-fact report of the events that lead up to Jesus' execution. On the contrary, he gives evidence throughout the story of the significance the executed Jesus has continued to have for him. In this the author of Mark is an outstanding example of someone who tells a story to make it mean something more than the events narrated. There can be no doubt that the author of Mark also wants to convince his readers of the importance Jesus still has for them.

Accordingly, the writer is clearly convinced that he is not writing about a fictitious figure, but about someone who really lived, acted and spoke, and who was killed in the end by people who had no use for him and disliked what he did and said. It is necessary to stress this point because this commentary might – because Mark is approached as a narrative – give the impression that Jesus is no more than a character in a book.

Of course, with this approach we do not in any way answer the question as to the exact historicity of what is quoted and said about Jesus in Mark: as to how far the words quoted were actually spoken by Jesus and the events related actually occurred. This is an important and complicated question and far from easy to answer in detail. However, it can hardly be considered in the present commentary which, as we have already stated, takes the book as it has come down to us, and consequently deals with it as a literary whole.

Not the Beads but the Necklace

Most gospel commentaries either follow the text line by line, sometimes almost word by word, or discuss it episode by episode. Even if a commentary and the text of Mark itself are divided into larger parts by means of subtitles, this method easily leads to a way of commenting and reading that emphasizes the separate episodes in themselves rather than their place and function in the whole of the book.

The present commentary, however, follows a different course in that its primary object is to do justice to the book as a whole. Of course, even then it would be possible to do equal justice to the smaller units, as anyone who has read *S/Z* by Roland Barthes on a story by Honoré de Balzac (Paris 1970) or *Maupassant* by A.J. Greimas (Paris 1976) knows. Analyzing one by one the five hundred and sixty-one units in which for the sake of discussion he divides Balzac's thirty-page story, and adding to these another ninety-three passages with methodological considerations and conclusions, Barthes had produced a difficult but fascinating book which, including the text of the story plus a number of appendices and indexes, runs to two hundred and seventy pages. In a book of about the same length and quality as Barthes', Greimas discusses a six-page short story by Maupsassant by analyzing the twelve 'sequences' into which he divides the story. If the methods employed by Barthes were applied to the sixty pages of Mark the result would be a very thick book indeed, and a commentary on Mark written in Greimas' way would probably become unreadable besides being too long for most readers.

I therefore prefer to adopt a middle course, which consists of discussing Mark in relatively large sections. These are not chosen at random but reflect a division recognizable in Mark itself, as we shall see in chapter 2. The advantage of this approach is that it is easier for me as a guide to show the reader wider panoramas. Its disadvantage is that it is less easy for the reader to look up everything about a particular pericope or episode because the relevant information is often scattered over different parts of a chapter. But it is perhaps even more inconvenient that quite a number are not dealt with separately at all. This is because a pericope is only discussed if it contributes to the message of the story, and not because it may be difficult to understand. So this commentary cannot really be used as a reference book on Mark, as, unlike other commentaries, it is primarily designed to open readers' eyes to what they miss if they only read bits and pieces of Mark.

Where does Mark End?

Up to now I have been speaking of the whole of the book or the whole of the story as if it were perfectly clear what that whole is or what it contains. But this is far from clear, at least not to the average reader of Mark. Some translations end the book at Mark 16:8 where the women run away from the tomb and say nothing to anybody. In other translations there follows, without comment or brackets, still another section, numbered 16:9-20, relating a number of appearances of the risen Jesus (The Authorized Version, The Douay Version). Some add a footnote to this section expressing doubts abut its authenticity (The Revized Standard Version). In a few cases Mark 16:8 is followed by an unnumbered 'shorter ending', which consists of only two sentences, and the 'longer ending' 16:9-20 (The New English Bible; The Jerusalem Bible gives the 'shorter ending' in a footnote). Finally, to make things even more complicated, all Churches have always considered the 'longer ending' – and not the 'shorter' – to be part of the canonically accepted body of inspired scripture. Such acceptance does not imply, however, a particular opinion about its authorship.

In fact, it is generally accepted that anything following 16:8 in the oldest extant Greek manuscript and in ancient and modern translations was not written by the author of Mark but added later. The oldest manuscripts, the codices Sinaiticus and Vaticanus, which are both from the fourth century, end with 16:8 while only more recent copies have either the 'longer' or 'shorter ending'. Quite part from this, the style and language of 16:9-20 are so different from chapters 1:1-16:8 of Mark that it must be by another hand. We may add that with regard to its content the 'longer ending' is really a brief summary of the narratives of the appearances of the risen Jesus found in the other gospels. But however much all experts agree in rejecting either ending as original, some find it equally impossible to accept 16:8 as the original conclusion of the book, which in their judgement could not have ended so abruptly at that point. They therefore argue that the original ending, written of course on the last page of the manuscript, must have been lost at an early date. I believe, however, that such a makeshift solution is only acceptable if it is absolutely impossible to regard 16:8 as the proper ending of the book. I therefore intend to interpret Mark as a unity comprising no more than 1:1–16:8. This, I believe, is very possible. The two additions are not discussed any further in this commentary, not just because they are not by the author of Mark and were added later, mainly because if they are read after Mark they (especially, the 'longer ending') radically change the character of the book.

The Exegete and the Readers of Mark

A literary critic or exegete can explain the meaning of a text from very divergent positions. He or she may, for instance, try and put themselves into the situation of the *author* and explain the meaning of the book in terms of what the author intended while he was writing it. The position is often taken up by exegetes who have given little or no thought to the problem of the different standpoints from which a text may be interpreted. That some exegetes almost naturally put themselves in the place of the author is understandable because they are so well informed and have at their disposal all sorts of information not given in the book itself. As a result they have not only formed an idea of the author, the intended readers, the book's intention and the way it came to be written, but also of the social, economic, cultural, religious or ecclesiastical circumstances in which it was produced. On this basis they believe, and not without reason, that they can somehow reconstruct the author's position. This does not alter the fact, however, that the exegete of a text must also have first appropriated it as a reader. Yet even then we can never know for certain whether the exegete's representation of the author's background is really in accordance with the facts.

For this reason, and because written texts are usually meant to be read in the absence of the author, other exegetes think they had better give up all attempts to jump from the text to the author. In that case there remain at least two possibilities.

The first is that exegetes confine themselves to dealing with the text in terms of its characteristic structure, which in the case of Mark is that of narrative which conveys meanings. To understand and interpret the book the commentator examines the way in which the signs and their meanings are related to one another, as well as the way in which these signs are related to those elements in the world outside the text to which they refer. By following this method an exegete can help readers see and understand things in a text that would otherwise escape them.

A second possibility is that exegetes go on to explicitly take the side of the reader and also regard themselves primarily as other readers. In this approach the text of the book is comparable to a musical score which must be realized to become music, and the readers to the musicians or singers who by realizing the score actually perform the music. To come to life the score needs a performer and the text a reader. The reading is part of the process that produces the meaning the author aimed at in his writing. As the interpretation is as much an essential part of this process as it is with music, it may within certain limits vary in the same way. The exegete is also one of the readers performing the text, but is a special and more skilful reader than most because of professional training and competence, and possibly knowledge of the theories of the nature and working of texts and the role of the reader. Exegetes could be called 'pre-readers' in the sense that they read the text to the best of their ability in order to show other readers the right way through the book.

Which Readers?

In the case of Mark which, like all biblical texts, was written a long time ago and intended for readers of that period, exegetes may carry out their task by attempting to put themselves into the place of those first readers. As they were once the ones actually addressed and taken into account by the author, the original readers were certainly in a privileged position compared with the readers of all subsequent generations. They not only had the same language as the author, but also shared with him all sorts of presuppositions about the world of their time and the people living in it. Most probably they also shared a number of ideas which made it unnecessary for the author to mention things with which they were already familiar. For the same reason the author could anticipate their reactions, which enabled him to move cautiously whenever he felt it his duty to speak of matters that were difficult for them to digest. A knowledgeable and competent exegete working along these lines can go a long way toward reconstructing the situation of the author's first readers.

Although the position we have just described is that of a reader, it is in fact not so different from the position assumed by exegetes who put themselves in the author's place. Being mutually dependent, author and intended reader reflect and are quite close to each other. But even if exegetes can put themselves to some extent in the position of the first readers, they will never be able to bring them really back to life. Yet, if it is their express aim to reconstruct what the text meant in its original historical setting, exegetes can only do so by attempting to enter into the ideas, convictions, feelings and mentality of the author and his intended readers.

The opposite possibility is that exegetes put themselves completely into the position of readers of today. They know of course that the text is not primarily addressed to them, yet are convinced that a text which has been preserved for so long and has been read and reread so often has something to say to readers of later generations as well. They will therefore interpret the text in terms of the questions, presuppositions and convictions of their contemporaries and take into account their cultural, social and economic circumstances. A clear example of this approach is the way the Bible is read within Latin-American Christian grass-roots communities, made up of men and women who are poor and denied human rights, and their supporters.

A third possibility is that exegetes quite clearly take the side of the reader, but concentrate neither on the original nor present-day readers. At first sight this may seem an unreal and abstract approach, but it is not necessarily so. On the one hand, exegetes start from the facts supplied by the author in the book itself and the presuppositions necessary to understand that information. They ignore any other knowledge as well as any other presuppositions the author might have had in common with his original readers. So in this case no attempt is made to reconstruct the outlook of the intended readers. On the other hand, such exegetes refrain from what is questionably called 'actualizing' the text, i.e. the attempt to connect it explicitly with specific situations of modern readers. Quite the contrary. They focus attention on those aspects which all approaches to the text have in common. It is in this way that they hope to reach the attitude which the text itself, independent of any concrete context, prescribes to all readers and every reading. If and in so far as they succeed, exegetes will represent and recreate the reader, sometimes called the 'implied reader', that the author has created through the way he wrote his book.

This is the role which I myself shall fulfil in this commentary as best I can. I would like to make two further observations about my position and the task of the reader. Firstly, it will be impossible for me never to act out of character. From time to time I will have to give readers of today information which is not found in Mark but was nevertheless common knowledge among its first readers. The author could take for granted, for example, knowledge about scribes and pharisees which is either unknown or inaccurately known by modern readers. Whenever such information is indispensable I have to change my role accordingly.

Secondly, if I give an explanation which disregards present-day questions and problems although it is in principle valid for every reading, I do so in the full conviction that readers of my exegesis cannot and will not stop there. They will, quite rightly, consciously or unconsciously connect what they read and understand of Mark with their present convictions and feelings, their attitudes, behaviour and plans, and through reading Mark enrich, adjust or completely change them, or perhaps only find them confirmed. Naturally I have also done that myself, and I challenge my readers to do the same, for it is equally their task to carry on and complete their interpretation of Mark.

Yet here too the exegete's guidance, even if it is offered with diffidence in this commentary, may be important and helpful. This is because a reader's personal interpretation cannot be considered to be the result of a proper understanding of Mark unless it is based on or at least not contradictory to a legitimate exegesis of the text. Thus, if and in so far as my exegesis is correct, the meanings I point out in Mark will indirectly help other readers to give meaning to their existence.

In the Light of the Old or First Testament

For the sake of present-day readers I have decided to read and discuss the text first as it stands, and only in the second instance consider it in the light of the Old Testament, or rather the First Testament as I prefer to call it (see Glossary p.16). As will appear from the following chapters, the text of Mark gains considerably in depth and meaning when it is read against the background of the First Testament. A certain acquaintance with the First Testament was undoubtedly part of the general knowledge of the intended readers taken for granted by the author. It would therefore be commonsense to pay attention to this aspect right from the start rather than read the text of Mark independently from its First Testament background. In spite of this, however, I opt for the present-day readers of Mark and therefore discuss the text first as we find it. Some of my readers, I am sure, know the First Testament well enough to relate Mark's quotations to their original context, but for those that do not have the required knowledge, I intend to discuss Mark in the light of the First Testament, be it only in the second instance.

Reading With Blinkers On

If, owing to the numerous quotations and allusions in Mark, we have to look back regularly to the First Testament, we deliberately do not refer to the other parts of the New or Second Testament, and least of all to the other gospels. The main reason for this is not that the other gospels were probably written after Mark, so that the intended readers could not possibly have known them; but rather the all-important principle already discussed, that Mark must be regarded as a book in its own right. As such it presents itself – no less than the other gospels – as an independent, self-contained unity consisting of language elements that primarily exist in relation to one another.

In practice, however, it is often far from easy to read and comment on Mark in this way. The influence of the other gospels appears to be so persistent that we must take special care not to read into Mark what simply cannot be found there but is in fact a suggestion of a parallel passage from another gospel. For instance, if Mark 8:27 has Peter confess that Jesus is the messiah, we re inclined to read into these words what Peter says according to Matthew 6:16, namely, that Jesus is the messiah, the son of the living God. Or to give another example, although there is in Mark 14:22-25 no instruction by Jesus to repeat what he is doing and saying, we tend to read it nevertheless as the institution of the Lord's Supper, simply because we do not realize that the instruction to repeat these actions is an echo of Luke 22:19 and 1 Corinthians 11:24-25. These examples show how difficult it is to let Mark be Mark, no more and no less.

Author, Time and Place of Origin

The book itself does not give us any direct information about these matters, so it would be consistent not to speak of them here either. But as readers of this commentary might think that these preliminary questions were left out by mistake, we had better discuss them briefly.

From the second century Mark has been named as the author of the book on the authority of the presbyter Papias, who is quoted by Eusebius in his *Church History* (III, 39, 15). It is, however, open to question whether he is the same as the John Mark who in Acts 12:12 and 13:5, 13 is called an assistant of Paul and in 1 Peter 5:13 an assistant of Peter. If he is not, the name is without importance. On the other hand, if the connection thus made with Peter and

Paul is intended, there is good reason to doubt its truth. It therefore seems best to take the book for what it is, an anonymous work. It was after all quite common in those days for authors themselves to ascribe their books to a more important name than their own in order to enhance the authority of their work. We do full justice to the fact that no such name was attached to Mark by its author if we accept and respect the anonymity of the book.

The *place* where the author wrote and the *audience* he had in view are not indicated in the book either. Of all the places suggested, Rome seems to be the least speculative, partly because it reflects an old tradition. But there is no real evidence.

Neither does the book itself give us information on the *date* of its appearance. There is every reason to think of a date just before or just after the destruction of the temple of Jerusalem in A.D.70. But difference of opinion on the question whether Mark was written shortly before or shortly after that event is persistent and likely to continue. The fact that the author time and time again warns his audience so seriously of the danger of persecutions says much about their situation but little or nothing about the time when the book was written.

Glossary

To prevent misunderstandings it may be helpful to give or repeat the meaning of a few terms used in this book.

* *Mark* does not refer to the author but to the book itself, and is therefore really an abbreviation of what is officially called 'the gospel according to Mark'.
* *Author, narrator, narratee, reader* are related terms. The anonymous writer is sometimes called author but usually narrator, according to the role I want to stress. When speaking of the reader(s) I do not mean the original readers intended by the author unless this is expressly stated, but everyone who reads or may read the book. I do not exclude myself. On the contrary, what I attribute to the reader is largely derived from my own experience of reading Mark.

* *First Testament and Second Testament* refer to the Old and New Testament. Like others I prefer to use 'first' and 'second' because they only indicate a sequence in time, whereas 'old' and 'new' may easily carry a value-judgement.
* *Characters* stands for the various persons and groups playing a part in the book. Besides Jesus, who throughout the book is the main figure and centre of the plot, there are a number of persons and groups that move round him in different circles. I have generally given them ordinary and functional names such as: *supporters, helpers, adversaries, the crowd, the temple authorities.* Only for the *demons* have I chosen a less ordinary name because if they seem strange to us they had better remain so.
* A *secondary meaning* is one that is based on or presupposes a *primary* or *first meaning.*
* *Parables* is used for all metaphors, similes and parable stories that are referred to in Mark by the same Greek word, *parabolē,* transcribed into English as 'parable'. The word *parable story,* however, refers exclusively to the two parables which also have the characteristics of a narrative, i.e. that of the sower (4:3-20) and that of the vineyard (12:1-9).

A Few Books to Which I Feel Particularly Indebted

In writing this commentary I was greatly helped by what I have studied and read over a great many years. Only extensive footnotes could do justice to the numerous colleagues to whom I am indebted. But I shall not give any here. Firstly, because they would almost certainly put off some readers and hardly interest most of the others. Secondly, because as far as this book is concerned, my dependence on other authors relates on the whole only to details and not to my basic approach.

I must, however, mention a few books. Heading the list are four by authors who have been specially stimulating and helpful. Of these the first may be too difficult, but the last three are recommended to all interested readers.

Yvan Almeida, *L'Opérativité Sémantique des Récits-Paraboles*, Louvain, 1978.

Frank Kermode, *The Genesis of Secrecy* Cambridge, Mass./ London, 1979.

David Rhoads and Donald Michie, *Mark as Story*, Philadelphia, 1982.

Ernest Best, *Mark, the Gospel as Story*, Edinburgh, 1983.

During my work on this commentary I kept some classical commentaries and two monographs within reach. They have helped me not to overlook things, but I have been careful not to follow their interpretation too easily. They are:

P. Benoit and M.-E. Boismard, *Synopse des Quatre Évangiles en Français II*, Paris, 1972.

Vincent Taylor, *The Gospel according to St Mark*, London, 1957.

Rudolf Pesch, *Das Markusevangelium*, Freiburg, 1976 and 1977.

Benoit Standaert, *L'Évangile selon Marc, Composition et Genre Littéraire*, Zevenbergen-Brugge, 1978.

Joachim Gnilka, *Das Evangelium nach Markus*, Zürich-Neukirchen, 1978 and 1979.

For everything connected with Judaica I regularly consulted:

Paul Billerbeck, *Kommentar zum Neuen Testament aus Talmud und Midrasch*, München, 1928.

Emil Schürer, Geza Vermes, Fergus Millar, Matthew Black, *The History of the Jewish People in the Age of Jesus Christ*, Edinburgh, 1973, 1979, 1986, 1987.

Geza Vermes, *Jesus the Jew*, London, 1973[1], 1983[2].

Jesus and the World of Judaism, London, 1983.

Two books that have been a great help to me with methods for analyzing such an extensive text as Mark:

Roland Barthes, *S/Z*, Paris, 1970.

Algirdas Julien Greimas, *Maupassant, La Sémiotique du texte; Exercices Pratiques*, Paris, 1976.

2

STRUCTURE AND COMPOSITION
Mark and This Commentary

The title of this chapter is ambiguous as it leaves undecided which book is meant. Mark or this commentary on Mark. This ambiguity is not due to negligence but intentional. Whether we think of the author of Mark or of the author of a commentary on Mark, both have the same reason for giving their book a structure and dividing it into a number of distinct parts. For it is difficult, if not impossible, to take in and really comprehend a text of any great length as a whole unless it is well arranged and the reader is led through the entire text part by part or chapter by chapter. In other words, the text is structured in order to structure the reading process. The longer the text, and consequently the more time required to read it, the greater the reader's need for a clear structure. Especially if a text is too long to be finished at one sitting, as is the case with this commentary (in contrast with Mark), a well structured division is thoroughly necessary.

Chapters and Verses

The reader of this book knows of course that Mark, like the other books of the Bible, is divided into chapters and verses. Thus Mark has sixteen chapters, each provided with a number and subdivided into verses whose numbers are usually printed alongside the text. In addition, smaller as well as larger episodes are generally provided with various headings. They are not by the author and are all of very recent date. No more is the division into chapters or verses the work of the author. The former dates only from the thirteenth century while the latter appeared for the first time in a Greek edition of 1551, produced by the famous Genevan printer Robert Estienne. Sometimes a chapter begins at an appropriate point, as with chapters 11 and 14, sometimes however, at a very inappropriate point (chapter 16), or at what only seems to be a good point (chapter 13). Neither division pretends to reflect the structure and composition of the book, but was introduced merely to facilitate speedy reference. So a commentator who intends to guide the reader through the whole of Mark's text has to examine how it is structured and by what text signals the reading of Mark should, or at least could, proceed.

Starting-Points

It seems to me that two kinds of text signals clearly present themselves to the reader. The first has to do with one of the elements that are of particular importance in a narrative text. The narrator usually creates a world in which the story takes place. This world is to a great extent defined by a system of indications of time and place. In Mark, then, the former are conspicuously rare in the first thirteen chapters, while they abound in the remainder of the book. For this reason they cannot be used for structuring the book as a whole. Indications of place, on the other hand, are quite numerous. Moreover, some of them are closely related to certain parts of the book and therefore offer a helpful starting-point for structuring the gospel.

Text signals of the second kind are of a completely different nature. They reveal the technique used by the author to connect episodes with one another. This consists in the incorporation of one story between the earlier and later parts of another, which is the reason why this device is sometimes called 'sandwich-construction' since the filling is not put on top, as is the case with Danish smørebrød, but in between two slices of bread. Two clear examples of this are the story about the healing of the woman suffering from haemorrhages (5:25-34), which is inserted between the two parts of the story about the little daughter of Jairus (5:21-24 and 35-44); and the story about the cleansing of the temple in Jerusalem (11:15-19), which is sandwiched between the two parts of the story about the cursing and withering of the fig tree (11:12-14 and 20-21). From a comparison with the other gospels it appears that this construction is characteristic of Mark. This naturally raises the question if the narrator employs it at macro-level as well as using at micro-level.

A Structured Build-Up

This question must be answered in the affirmative, as further investigation shows that the whole book is structured by means of sandwich construction. This can be seen most clearly in the way the device is applied to the different locations in the story.

In this way the book can – as I have tried to demonstrate more extensively and more technically elsewhere – be structured at the level of the total text as follows:

> *Title* (1:1)
> **(A1) In the desert** (1:2-13)
>   (y1) first hinge (1:14-15)
>   **(B1) In Galilee** (1:16-8:21)
>   (z1) blindness → sight (8:22-26)
>   **'C) On the way** (8:27-10:45)
>   (z2) blindness → sight (10:46-52)
>   **(B2) In Jerusalem** (11:1-15:39)
>   (y2) second hinge (15:40-41)
> **(A2) At the tomb** (15:42-16:8)

Desert and Tomb (1:2-13 and 15:42-16:8)

The two outer parts of the book take place in the desert and at the tomb. The words 'desert' and 'tomb' refer to places which in the experience of the reader are in many ways interrelated: they do not form part of the inhabited world, people do not settle in them, and they are therefore pre-eminently suitable as dwelling-places for demons. It is no accident that Jesus is tempted by Satan in the desert and that the Gerasene demoniac is staying in barren surr-oundings where he lives in caves and tombs (5:2–5). They are in places of death and destruction. In another respect they are each other's opposites, for the desert is a place one travels through, whereas the grave is a place where the dead rest for ever. But not only are the places referred to by the words 'desert' and 'tomb' related to each other; both parts of the story taking place there show some remarkable similarities. In both a messenger appears, John and a young man, whose dress is mentioned in each case (which is exceptional in Mark), and both speak of local move-ments of Jesus, his coming after the baptist and his going on before the disciples, respectively. In both parts also the 'way' of Jesus is an important theme, referred to in the former through the quotations in 1:2–3 and in the latter through Jesus going on before his disciples to Galilee (16:1). Finally both stories tell how new life springs up in these places of death, in the first through the baptism, in the second through the resurrection from the dead (and Romans 6:45 shows that the baptismal font and the tomb can, or perhaps even should be, seen in direct connection with each other).

The Two Hinges (1:14–15 and 15:40–41)

These two pieces connect the outer with the next inner parts of the text, blending more or less into them. For this reason we call them hinges or transitional links, which accordingly are joined to and discussed with both of their parts in this commentary. The first (1:14–15) gives in broad outline what Jesus proclaims in Galilee, and thus looks forward to the whole of the section devoted to Galilee. At the same time, it twice repeats the word 'gospel' (meaning 'glad tidings') from the title of the book. The second (15:40–41) also looks forward and backward. In a flashback it tells the reader that the women who are watching the crucifixion from a distance followed and served Jesus in Galilee, and that many other women have accompanied him to Jerusalem. At the same time it introduces the women who will play a leading part in the next, final, part of the book. It is not without significance that at this particular point the narrator himself sums up the three central parts given above in our outline of the overall structure of the book: Galilee, Jerusalem, and the way to Jerusalem.

Galilee and Jerusalem (1:16–8:21 and 11:1– 15:39)

These two parts have long been known to be interrelated. But generally no mention is made of this being connected with the narrator's compositional technique. A certain opposition between Jerusalem and Galilee is already given with the geographical references themselves. Jerusalem is the centre and capital of the country, the seat also of political power and the temple authorities. Galilee, on the other hand, is on the periphery, a faraway province whose inhabitants are looked upon with suspicion by Jerusalem, partly because of their being mixed with non-Jewish populations. In the two parts of Mark we are considering, this contrast is carried through in various ways, including explicit discussion. When Jesus is active in Galilee, his opponents come from Jerusalem (3:22; 7:1). And the other way round, when Jesus stands trial in Jerusalem, a servant-girl says to Peter: 'Surely you are one of them. You must be: you are a Galilean' (14:70). The inherent contrasts between Galilee and Jerusalem are considerably reinforced by what the story locates in each. In Galilee Jesus is very active: he makes a new beginning, finds a number of supporters, gets response, helps the sick and handicapped, casts out demons, and resists his adversaries. Jerusalem is the scene of the passion narrative, in which Jesus plays a passive rather than an active part; here he announces the end of the temple and the world, loses his supporters, fails to get a hearing, cures no one, does not cast out any demons, and is defeated by his adversaries.

The Framework Around the Central Part (8:22–26 and 10:46–52)

Of all the frameworks in the book, the ones that most clearly illustrate their function of effecting a transition from what is inside to what is outside the frame are the only two stories about the healing of a blind man. The scene of the first story is therefore still in a town in Galilee, in Bethsaida. In addition, it carries further the basic theme of the preceding part, which is summarized in 8:15-18 where Jesus says to his disciples that they have eyes but do not see, and calls upon them to watch and look carefully. The blind man whom he then cures resembles the disciples and is at the same time their counterpart. The story makes one expect that Jesus will sooner or later heal their blindness too, but this expectation is not realized within the story itself. There is only the promise, at the very end of the book, that they will see in the future (16:7).

The second story also effects a transition to what happens outside the frame. After Jesus, on leaving Jericho, has cured his blindness, Bartimaeus follows him 'on the way' (10:52). This phrase not only stresses the thematic keyword of the foregoing part but also recalls 10:32, from which the reader has already learned that this way leads to Jerusalem, and thus points forward to 11:1 where Jesus arrives in the immediate surroundings of that city. It so happens that of the followers of Jesus the beggar from Jericho is the only one who is no longer blind but sees.

The Way (8:27-10:45)

Like 'the desert' and 'the tomb', 'the way' is not a geographical reference, and must therefore be distinguished from 'Galilee' and 'Jerusalem', which both, as places and as parts of Mark, are connected by this 'way'. In this part of the book Jesus is continually en route with his disciples, as the reader is regularly reminded by the words 'on the road' or 'on the way' (8:27, 9:33-34, 10:32 and 10:52 as against 10:46). To define this part of the book, however, we cannot confine 'the way' to this literal meaning, for location and theme reflect each other here. On the way Jesus speaks time and again of his own way of life. He tries to make it clear to his disciples that in view of the programme he is to carry out by God's order on the one hand and the plans of his adversaries to get rid of him on the other, he has to chose between unfaithfulness to his mission and the risk of his life, and that as a consequence he will go and meet his execution in Jerusalem. He also tries to make them see that his own way of life cannot remain without consequence for his followers. In this figurative sense of 'the way', this part not only takes up the central position in the book, but also forms the central and prominent theme upon which the narrator wants to focus attention. Accordingly the reader understands why it is precisely this aspect to which attention is called by the sentences beginning and ending the book (1:2-3 and 16:7).

Identical Substructures

Due to their length the two longest parts of the book, which take place in Galilee and Jerusalem respectively, are more difficult to grasp as wholes for both the commentator and the reader. Fortunately, here too the text appears to be structured and, what is specially helpful, structured identically in both parts. In the centre of each part stands one of the only two rather long discourses in Mark: the parable discourse set in Galilee (4:1-35) and the so-

(13:3-37), which are each sandwiched between the two remaining subsections. So the reader is helped once more by the narrator's framing technique which has structured his narrative and made its joints visible.

Turning next to the four passages framing the two discourses, the reader will see that each one of them is composed according to the same technique. Thus the subsection before the parable discourse is framed on one side by the calling of the first four followers (1:16-20) and on the other by the provisional completion of what I would like to call 'the new family of Jesus' (3:31-35). The subsection after this discourse is sandwiched between the first (4:35-41) and the last crossing of the lake (8:13-21). The subsection before the apocalyptic discourse is framed on one side by Jesus arriving in the temple and observing the whole scene (11:1-11) and on the other by Jesus observing the people who drop their money into the alms box and his leaving the temple (12:41-13:2); the subsection that follows is sandwiched between two stories, of which the first prepares for the burial of Jesus and the second relates it (14:1-9 and 15:42-47). The parallel structure of the two parts may be illustrated by the following outline:

Galilee	Jerusalem
(A1) The first followers (1:16-20)	**(A1) Arrival→observing** (11:1-11)
(b) a man of authority (1:21-3:30)	(b) lasting authority (11:12-12:40)
(A2) The new family (3:31-35)	**(A2) Observing→departure** (12:41-13:2)
(C) Parable discourse (4:1-34)	**(C) Apocalyptic discourse** (13:3-27)
(D1) The first crossing (4:35-41)	**(D1) Anointed for burial** (14:1-9)
(c) misunderstood (5:1-8:9)	(c) killed (14:10-15:39)
(D2) The last crossing (8:10-21)	**(D) Burial** (15:40-16:8)

The outline brings out one or two more similarities between the two main parts of the book. Both in Galilee and in Jerusalem the part before the discourse is determined by the theme of Jesus' authority (b). In Galilee, where it shows clearly in what he says and does, Jesus' authority is acknowledged by his followers, the crowd and the demons, although it gives rise to the opposition of his adversaries. In Jerusalem his authority cannot be undermined by his adversaries, as can be seen from the way he argues with them in the temple. In the central parts after the discourse (e) the principal theme is either the first or the second of the two plots governing the two parts, Galilee and Jerusalem, to which we shall return later. In the first of these central parts the plot is that Jesus is misunderstood by his followers, and in the second that Jesus is killed by his adversaries.

It may seem a problem that 15:40-41, which introduces the three women, has a somewhat different place in the above outline of the substructure than in that of the book as a whole, where this passage is considered to have the function of a hinge comparable to 1:14-15 (see p.21). This double function may, on the other hand, may corroborate by the curious, only partly identical repetitions of the names of the women (15:40; 15:47 and 16:1). It is, moreover, not too difficult to imagine that the effect of such text elements is different on the more easily surveyable level of smaller units than on the level of the overall text. After all, in the borderland between two states or counties there are always signposts directing the traveller to places on the other side of the

border, and borders themselves often run through the middle of a
residential quarter or even a street.

To a certain extent the same also applies to the part that follows
15:40-41, namely 15:42 – 16:8. In the composition of the whole
book it functions as a separate part which, taking place at the
tomb of Jesus, is distinguished from the part taking place in
Jerusalem. In the division of the substructures, however, these
two parts are not distinguished. This is not so strange as it may
appear at first sight. The panoramic view of a town sometimes
allows us to see structures which we perceive differently or not at
all from a lower point or from the street.

Division of This Commentary

After the foregoing the division of this commentary is more or
less self-evident. Each of the shorter parts (the desert, the way,
and the tomb) is deal with in one chapter (chapters 3, 7 and 11).
For the intermediate longer parts (Galilee and Jerusalem) more
space is needed, so three chapters are devoted to each (chapters 4,
5, 6 and 8, 9, 10). These follow the threefold division given in the
outline above: what precedes the discourse (chapters 4 and 8), the
discourse itself (chapters 5 and 9), and what follows it (chapters 6
and 10). Chapter 6, entitled 'Greater Signs, Growing
Misunderstanding' , is considerably, perhaps irritatingly, longer
than any of the others. I am sorry that this must be so; it simply
cannot be split up without spoiling the unity of the part
concerned.

Other Places

The world where the narrator locates the story is naturally
defined by the places to which he takes his characters and
consequently his readers. But the world referred to and brought
into play by the story is nevertheless much larger. In 3:7-8, for
instance, the narrator mentions Galilee, Jerusalem, Idumaea,
Transjordan and the region of Tyre and Sidon. To be sure, the

reader is taken to most of these places, but not to all. Apart from this reference Idumaea does not occur anywhere else in the book. So the world of the story is only part of a larger world which in fact comprises the whole inhabited world (14:9).

But the narrator's world extends even further, for the book also refers to heaven. This is the vault enclosing the earth, the overhanging firmament where the sun, the moon and the stars have their places (13:25), along which the clouds move (14:62) and below which the birds fly through the air (4:4; 4:32). But it is also the heavens which may suddenly tear open to let the spirit of God pass through (1:10) and from where the voice of God is heard (1:11; 9:7). The one who speaks from there is named by Jesus 'your father in heaven' (11:25-26), while he himself sometimes looks up to that heaven, for instance when saying a blessing (6:41). The mysterious messengers who look after Jesus when he has overcome temptation in the desert (1:13) appear to belong to that same heaven (12:25; 13:32). Next, people can be authorized to do something not only by other people, but also by someone in heaven (8:11; 11:30-31). And finally, people may acquire treasure in heaven (10:21), which is perhaps the same as what is called elsewhere 'eternal life' (10:17; 10:31). In other words, there is according to Markan cosmology another space above the earth and the firmament which is the dwelling-place of God as well as the home of his messengers, and to which mankind can also gain access.

Corresponding with this regularly-mentioned place on high is another place deep below which is mentioned in one passage only: the deep ravine called Gehenna, a place of death, inextinguishable fire, and a forever-gnawing worm (9:42-48). There too people may end up. The book does not say that this is also the home of Satan and the demons, the opponents of God and his messengers. In 3:27 Mark has Jesus say that no one can enter 'the house of the strong one' and make off with his goods unless one has tied up the strong one first. But that house is better situated on the other side of the lake where there is, we are told, a frighteningly dense concentration of demons (5:1-20).

It is obvious that the narrator presumes that the reader shares his cosmology. But this does not mean that it is absolutely necessary for the modern reader to adopt every single image and detail of his view of the universe. What every reader should accept, however, is that with all visible and audible things taking place under heaven, not everything that may be important to mankind can be seen or heard.

Diverse Times

Besides this network of places which covers as well as extends beyond the locations of the story, there is a pattern of times within which the respective positions of characters and readers call for further clarification. The time-span of the story is comparatively short, and it is covered at quite a high speed. The repeated usage of the Greek adverb *euthus* (translated as 'at once', 'immediately', 'directly', 'straight', 'without delay', etc.), especially in the first part of the book, speeds up the pace of the story and – if the reader allows himself or herself to be influenced by it – of the reading as well. For the characters, the period spanned by the story coincides roughly with their 'now', the time *present*, and only with a small part of their future, which within the story is very limited (e.g. 11:2-5 and 14:13-16), and in no single case exceeds the third day after Jesus' death. For the readers, on the other hand, the time spanned by the story is clearly 'formerly', time *past*.

But just as the world extends beyond the locations where the characters and readers are taken by the narrator, so the time of the story stretches before and after the period within which the characters play their part. Thus both the main character, Jesus, and the narrator himself evoke the distant past, be it in a different way: Jesus, for example, by referring to what David did (2:25-26), by quoting what was written by Moses (12:26), Isaiah (7:6-7) and David (12:36; 12:10), and by mentioning in the parable of the vineyard the many servants whom the owner had sent first before he sent his only son (12:2-5); the narrator, for example, by inserting after the title of his book a motto which he says he has borrowed from the prophet Isaiah (1:2-3). Again, they both connect the preceding time with the time at which the story takes place, describing the latter as the beginning of the end time. The narrator does this, for example, by dressing the forerunner, John, as the prophet Elijah, who is expected to return before the end time comes (1:6), and with Jesus by beginning his appearance with the announcement that the time has expired and God's kingdom is close at hand (1:15). Thus the narrator has both his characters and his readers connect the story of Jesus with the past in a similar way.

Particularly complex are the relative positions of characters and readers with regard to the future beyond the time of the story. The narrator himself does not speak of that future (which is quite understandable in a story looking back to what has happened), but again and again he has the most authoritative speaker of the book, Jesus himself, raise the subject. For the characters, everything happening after the time at which the story takes place is future: for example, the fasting when the bridegroom has been taken away (2:20), the coming in power of God's kingdom (9:1), Jesus going before his disciples to Galilee (16:7) and the proclamation of the gospel in all the world (14:9). This applies in particular to everything said by Jesus in chapter 13 about the destruction of the temple, the appearance of impostors, the outbreak of wars and persecutions, the horrible days following on the setting-up of 'the disastrous abomination where it ought not to be' (i.e. in the temple), the appearance of pseudo-messiahs and the coming of the son of man, announced also in 14:62.

But what exactly is the position of the readers with regard to the time of these events? Clearly, it is here more important than ever to differentiate between the readers intended by the author and other readers. Could what is future in Mark 13 be present time to the intended readers? This is very possible. And if this is not so, it seems clear that the events mentioned are at least imminent and easily foreseeable. For all later readers of the book, at least part of that present or immediate future has already become past. This is true of the destruction of the temple of Jerusalem and of the 'disastrous abomination' set up in it, both being unrepeatable events. But is it equally true of the other future events? Precisely because they do not have that same historical uniqueness, the other events, especially the appearance of impostors and the outbreak of persecutions, may become present also for later readers.

In one respect, however, the position of characters and readers is identical, namely with regard to the coming of the son of man. In Mark it remains obscure how this is related in time to the coming in power of God's kingdom (9:1) and the drinking of new wine in the kingdom of God (14:25). But these two events are, in the book, future for the characters as well as the readers. On the question whether time will come to an end with this or not, the book is also quite explicit. Mark has Jesus make it clear in 10:40 that there are people for whom it has been assigned to sit at the right or left of the son of man, and in 10:30 that there is yet an age to come, which will bring eternal life with it.

3

SETTING THE SCENE
1:1-15

Context and Structure

The place of this section within the whole book cannot be described more simply and accurately than by the word with which it opens: 'beginning'. This also applies, although not in the same way and to the same degree, to each of the subsections distinguishable within this part of the text: the title (1:1), the motto (1:2-3), the appearance of the baptist (1:4-8), the installation and temptation of Jesus (1:9-13), and the summary of his proclamation (1:14-15).

Of these six subsections the title, 'beginning of the good news of Jesus messiah (son of God)' – the words in brackets were possibly added in later manuscripts – refers most clearly and directly to the whole book, and not just to the prelude. Apparently the good news about Jesus is only proclaimed on the last page of the book when it rings out in the words of the young man who, sitting in the open tomb, tells the women that Jesus has risen. For that reason all that precedes the last page is part of the beginning. On account of its connection with the end of the book, I regard the first line as its title, intended to put the reader on the right track from the start.

As is often the case with mottos prefixed to a book, the motto in question consists of a quotation (1:2-3) which, although its first half is from the book of Malachi, is ascribed by the author to Isaiah. After the title, it is the second way of making it clear at the outset how what follows should be read. Syntactically the words 'as it is written' form the beginning of a subordinate clause which is followed by the main clause that starts in verse 4 to tell the story of John's appearance. Thus the quotation directly throws light on the conduct of the baptist. This is supported not only by the emphasis laid on the desert in both the quotation itself and the story of the baptist, but also by the circumstance that this is the only voice making itself heard there, whereas the voice from heaven speaks at the River Jordan from where Jesus is driven out into the desert.

It would, however, be short-sighted to confine the significance of the quotation to the appearance of John. In that case one would overlook certain elements of the text which demand equal attention. First, the quotation is not about one but about two persons: one who appears as a herald and another whose arrival he announces. Of the two the latter is doubtless the more important. It is *his* way which is prepared by the herald (1:2) and which, according to the second half of the quotation, must likewise be prepared by his listeners (1:3). Thus, in a roundabout way the quotation bears equally, perhaps even primarily, on Jesus.

The second element is perhaps even more important. As noted above, the word 'desert' occurs both in the quotation and in the story of the baptist. But this is not the only repetition. In the quotation itself the word 'way' occurs twice, and the word 'path' is used in addition, which certainly, at a time when only the Roman highways were metalled, was synonymous with 'way'. So already in the motto the theme which is central to the whole book is clearly stated: the way of Jesus, the appointed and only way also for everyone who wants to follow him. Accordingly there is, I think, every reason to take the motto, as well as the title, to refer to the whole book and not just to the first part.

Similarly, the section following the motto (1:4-13) can still in the full sense of the word be called the beginning, namely, the beginning of the narrative proper of Jesus' doings, his pronouncements and stories, his activities and experiences. It tells of John addressing and baptizing all the inhabitants of Judaea and Jerusalem, and rounds off his appearance with the baptism of that one man from Galilee and with what the latter experiences on that occasion.

The summary of Jesus' proclamation (1:14-15) is also a

beginning, but in a different sense again. In contrast with most other episodes in the book it is not concerned with a particular incident. It is rather intent on stating in a few words what is taught by Jesus on his journeys through Galilee, that is, up to 8:21 or 8:26 where the Galilean cycle ends. The reader should constantly bear these words of Jesus in mind when reading that whole section.

Installations

We can speak of a distinct beginning in another sense also, for it is in this part that the author sets up himself and the reader as the narrator and the narratee of the story (see page 4 above). This is done through the title which, placed at the beginning, functions as a signpost. Although anonymous, the narrator is by no means invisible. Assuming as it were the cloak of the speaker, he steps on to the stage before the curtain rises in order to recite the prologue, telling the audience how he wants the play to be understood. As a second hint the motto is added, for the quotation is not spoken by one of the characters but again by the narrator himself. Thus, by implication, the narratee, being the logical counterpart of the narrator, is set in his place and told briefly how he ought to listen to the story.

Pursuing the same approach, we can say that the narrator also puts the main character of the story in context. This he does directly by calling Jesus in the very first line the one to whom the good news refers, describing him for the time being as 'messiah' (and possibly 'son of God') and in the quotation of 1:2-3 as 'the Lord', whose way is the subject of the book. And he does it indirectly through the other characters. In this respect the pronouncement of John that the one who comes after him is greater and mightier than he is himself clearly has a preliminary function. The installation proper takes place after Jesus' baptism when the voice from heaven calls him 'my dear son'. That Jesus holds out against Satan, God's adversary, when put to the test in the desert, shows that the installation has been crowned with success and that God's spirit has not moved him just temporarily.

It is noteworthy that no other characters are introduced to the reader in this prologue. Those acting a part in the book, such as followers and adversaries, the anonymous crowd and certain individuals, are not yet mentioned and stay in the wings for the time being. The ones that are mentioned beside Jesus – John, God, the spirit, the wild beasts, Satan and God's messengers – can hardly be regarded as proper characters. John, it is true, is regularly referred to by other characters – and it is in connection with one such reference that his execution is later told in a flashback (6:17- 29) – but after his arrest (1:14) he really no longer plays a part in the book as a character. Although God makes his voice heard a second time (9:7), he also remains behind the scenes as the one whose kingdom is proclaimed and made visible by Jesus through the way he acts and lives. The reader cannot fail to be affected by the fact that all the characters placed on the stage in the prelude apart from Jesus are normally active behind the scenes. He will come to see that those who play a part in the rest of the book are not really the main characters in the drama about Jesus, but that hidden behind them there is another and more important struggle, of which the main figures are God and Satan. What the reader realizes only later is that this means that the characters other than Jesus who play a part in the book have not witnessed what is said on the first page, and are consequently deprived of essential information relating to the identity of both the baptist and Jesus himself.

With Words from the First Testament

This first part of the text introduces the main character, Jesus, and begins to record God's good news, Jesus himself being both its messenger *and* its message, the medium and the content of the proclamation. What is said of him here is so much couched in terms quoted from or at least referring to the First Testament that it is hardly feasible to distinguish between the level of first meanings and that of First Testament references. In addition to the quotation already mentioned, from Isaiah and Malachi, which is prefixed as a motto to the book, the description in verse 6 of the way John the baptist is dressed must likewise be regarded as a quotation from the First Testament. It is from 2 Kings 1:8 and describes the appearance by which the prophet Elijah is recognized. Similarly the words spoken by the voice from heaven are derived from Psalm 2:7 and Isaiah 42:1, and must therefore be interpreted against that background. Finally, verse 13 also is full of First Testament references: Jesus going into the desert, his forty-day stay in the desert, and his being looked after by heavenly messengers; each incident has one or more parallels with events related in the First Testament. For this reason it is impossible to really understand this part of the narrative if one overlooks how deeply it is anchored in the First Testament.

The Time

Before presenting Jesus himself and telling the reader who he is, the book locates him in time. The time of Jesus succeeds the time of John the baptist. After he has been announced by John as superior to him and after he has submitted himself to John's baptism (a traditional rite of conversion and purification), Jesus steps on to the scene as the protagonist in the story when the baptist has been eliminated. So in a few words Jesus and his time are both connected with and separated from John and his time. But this does not merely mean that John and Jesus are placed in the correct chronological order. That something of far greater importance is intended here appears from the quotation in 1:2-3 as well as from the way in which the baptist is described by the narrator.

The time in which the baptist and Jesus appear is related to what in Malachi 4:5 is called 'the day of JHWH'. In Malachi 3:1 the prophet quotes God as saying: 'Look, I send my messenger to prepare a way before me.' Only in Malachi 4:5 does it appear that the messenger is not an anonymous person but no other than the prophet Elijah, who was thought to return before the end time, before 'the day of JHWH, that great and terrible day'. The author of Mark does not quite quote the text to the letter, but slightly changes the 'messenger who prepares a way before *me*' to a 'messenger who prepares a way before *you*', without it being immediately clear to whom the personal pronoun 'you' refers. But this is clarified both by the relation of the quotation with the title of the book and by the subsequent part of the narrative, recording how the baptist appears as Jesus' messenger who paves the way for him. Consequently, the time of Jesus is described as the terrible end time, while the use of 'you' instead of 'me' suggests that the one who is to come on the day of JHWH could be Jesus himself.

The second half of the quotation is, with a slight alteration, derived from Isaiah 40:3. Whereas Isaiah has 'make the paths straight of *our God*', the quotation reads 'make *his* paths straight', which, referring to the paths of 'the Lord', at least allows it to be applied to Jesus. However, it is only by reading the whole of Isaiah 40 that we come to understand how the quotation really describes the time in which the baptist and Jesus appear. For in that chapter there also mention of a joyful messenger (in Greek *euaggelizomenos* – hence evangelist in English, derived from *euaggelion*), and it seems no exaggeration to say that the word 'good news' (*euaggelion*) used in the title of Mark refers to it. ('Gospel', most probably from Old English *god spell* – *god* meaning 'good' and *spellian* meaning 'tell' – has the same etymological sense of 'good tidings.) The message of the messenger in Isaiah runs as follows: 'Your God is here. Here is the Lord JHWH coming in might, coming to rule with his right arm . . . He will tend his flock like a shepherd and gather them together with his arm: he will carry the lambs in his bosom and lead the ewes to water' (Isaiah 40:9-11). A few things are noticeable here.

First, the time is no longer described as a time of fear and trembling, but on the contrary, as a time of joy and happiness, for good and joyful news has been announced. This has to do with the way in which JHWH comes: true, with power and sovereignty, but they are now applied as a shepherd applies them, namely, to protect the flock, bring it to a place of safety and there watch over it, and take special care of the helpless and the weak. Second, the quotation describes not only the time but also the person announced, JHWH himself, who is said to conduct himself like a shepherd. Thus the quotation prefigures Jesus, as he is conceived in several places in Mark (6:34-44; 14:23; 16:7). So what is said of the time of John and Jesus gradually blends into what is said of Jesus himself.

Places

The beginning of the story is set in the desert and at the river Jordan, two scenes charged with meanings from the First Testament. In addition to what was said about the desert earlier the informed reader will no doubt remember that the desert was marked from ancient times as the place where the old Israel experienced God's special affection through numerous remarkable events, but at the same time was punished by him and put to the test. The desert has always been the place of retreat for pious and law-abiding people wishing to dissociate themselves from the course of things in the Jewish society of their day. A clear example of this are the Essenes, who withdrew to Qumran on the shore of the Dead Sea partly as a protest against the temple authorities in Jerusalem who, in their view, had come into power unlawfully. In the desert they wanted to establish a new Jewish community which would be agreeable to God. People claiming to be the messiah also migrated with their followers to the desert in order to start messianic liberation movements. The desert is, in short, a place where people of a kindred spirit assemble for the sake of pursuing a new way of life together.

The place in which events are set is of similar importance in the account of Jesus in the desert (1:13). The meaning of his sojourning among wild beasts is uncertain. It could imply a reference to the restoration of the state of paradise in the messianic age as it is pictured in Isaiah 11:1-9, but this state is hardly conceivable in the barren desert suggested by Mark. It seems, therefore, more plausible to take the wild animals as belonging to the normal environment of the desert. The forty days' trial is a repetition in condensed form of Israel's forty-year ordeal in the desert (e.g. Deuteronomy 8). The relief and care provided by the heavenly messengers is especially reminiscent of the way in which a similar messenger supplied Elijah with provisions before he set out on his forty-day journey to Horeb (1 Kings 19:4-8). Thus the narrator evokes the experiences of the old Israel, and in particular of her prophets, in order to enable the reader to link Jesus with the memorable events of Israel's past.

The Jordan too is a place full of reminders. Apart from the Jordan itself, and the two inland lakes and the Mediterranean, there were in both Judaea and Galilee a good many brooks that were quite suitable for immersion. The choice of the Jordan reminds the reader that from time immemorial the Jordan has been honoured as the river which the old Israel crossed before entering the land where it was able to build up a new existence. In the First Testament there are numerous references, especially in Numbers and Deuteronomy, testifying to the importance of the Jordan as a boundary-crossing. Joshua 3-4 relates how the Israelites, led by the ark of the covenant, crossed the Jordan dry-shod because its waters were halted, just as they had crossed the Sea of Reeds forty years before, and that afterwards a memorial consisting of a circle of twelve big stones was erected on the river at Gilgal. So when people go down with John into the Jordan, there to be immersed by him, it is a place eminently suited to serve as a rite of passage signifying conversion and change of life.

Persons

The prelude deals, however, first of all with the characters, in particular with the principal character of the book, Jesus from Nazareth in Galilee. In the strictest sense of the word he is put on the stage, the stage being Galilee, which he leaves in order to be converted, baptized and installed at the Jordan, and to which he returns by way of the desert, where he is tried by Satan. The one who baptizes him is really the long-awaited prophet Elijah, who does not hesitate to proclaim in unequivocal terms that in spite of being Elijah come back he is not fit to hold a candle to Jesus. Jesus' power is as much greater than his as wind is stronger than water, and the moulding spirit more vigorous than the primordial chaos.

Being greater than the baptist, Jesus is allowed to see and hear what is not seen and heard by anyone else: the breaking open of the heavens, the spirit descending, and the voice speaking from heaven.

What the voice from heaven says is undoubtedly the climax of the prelude. These words too are a combination of two passages from the First Testament. The first is Psalm 2:7: 'You are my son, this day I become your father', a pronouncement of God cited at the installation of the king in Jerusalem and probably belonging to the rite of enthronement. The words 'this day I become your father' speak about the king's installation in a metaphorical way. The second passage from the First Testament is Isaiah 42:1, where the prophet has God say about his servant: 'Here is my servant whom I uphold, my chosen one in whom I delight, I have bestowed my spirit upon him . . . ' Although Mark speaks of God, his son, and the spirit, one cannot conclude that it is the narrator's intention to refer to a trinitarian conception of God. It is rather the other way round, in the sense that passages like this one have given rise to trinitarian understandings of God. In this story the voice from heaven designates Jesus as messianic king and as the servant of God *par excellence*.

The second of the two aspects just mentioned – the servant endowed with God's spirit – implies that Jesus is designated a prophet as well as messianic king. In this connection is it is important to point out that the story of Jesus' baptism and installation both agrees with and differs from accounts of prophetic calling in the First Testament. There are great similarities with the call of Ezekiel, as appears from his own description in the first chapters of the book bearing his name (Ezekiel 1-3). The event takes place on the bank of a river, winged beings appear in the sky, a voice speaks from heaven, and the prophet is moved by the spirit who carries him off to another place. Remarkable differences, however, are that with Ezekiel there appears a human figure sitting on a throne above the firmament, that the prophet is addressed as 'man' (in Hebrew and Greek: 'son of man'), and in particular that Ezekiel is clearly commissioned to go to the rebellious people of Israel with a message which he is told to assimilate by eating a scroll (as in

Revelation 10:8-11). Similarly in the accounts recording the calling of Isaiah and of Jeremiah (Isaiah 6; Jeremiah 1). It is precisely this central element in the prophet's calling that is entirely absent from the story about Jesus. He is sent by no one, not even by the voice from heaven, nor is he told what he must say or do. It appears that Jesus' authority as messianic son of God does not derive from a higher authority, but is due to him as a matter of course.

End and Beginning

The last two verses of the prelude (1:14-15) conclude what has gone before and at the same time pave the way for what is to come. Their terminating character is underlined by three elements. First, mention of the arrest of John brings this part of the story to an end, for, as we have seen, he will not reappear in the book except as a topic of conversation. Second, the time is said to have expired or run its course, which emphasizes that a period has come to a close. Finally, with the twofold repetition of the term 'good news' from the title, the preliminary presentation of the theme is likewise rounded off. As the prologue both begins and ends with the same word, it is framed by the term 'good news'.

That 1:14-15 opens a new part of the story is not only apparent from Jesus' going back to Galilee in order to start his ministry, and from the content of the message that the day of God's kingdom is dawning, but also because, so far from being a piece of incidental information, the words of Jesus are like the announcement of a programme which actually governs his teaching activity during a great part of the book.

At least two of the expressions used here need some further clarification: 'the good news of God' and 'God's kingdom'. As already noted, the term 'good news', occurring in the first and last line, rounds off this part of the text. It is noteworthy, however, that it appears in three different combinations. The last line simply has 'good news' without any addition, but in the other two cases the term is followed by a genitive, in the first line by 'of (about) Jesus messiah' and in the last but one by 'of God'. This difference is probably due to a shift of the point of view. In the first line we hear the voice of the narrator himself, who prefaces his narrative with this particular title to present the reader with a clue to how the whole book should be understood. In 1:14 it is once more the narrator speaking, but now he summarizes what Jesus proclaims, namely, the good news of God. Finally, in the last line the narrator quotes Jesus by repeating his words in direct speech. So the narrator makes a distinction between the good news he announces and the good news proclaimed by Jesus.

The good news brought by the narrator concerns Jesus, his way of life, his death and resurrection, and his abiding influence. Before Mark was written, the core of this message had already been formulated in some such form as the ancient creed quoted by Paul with the introduction: 'I remind you of the good news that I preached to you' (1 Corinthians 15:1), and which must have run as follows:

'(I believe)
that Christ died for our sins, in accordance with the scriptures;
that he was buried;
and that he rose on the third day, according to the scriptures;
and that he appeared to Cephas'
(1 Corinthians 15:3-5).

It is the origin of this message, then, or the way the proclamation of the good news about Jesus messiah began, that the book relates. Jesus is the one to whom this good news refers. But in the book Jesus is also the herald of good news. This is, in the narrator's view as well, not the news of his own death and resurrection, although Jesus refers to them repeatedly in the second half of the book. The good news announced by Jesus is rather the news that God's kingdom is at hand.

With this we have come to the second important expression. 'God's kingdom (or kingship) is close at hand' – the term 'kingdom of heaven', a Jewish synonym for 'God's kingdom', does not occur in Mark. If this expression is an apt phrase to summarize such a central theme of Jesus' message, one would naturally want its meaning defined in a few clear and simple terms. Such a definition, however, is hard to give, for the simple reason that the expression 'God's kingdom' is mainly used for its evocative power, both by Jesus in his reported proclamation and the narrator, with the result that it has various meanings. It refers to a future event as yet unknown, as well as to a present reality one may already accept. In order to enter God's kingdom there are things in life you must do and other things you must leave undone, and in that sense it is intimately connected with the theme of 'the way'. The kingdom can be recognized but it is at the same time hidden. Likewise, it is closely bound up with Jesus' presence and activity, his speaking and doing, and at the same time with the son of man who is to come when the end time, begun in Jesus, is one day fulfilled. So it is no accident that Jesus employs the language of parable, simile and metaphor when speaking about the kingdom of God.

The Initiated Reader

After reading just one page of Mark the reader has become an initiate, already knowing much more than most characters will ever get to know in the course of the story. Reading further, he or she will realize that most of them appear to be ignorant of Jesus' identity and will actually remain so. The only exception is the demons, who time and again make it known who Jesus is, but who are equally often commanded to be silent. Readers, on the other hand, know from the beginning that Jesus is the son of God, and that no one else knows that apart from the demons. Thus they have been initiated into a secret unknown to Jesus' followers as well as the crowd and Jesus' adversaries. This lends a particular tension to the reading of the book. As they have been told what the voice from heaven says to Jesus, readers share to a certain extent in the knowledge of the omniscient author and of Jesus himself. It would seem that this means that any reader knows everything there is to know about Jesus' identity, but this can hardly be expected. Jesus' identity turns out to be so prominent a theme in Mark that it is unlikely to be fully disclosed on the very first page of the book.

4

A MAN OF AUTHORITY

1:14 – 3:35

Main Outline of Events

After placing his main character, his readers and himself on the stage, and summarizing Jesus' message, the narrator goes on to relate what happens to Jesus when he starts to proclaim the good news and what complications arise from his teaching. This part of the story can be summarized as follows.

Back in Galilee Jesus proclaims that the kingdom of God is at hand. At the outset four fishermen join him. On the sabbath his teaching in the synagogue of Capernaum makes a deep impression, as does his action of casting out an aggressive demon with a single word. On the same sabbath he cures the mother-in-law of Simon – one of the four – and after the day of rest is over he heals many others besides, until far into the night. Then Jesus withdraws from the bustle around him to pray and reflect, coming to the conclusion that it is his task to do all this throughout Galilee. So he travels the entire neighbourhood, preaching and casting out demons, and even cures a leper by one mere touch of his hand.

Back again in Capernaum, he astonishes the public when he cures a paralytic by giving him back the use of his limbs, but antagonizes some lawyers when he assures the man of the remission of his sins. The group of followers is joined by a tax-gatherer. When Jesus goes to table with some of these tax-gatherers and their friends, pharisee scribes object. He then becomes involved with them in a heated debate on the rules about sabbath observance and fasting, which his followers disregard.

Not put off by their presence, Jesus heals a man with a withered arm on the sabbath. As a result the pharisees and Herodians start consulting together about how to get rid of him.

Meanwhile Jesus cures more and more people, while demons shout unusual but significant names at him. While in the hill-country, Jesus appoints from the company of his followers and supporters a smaller group of twelve men to act as his close helpers. He sharply protests against the imputation of scribes from Jerusalem that he must have made a pact with Satan. When even his closest relatives try to put him out of action, he breaks off all family relations and declares those who do the will of God are his true family.

This main outline is elaborated and amplified with narrative text of two kinds. Firstly there are number of sub-stories complete in themselves, which are strung together as episodes. Secondly there are passages that summarize what happens frequently or regularly. In addition to these there are comments on the events related. We will now look at these different elements of the text by considering each of them in turn.

Movements

The book takes the readers and Jesus to Galilee from the desert, where he will continue to be active until he sets out for Jerusalem. Jesus is en route most of the time. The story begins at an indefinite place on the shore of what is called *the lake of Galilee*, a name probably devised by the narrator. It is possible that he uses it rather than the current names 'lake of Gennesaret' and 'lake of Kinneret' to emphasize that the scene of action is Galilee whenever he mentions the lake. Although the shore is not speci-fied, we may say that for both the narrator and his readers it lies on their own side, the side which is familiar and secure. It is here that most of the events set by the lake or on the shore take place: the calling of the four fishermen, the calling of the tax-gatherer, and the discourse from a small boat. In this part of the book there is no sailing yet. This will not come until later, so it seems obvious that only then will the other side of the lake be visited (although it is quite possible to walk round to certain parts on the other side and arrive there sooner than by boat, 6:33). Both the people Jesus asks to follow him and those addressed by him readily respond to his call and message. They come to him in great numbers from Galilee and Judaea, but also from more distant areas where the population is not predominantly Jewish (3:8).

Even if the scene of action in this part of the book is specified, it is never far from the lake. Perhaps it is always the same village *Capernaum*. After his departure from Nazareth Jesus seems to have found a home in the *house* where the two brothers Simon and Andrew live with their mother-in-law. Several scenes which take place around, in front of and inside the house are all related to what Jesus preaches and does for people. The difference between those who are inside and those who remain outside is stressed more than once in the book, which invariably describes the state of the former as positive and that of the latter as negative, a description which also seems relevant to the reader's position. Twice in this part of the book Jesus visits the village *synagogue* to attend as a matter of course the sabbath service of worship with his fellow Jews. Other events such as the walk through *cornfields*, the appointment of the twelve in *the hill-country* or the search for privacy at a *lonely spot*, take place in the surrounding area at locations only partly specified. But in Capernaum and its environs, as with the events situated at the lake, success prevails. It is indeed not too much to say that Jesus is successful.

Had the matter rested with these parts of the text – especially since according to a number of old manuscripts verse 3:1 should be read as having *the* synagogue instead of *a* synagogue – Jesus' activities would have had a very limited range indeed, restricted in fact to one single village with a lake, some fields and a nearby mountain. But this impression is corrected and amplified by a constant string of references to the rapidly-spreading fame of Jesus, his many journeys through *the whole of Galilee*, his appearances in nearly every place, and finally to the onrush of vast crowds wherever he appears. Thus the image is created of a man wandering restlessly about, forever in search of an audience for his message, continually troubled by the handicapped and the sick, attracting crowds wherever he goes, and only exceptionally able to go to Capernaum, where he is not to be left in peace either.

Supporters and Helpers

In this part of Mark a great number of characters are introduced who play an important part in the book. The first category is made up of the *supporters* and helpers who are placed in context in this section. Right at the beginning, practically before Jesus has done and – if we do not count the introductory summary of his preaching in 1:15 – before he has said anything, he twice asks two fishermen and their brothers, Simon and Andrew, James and John, to join him (1:16-20). This is related in two short, almost identical, stories, which are constructed in exactly the same way. The same structure is to be found in the story about the fifth man whom Jesus asks to go with him, a tax-gatherer by the name of Levi (2:14). This structure is like a circle or spiral in that the interrelated extreme or outer elements are arranged around the centre as in the figure below:

- Jesus passes by
  - ★ Jesus sees people working at their trade
  - ○ Jesus asks them to join him
  - ★ They leave (their homes) and give up their livelihood
- They go with Jesus

It is noticeable that four men are taken on at the same time, so that there is a small group from the start. With the events taking place at the lakeside, it is not very surprising that the first four are fishermen by trade. That the fifth, Levi, is a tax-gatherer, is not only somewhat unexpected but also problematic. Unlike fishermen, tax-gatherers were often well-to-do. They had acquired the leasehold of a toll – often directly or indirectly from the Roman authorities – and usually saw to it that the taxes they levied were such as to leave them with a considerable income. They were, in fact, respected by no one, and therefore little suited to further Jesus' prestige and promote his cause. Yet Jesus' invitation was no mistake, as the book clearly shows us. When his adversaries trouble him about his choice he gives them the rough edge of his tongue (2:16-17). In this context the book adds almost casually that meanwhile there were many following Jesus (2:15), and the narrator gives the impression that Levi is not the only one who is questionable or suspect to Jesus' adversaries.

Out of the large number of supporters *twelve* are selected and appointed by Jesus as his *helpers* (3:13-19). The number twelve is probably connected with the twelve patriarchs of Israel, in which case it indicates that here a new beginning is made. The twelve are called by name, some even by their nicknames. The tax-gatherer Levi, however, is not among them, neither is he mentioned in the rest of the book, whereas the four fishermen appear to belong to the group of twelve. Simon is named first on his own this time and apart from his brother Andrew. Jesus gives him a new name, Peter, of which the meaning is not explained. He will regularly appear first in Mark and act as spokesman for the others, ranking as the most important man in Jesus' company. From now on the narrator will always call him Peter, except for the one occasion in Gethsemane when Jesus calls him Simon again (14:17). James and John also have another name, of which the origin is ascribed to Jesus himself. They are nicknamed Boanerges, sons of thunder, for apparently they are no darlings. The other Simon has a second name, too, and is called the zealot. But the most caustic explanation is no doubt the one added to the last name on the list, Judas Iscariot, who – the reader is told – betrayed Jesus. In this way the narrator forewarns the reader of a bad ending. The idyllic atmosphere pervading the first chapter is not going to last and may even prove deceptive. One of the supporters whom Jesus has chosen as a close helper will make common cause with his adversaries.

Yet the mood that prevails at the end of this section is one of optimism. This is true even though Jesus' relatives have come to the conclusion that he is out of his mind and set out to take him back to Nazareth (3:21). With this incident the part beginning with Jesus' departure from Nazareth (1:9) is more or less concluded. When his former companions arrive at the house where Jesus is preoccupied with the crowd around him, they remain outside, realizing they do not belong there, and send someone to 'call' him (3:31). This is a suggestive word to use here, because everywhere else in the book 'call' in its active form is only employed to mean the appeal Jesus makes to people to join him. There is a sharp contrast between this meaning and the conduct of Jesus' relatives, who, so far from going up to him, keep themselves aloof and then must send someone else to call him. Here 'to call' is not aimed at establishing community, but at destroying it. Jesus' reply admits of no doubt. Pointing at the people around him, he declares that they are his new and true family (3:34-35). So what began with four fishermen leaving their father as well as their nets and boats in order to go with Jesus is brought to a conclusion in this house. Jesus' reply refers to all those that are listening to him then and there, including the twelve who after 3:13 may be taken to have been present at this event, but as the emphasis lies on *whoever* does the will of God, the intention of Jesus' pronouncement extends to the readers of the book as well.

Incidentally, Jesus does not only speak of brothers in his reply, but also of sisters. Thus attention is subtly called to the fact that although no mention has been made so far of any women following Jesus, there are also women among his supporters, and that naturally there is an equal place for them within the new family.

Adversaries

Besides supporters and helpers, the book introduces adversaries. Unlike the supporters, who are there from the beginning, the adversaries do not appear until a number of remarkable works accomplished by Jesus and a tour through Galilee have been recorded. On his return to the house in Capernaum, which is his base there, he cures a paralytic. With a story-teller's *tour de force* the narrator introduces a few adversaries into the story by making room for them inside the house where Jesus performs the cure. They are presented as *scribes*, *doctors of the law* or *lawyers*.

Of course, these people are not scholars in the modern sense of the word. They do not pursue studies, nor do they conduct research the way we do today. They were usually trained by their predecessors, who taught them to be true to the oral traditions which expound the Torah and regulate its applications. They were the undisputed religious leaders and, as such, considered it their task to interpret the Torah for present-day situations, to instruct younger pupils, and to be members of the courts of justice. Their centre was Jerusalem, although they were very critical of the priests officiating there. As to their mentality and outlook, most of them, but not all, held the pharisaic view. In Mark they are usually mentioned together with the pharisees or the chief priests and elders. It is not clear, however, if the narrator really wants to differentiate between these groups or not. With one exception (12:28-34), they are always represented unfavourably in the book, and always act as Jesus' adversaries. It is obviously a stereotyped presentation, and modern readers should guard against the idea that they are given a truthful and complete picture of the scribes in the days of Jesus.

When they appear for the first time, the reader has already heard that there is a striking difference between their way of teaching and that of Jesus (1:22). From the fact that Jesus' teaching in the synagogue at Capernaum astonishes his hearers because it bears the stamp of his personal authority, one could deduce that the narrator represents the teaching of the scribes as predominantly based on traditional authorities. As Jesus' authority is borne out by his competence and power to subdue and control unclean spirits, the reader realizes what the people in the synagogue at Capernaum cannot know: Jesus derives this power from the holy spirit whom he saw descending upon him after his baptism.

After having read what Jesus did in the synagogue at Capernaum, attentive readers must expect that an encounter between Jesus and the scribes is bound to cause problems. When they do arise, they lead straight to the heart of the matter. The scene of the action is the house in Capernaum where the paralytic is brought to Jesus. His companions, who by hook or crook have managed to get their friend into the house, expect as a matter of course that Jesus will give him back the use of his limbs. And the reader expects the same. However, at the stage where in similar stories the healing is related, the goalposts are moved, so to speak, and Jesus says, unasked and for no apparent reason, to the paralytic, 'My friend, your sins are forgiven.' To be sure, there are usually quite a few things people may have to forgive each other, but the forgiving of *sins* is – at least outside the sphere of ritual and sacrifices of atonement – the exclusive right of God himself, a matter on which all Jews are agreed. It is therefore not at all surprising that the scribes present do not believe their ears. What is at stake here is their holiest conviction that God is unique; a belief that is professed three times a day in the *Shema*: 'Hear, O Israel, the Lord is our God, one Lord' (Deuteronomy 6:4). Hence their shock reaction, 'He is blaspheming!', a phrase spoken out loud at the end of the book by the high priest to justify the death penalty for Jesus (14:64). Although the scribes do not utter that conclusion, Jesus, who can read their hearts, knows what they are thinking. The reader meets here not only with an all-knowing narrator, which is, after all, no unusual phenomenon, but also with a character who knows more than is usually given to human beings. Jesus responds to their silent reproach with an overt action. First he makes them understand that he knows the drift of their thoughts, and then proves to them the power of his word, telling the paralytic to take up his sleeping–mat and go home on foot. That the cure is effective indicates that Jesus simply cannot be judged according to the standards applied by the scribes. In his comment on the story the narrator stresses this point again, saying that Jesus cured the paralytic to demonstrate that he, as son of man, has indeed the power on earth to forgive sins. This must for the present lead to the conclusion that the unspoken allegation of blasphemy, however valid from the Jewish point of view at the time, does not apply to Jesus if we consider who this 'son of man' really is.

In the next episode we come across the scribes again, this time called 'pharisee scribes' (2:13-17). They object to Jesus mixing freely with tax-gatherers and law-breakers, but again Jesus pays them in kind. When they appear for the third time in this part, they are once more described, but now as the scribes 'who had come down from Jerusalem' (3:22), a phrase based, no doubt, on the assumption that they are credited with greater authority than the scribes from the village or district. The scribes from Jerusalem are the ones who spread the rumour in Capernaum that Jesus is dominated by the prince of the demons, enabling him to eliminate the ordinary demons. The reader of course knows better. It is the spirit of God himself who gives him this extraordinary power.

Jesus refutes these scribes by pointing out the contradiction contained in what they bring against him (3:23-27) and by laying the blame of blasphemy at their door: they blaspheme the holy spirit, and that is the one sin that is unforgivable (3:28-30). Besides the scribes a second category of adversaries is introduced, the *pharisees*. Like the scribes, they are first compared to Jesus (2:18) before appearing on the stage themselves (2:23). To what extent the two groups as represented in the book must be distinguished from each other is far from clear, the more so since most scribes belonged, in fact, to the pharisees. The term used to describe them means 'the separated' or 'the ones set apart', but this hardly expresses what was characteristic of them. They were organized in a kind of association which one could only join if one met certain requirements, in particular the scrupulous observance of the Torah, including the prescriptions regarding cleanliness, which really applied to priests on duty performing sacrificial rites. In present-day terms one could perhaps say that the pharisees were laymen practising a clerical spirituality. Their aim was to live a life of the strictest purity and special holiness. Consequently it was really impossible for anyone to belong to the pharisees unless he knew in detail not only the relevant rules of the Torah, but also their subsequent interpretations and all related casuistry. As a result, the pharisees adopted an ambivalent attitude towards the average Jew. Being a lay movement, pharisaism originally had a certain affinity with the common people. On the other hand, pharisees were inclined to look down on their less-educated fellow-men, for they thought them unable to know the Torah and its traditions well enough to put them into practice and live up to the high-minded ideal of purity held by pharisees. In Mark they are always seen as a homogeneous group of like-minded people, a view which, historically speaking, is certainly incorrect, but may be ascribed to the strongly-stereotyped way in which they are presented in the book.

In this part of Mark the pharisees appear three times, just like the scribes. First they are described as having pupils who, unlike those of Jesus, fast on certain days (2:18). The fact that Jesus' followers do not fast is, as it were, the introduction to the next story, where we see them plucking ears of corn on the sabbath day to satisfy their hunger (2:23). The pharisees insist on interpreting this casual act as a gross violation of the Law, calling Jesus to account for it. They appear the third time to witness a cure in the Capernaum synagogue (3:1-6). The point at issue is once again the rules about time. The sabbath-prohibition from working on behalf of a sick or disabled person is only suspended in a case where life is at stake. So when Jesus, openly, and in the synagogue, of all places, cures a man whose only ailment is that he has a deformed arm, they have occasion to contrive plans for Jesus' downfall. This third fragment fully reveals the part played by the pharisees in the book. Unlike the scribes in the house at Capernaum, the pharisees are not in the synagogue by accident. On the contrary, they have come – be it with the anonymity suggested by the impersonal plural 'they' – in the hope of catching Jesus violating the sabbath himself so that they can indict him on that ground. The only thing missing is that they should have arranged for the presence of someone whose handicap was slight enough to prove the justice of a charge. In the story Jesus reveals in a subtle yet clear way what they are after and what sort of people they are. To this end he asks, 'Is it permitted to do good or to do evil on the sabbath, to save life or to destroy life?' The question makes it clear at the same time that when the pharisees start discussing with the Herodians how to dispose of Jesus, they are plotting a murder. They are murderers, doing on the sabbath what is not permitted on any day, let alone on the sabbath. They themselves are guilty of violating the sabbath, the very sin they want to expose in Jesus. From what the narrator tells us here about the conduct of Jesus' adversaries, we understand that even within the framework of what is apparently a success story, his murderers have their weapons ready.

The Sick and Suffering

Apart from Jesus' supporters or helpers and his adversaries, characterized by their own actions, a third group is put on the stage whose members are characterized instead by being the object of the actions of others, namely the innumerable sufferers needing healing. Some have a specific part of the story devoted to them in which they play a leading part. As a rule these brief, self-contained stories have an identical structure whose principal elements are the following:

- The sufferer turns to Jesus or is brought to him
- Jesus performs the healing act or speaks the healing word
- An act by the sufferer or the acclamations of those present show that the intervention has been successful

Within this structure there is room for different kinds of supplementary information. Those who are not given their own story appear in one of the summaries, where they play a supporting rather than a leading part.

The first to figure in his own story is the man possessed by an unclean spirit (1:23-26). About the unclean spirits themselves we will have to speak later on in this chapter. Although the man in question may certainly be regarded as someone who needs to be healed, the story does not do so. The narrator shows no interest whatever in his well-being, but is entirely taken up with Jesus' confrontation with the demon. The second individual needing healing – but to the narrator really the first – is Simon's mother-in-law, who, bedridden with fever, is cured by Jesus on his return from the sabbath service in the synagogue (1:29-31). Also, on account of its brevity, this is the clearest model of all healing stories in the book. The cure is effected in the privacy of the house, with no other witnesses present except Simon and his three companions who have just before decided to join Jesus. It is the sabbath, but this is not stressed in any way. It is, however, clear from the information given that the four men have just come home from the sabbath service, and this is confirmed by the fact that all those needing to be healed and those possessed by evil spirits are brought together at the door of the house after sunset, the moment when the sabbath is past (1:32). Their healing is reported in 1:32-34. As this is a passage dealing with a specific event that happens at a particular place and time, it cannot be called a real summary in the sense defined at the beginning of this section. On the other hand, the collective nature of the healing makes the passage something of a summary. Be that as it may, the story says that Jesus cures many. It would be wrong to conclude from the word 'many' that some of the sufferers are not cured. The transition that matters here is from one to many. This generalization is completed with the one single sentence, which says that Jesus went through all Galilee, preaching in their synagogues and casting out *the* evil spirits (1:39).

The next individual who turns to Jesus is a leper (1:40-45). Just as in the case of Simon's mother-in-law, the healing is partly done through Jesus touching the patient. This is of particular interest in this story because lepers were obliged to take precautions in order to prevent physical contact and the resultant contagion as far as possible under the circumstances. Leprosy was, moreover, looked upon as a state of uncleanness brought on by the sufferer's sin, excluding them from participation in any form of ritual worship. In the story the touching has both a therapeutic and a communicative function, for it restores the normal social contact from which lepers were excluded. The sufferer was only permitted to resume normal contact with people after a priest had pronounced him clean and the prescribed purification rites had been performed in the temple.

While in the case of the leper the connection between sickness and sin remains implicit, the two are explicitly connected in the fourth case, that of the paralytic who is carried to Jesus in Capernaum (2:1-12). Both the way in which the scribes are brought into the story and the combination of the two different themes of sickness and sin or healing and forgiveness have something artificial about them. But it is precisely this artificiality which may be considered to indicate how anxious the narrator is to combine the two. Yet it is not easily explained what connection between the two is really intended in the story. On no account should we presume too lightly that the symptoms of paralysis are regarded here as due to a moral lapse either of the man in question or of someone else, which would mean that the story suggests a causal connection between sin and sickness, a supposition for which there is no sufficient evidence in the text. So there is nothing for it but to accept that we cannot answer the question whether such a connection is intended here and, even if such were the case, what the precise relationship would be between sin and sickness, forgiveness and healing.

There are, however, two other relationships which perhaps escape our attention but may have some bearing on the matter. The first is that between the inactivity of the paralytic and the activities of his friends, the second that between *their* faith and *his* sin. Their correlation is made explicit at the moment the standpoint shifts towards the theme of sin: 'When Jesus saw their faith, he said to the paralysed man. "My friend, your sins are forgiven" ' (2:5). Inactivity and activity seem to relate to each other in the same way as sin and faith. This is to some extent confirmed by two stories of healing further on in the book, where Jesus addresses a woman (5:34) and a man (10:52) who have both exerted themselves to find healing, with the identical words: 'Your faith has cured you.' Whatever the precise nature of that relationship, two things are certain, first that the story presents the healing as an indication that the man's sins are forgiven too, and second that the story wants to make it clear that the son of man, Jesus, can forgive sins on earth.

Also in the final case in this section of Mark, the theme of healing is secondary to another motive (3:1-6), as is clear from the mere facts of the time and place of the event; for it is not without reason that the man with the withered arm is cured on the sabbath, in the synagogue, and under the watchful eyes of the men bent on finding incriminating evidence. But we have said enough about this when discussing Jesus' adversaries.

Demons

Supporters, helpers, various adversaries and sufferers needing healing are characters in Mark who also appear in our own everyday world. But there are other characters in the book with whom we are no longer acquainted in the western world, such as demons, also called unclean or evil spirits. They cannot quite compare with the other categories, if only because they seem to be unable to do anything until they have taken possession of a human being who is both their victim and their instrument. We who have grown up in a scientific culture have an image of man and the world in which there is no room for such creatures. Yet there can be no doubt that in the environment and situation in which Mark was written even educated people accepted the existence of demons. Nor is there any reason to think that the author of the book or even Jesus himself did not share this view. In these circumstances it would have been rather surprising if the book had not contained stories about the casting-out of demons.

How then did people imagine these demons? Invisible, unpredictable, evil and dangerous spirits who preferred to stay in lonely places like ruins, deserts and graveyards. They were seen as enemies of God, but also of human beings, whom they liked to harm both physically and morally, by taking possession of them and making them suffer and sin. They were believed to be in the service of the prince of the demons, named Beelzebub or Satan, who carried out his godless activities with the help of his subordinates. They could make people ill, but also cause natural disasters. Speculations about their origin in Jewish thought of the pre-Christian era had already suggested the idea that they were fallen angels. It is not surprising that they were seen at work especially in people who in a schizophrenic state considered themselves to be in the power of an unclean spirit, and consequently felt that they were the victim as well as the instrument of the demon living inside them.

In this part of Mark there is only one story that records how Jesus casts out a demon. Such stories tend to resemble stories of healing, but differ from them mainly in concentrating on the struggle between demon and exorcist. It is certainly not without significance that the first activity mentioned after the calling of the first four supporters is the expulsion of an unclean spirit (1:21-27). How much stronger the demon is than men usually are appears at once from his superhuman knowledge of the true status of Jesus. He loudly calls him by the name of 'the holy one of God', a term reminiscent of the way the First Testament refers to the Nazarite Samson, as well as to Moses and the prophets Elijah and Elisha. From the demon's address it is clear that by using this name he classifies Jesus as one who is on the side of God and, by calling him *holy*, as an enemy of the *unclean* spirits. Not for nothing does the demon shout that Jesus has come to destroy the unclean spirits. In the story it is not Jesus but the demon who takes the initiative. The calling out of Jesus' name can be regarded as equivalent to handling a lethal weapon; for in those days it was a common conviction, as it still is today in animistic cultures, that he who knows a person's name can use it magically and thereby get power over him. But the weapon fails. Jesus silences the demon, forcing him to leave his victim and instrument. That this only happens after one more spastic movement and a loud scream is typical of stories of this kind. The demon's action in shouting Jesus' name and Jesus' reaction of commanding him to be silent have yet another function in the context of the book as a whole besides the one they have in this individual story, but that will be discussed later (see p.67).

The sub-story about the demon's expulsion makes it clear from the very start that the kingdom of God is absolutely incompatible with the tyranny of enslaving demonic powers. For, as is shown by the end of the story, what we have here is more than a chance incident. The people present conclude that Jesus is more powerful than *the* demons, thus generalizing the meaning of what has happened here. In addition to this, they conclude from Jesus' superior power that his teaching also is based on a different kind of authority to that of the scribes. The narrator stresses the generalization yet again by explicitly stating in two place that the unclean spirits cannot but acknowledge Jesus' superiority (1:32-34 and 3:11-12). The image the narrator has so far given of Jesus must therefore be amplified. He is not only a man who wanders restlessly about and tirelessly proclaims his message everywhere, meanwhile healing innumerable sufferers, but he is also a successful exorcist whose powers no evil spirit can resist. Yet at the same time Jesus appears to be unable to silence them. If one of them falls silent, the next one takes over.

About the scribes' charge that Jesus is only able to cast out demons because he is in alliance with Satan and must therefore accommodate an unclean spirit himself, as well as about Jesus' refutation of this allegation (3:22-30), we have already spoken (see p.44).

The Crowd

Apart from these diverse specific characters there is one that is wholly collective and anonymous, appearing in a great number of places: the crowd (in translation often referred to as 'the people'). It is mentioned for the first time in 2:4 on Jesus' return from Capernaum. So many people have gathered in front of the house where Jesus is staying that there is no room left, and the crowd is so dense that it is impossible to pass through. This shows immediately the ambiguity of the crowd. It is on the one hand living evidence of the response to Jesus' word (1:28), and on the other a nuisance and sometimes even a danger. As the people start to come from even farther away, we clearly have to do with a snowball effect. First they come from the whole of Galilee (1:39-45), and later even from Judaea and Jerusalem, Idumaea and Transjordan, and the region of Tyre and Sidon (3:7-8), in short from far and wide. (Strangely enough, Samaria is not mentioned and does not appear elsewhere in the book either; it almost seems as if the narrator does not know of its existence.) The crowd comes to Jesus to listen to him (2:13), and follows him as he moves on (3:7). Sometimes it is even necessary for Jesus to take precautions so as not to be crushed by it (3:9-10). When he enters a house, the crowd is so close upon his heels that he does not get a chance to eat (3:20).

Yet Jesus does not try to ward it off or defend himself against it. On the contrary. The crowd is sitting round him at the time his relatives send someone inside the house to call him – do not wonder how we are to picture a crowd inside a modest house, for a lot more is possible in the story than in reality (3:32). And they are the very people Jesus points at when he says, 'Here are my mother and my brothers. Whoever does the will of God is my brother, my sister, my mother' (3:34-35). The crowd is therefore much more than a vague mass which merely serves as a background against which the narrator can set individuals and specific groups. The crowd has its own character, and consists of the many people who are deeply impressed by what Jesus says and does, who want to see and hear him for themselves, and who take their sick and handicapped to him. In short, they are the people who allow themselves to be influenced by this exceptional man from Nazareth without as yet wholly committing themselves to him.

Time and Sequence

A few things have already been said in the previous chapter about the relationship between John the baptist and Jesus. Suffice it to observe here that the only specific indication of time in this part of the book, if there is one at all, is in 1:14, 'after John had been delivered up'. Certainly this opening line draws a bold line between John and Jesus. The latter only steps on to the scene after the former has been carried off as a prisoner. On the other hand, the words 'delivered up' underline at the same time that Jesus and the baptist have a lot in common. In so far as it relates to persons, 'delivered up' is only used in Mark for what happens to Jesus in Jerusalem and for what will happen to his followers later, thus uniting the baptist, Jesus and persecuted Christians in their common destiny of martyrdom.

Apart from the one just mentioned, there are a few general indications of time in this section of Mark. After the narrator has recorded the baptist's arrest and summarized Jesus' message the passage of time is left rather vague. In the first series of events it only seems important whether they take place on the sabbath (1:21; 2:23; 3:2) or after the sabbath is over (1:32). For the rest the story only mentions an interval of a few days (2:1), and places the praying of Jesus early in the morning after a night's hard work (1:35). It looks therefore as if the narrator confines himself in anchoring his story in time with the baptist's arrest, and does not think that the chronological order of events is of any real importance.

By and large this is true, but it does not apply to the sequence of the various episodes and summaries, which is far from arbitrary. The healing of Simon's mother-in-law, for instance, cannot really be related before Simon himself has been mentioned, and Jesus cannot very well decide that it is his mission to go and proclaim his message elsewhere in Galilee unless he has already started at some particular place in the region. It is likewise important that before Jesus starts fighting demons he should have been attacked by one first. On initial reflection it seems that the healing of the leper is an episode which might have been found an appropriate place at several other points in the story, but this too is deceptive. For it is precisely on his long journey to the priests in Jerusalem that the man tells everywhere what has happened to him. As a result Jesus becomes so well-known that he can no longer enter a town openly, but has to conceal himself (1:45). It is again in consequence of his reputation that Jesus attracts such a big crowd on his return to Capernaum that the paralytic cannot simply be carried through the door of the house where Jesus is staying. The fact that Jesus' adversaries do not make their first appearance until this sub-story shows equal evidence of careful composition. After all, Jesus cannot encounter resistance unless he has first made himself sufficiently known. Attesting to the same carefulness is the way in which the company of supporters and helpers is steadily extended, and at the same time the opposition of the adversaries is built up to the climax of 3:6.

But this sequence is even more important for the effect it has on the reader. The image of a man equipped with exceptional authority, unusual healing-power and superhuman control over the forces of demons and sin is built up so skilfully that it is almost impossible not to be deeply impressed. Besides, the acceptance of his authority by the vast majority of the people who came in touch with him appears to be so convincing that the reader can hardly fail to be won over. Finally, the objections of Jesus' adversaries, which sound reasonable at first (cf. 2:1-12), turn so obviously into straight contradictions and dishonest attacks in the course of the story (3:22-30) that the reader is only too happy to reject their way of thinking. In other words, the narrator has established Jesus as a man of authority who cannot easily be bypassed by the reader either.

From the First Testament

In comparison with the earlier section of the book, the passages that receive special light from the First Testament are less numerous. The first of these deals with the *calling* of the four fishermen and the tax-gatherer. The words 'come with me', with which Jesus asks them to join him (1:17), are sometimes connected with 2 Kings 6:19, where the same words are spoken by Elisha. But as they apply to a completely different situation I am inclined not to attach any great importance to them. The same holds good for Jesus' promise 'I will make you fishers of men', when it is related to a passage like Jeremiah 16:16, where to fish and hunt men clearly means to hunt them down and to prosecute them. It seems to be more rewarding to turn to 1 Kings 19:19-21, which tells the story of Elisha's call by his predecessor Elijah and is likely to have served as a model for Mark's story. All the elements found in the latter can be traced back to the former, although Elisha's reaction to the call of the prophet is rather more drastic than that of the men who decide to follow Jesus. Elijah walks by and, seeing Elisha at work with oxen and plough, throws his prophet's cloak over him as an invitation to join him, whereupon Elisha slaughters the oxen and destroys the plough and, having thus renounced his livelihood, takes leave of his parents and follows him. In this way the narrator parallels the relationship between Elijah and Elisha with that between Jesus and his helpers. This is important because in some other stories as well, it is not John (as on the first page of Mark) but Jesus who is drawn with features borrowed from the 'prophetic duo' Elijah and Elisha.

One such story is that of the cure of the *leper* (1:40-45), which is connected with Elisha's cure of a leper (2 Kings 5:8-14). At first sight the two stories seem to differ so much that they seem hardly related to one another. The Aramaean army commander Naaman is healed not through any direct intervention of Elisha, but after he, on the prophet's advice, has bathed seven times in the Jordan. But after receiving Elisha's advice Naaman becomes extremely angry and says: 'I thought he would at least have come out and stood, and invoked JHWH his God by name, waved his hand over the place and so rid me of the disease' (v.11). This sentence is the key to what connects and separates the two stories. What Naaman expects but Elisha does not do is done by Jesus, at least partly. He touches the leper with his hand and cures him. But he does not call on JHWH, for he received permanent power to heal when the spirit of God moved him. Thus the story underlines the fact that Jesus follows in the footsteps of Elijah and Elisha, doing the things they did, but is nevertheless – as has already been said by the baptist – more powerful than they are.

The First Testament may also add another dimension to the thought that strikes the scribes when they hear Jesus say that the *sins* of the paralytic are *forgiven* (2:5). As it is worded, their question, 'Who but God alone can forgive sins?', echoes a statement which Isaiah puts into the mouth of JHWH: 'I alone, I am He, who for his own sake wipes out your transgressions, who will remember your sins no more' (Isaiah 43:25). In other words, Jesus' adversaries are initially proved right by the same prophetic voice which according to the beginning of the book carries so much weight with the narrator. The least we can say of this is that it adds relish to the situation.

The third story which gains in perspective if we put it against the background of the First Testament is the one about Jesus' disciples picking corn on the sabbath (2:23-26). When the pharisees trouble him about this Jesus gives as good as he gets by asking them if they have never read that David went into the house of God, in the time of Abiathar the high priest, and ate of the sacred bread which only the priests are allowed to eat, and even gave it to his men. There is some piquancy in the fact that the very question asking the pharisees if they have ever read the passage concerned is followed by a summary of David's conduct which is not consistent with the facts as 1 Samuel 21 has them. According to 1 Samuel 21:1-7 it was not the high priest Abiathar but his father Ahimelech who spoke to David in the sanctuary. Besides, in Samuel David asks for bread only for his soldiers, whereas the narrator has Jesus say that David himself ate of the loaves and then gave them to the men who were with him. Abiathar is probably the kind of mistake made by someone who thinks he knows the scriptures well enough to rely on his memory. Whether this is also true of David eating with his men is another question, for Mark will tell us later that Jesus eats with those who are with him. And it is possible too that the narrator thinks it important that his readers should be made sensitive to a sequence which in another place and at another level of the book serves as a key, namely the otherwise obvious sequence: gather corn . . . eat bread with companions.

The Development of the Story

After the protagonist has been placed in the desert, where the first part of the book is set, and the reader has learned who he really is and what his true background and his mission are, Jesus returns to Galilee. Here a number of characters are put on the stage around him, such as followers, twelve of whom are designated his close helpers, adversaries; the sick and the suffering, some of whom are in the power of a malevolent spirit; and finally the crowd. At some point some relatives of Jesus show up, but they are rejected so firmly that it is hardly to be expected that we shall hear of them again. Scarcely have the various characters established themselves by virtue of their actions as belonging to one of the categories mentioned, when they begin a process that can only develop along predictable lines. The reader anticipates that unless the story takes an unexpected turn, Jesus' adversaries will sooner or later move into action, and that his supporters and helpers, more than the others, will grow to understand Jesus better simply because they are in closer touch with him.

With regard to Jesus himself, the reader now knows more or less what his message contains and that he proclaims it everywhere in Galilee, especially in the local synagogues, where Jews come together to pray and learn from the scriptures as well as from one another. As soon as the news gets about that he also has the gift of healing the sick and the handicapped, there is a rush of people who want to benefit from it, so that Jesus often acts as a healer. And wherever demons manifest themselves, Jesus fights them.

But what contributes to the development of the story far more than anything else is the fact that a complication arises, caused by the reaction of the scribes and pharisees. Alarmed by what is generally said about Jesus, they decide to make sure themselves.

They find that he claims the right to say to people that their sins are forgiven, whereas they are of the opinion that he thereby arrogates to himself what is commonly believed to be the exclusive right of God. They themselves witness as well that he breaks the sabbath by curing someone with a negligible handicap, which induces them to consider measures to put a stop to his activity and liquidate him.

After this complication has been dealt with, the reader expects that the story will go on to relate the execution of these plans. But that is not the way it goes. In fact, the liquidation does not take place until much later, because besides telling the story, the narrator also wants to say something with it. Like many a story-teller, the narrator uses delaying tactics that keep the reader in suspense.

Additional Comments

The events recounted in the book are frequently accompanied by comments which the narrator puts into the mouth of an authoritative speaker within the story – usually Jesus – or which he adds himself in his own voice. Sometimes it is only a relatively unimportant addition. Words like 'for they were fishermen' in 1:16 are a case in point unless there is proof to the contrary. Sometimes such a comment is of the utmost importance because it underlines connections between certain themes, and thus reveals particular lines or tendencies in the story, or because it says how the narrator means the story to be understood.

Comments made by the narrator are fairly often found in summarizing passages or explanatory sentences, like the one just mentioned. Within the scope of this book we must confine ourselves to a few cases of greater importance. One of these is to be found at the end of 1:34: 'He would not let the demons speak, *because they knew who he was*'. In a manner typical of him, the narrator uses these words to pose the question why Jesus again and again enjoins secrecy on the evil spirits. We shall go more deeply into this in the next section, Speaking and Silence. One of the most remarkable comments from the narrator occurs in 2:10:

'But to convince you that the son of man has the right on earth to forgive sins – he turned to the paralysed man . . . ' In the same way as he will later interrupt a discourse by Jesus to address himself directly to the reader (13:14), the narrator interrupts the present story to point out how extremely significant it is for the reader to really understand that Jesus has the authority to forgive sins on earth.

Similar comments are also found in a number of Jesus' own sayings. Two cases in point are 1:15, which we have already discussed in the previous chapter, and 1:38, which, however, does not add much to the story itself. It is different with Jesus' words in 2:17: 'It is not the healthy that need a doctor, but the sick; I did not come to invite virtuous people, but sinners.' In the context of the book the last word should be taken to refer to people who are sinners in the eyes of scribes and pharisees, people therefore who do not live up to the Torah, including the observances regarding cleanliness, and so are considered ritually unclean. And since unclean people are, as it were, contagious, one certainly does not eat with them. That must be the reason why this saying of Jesus rounds off a scene which portrays Jesus as being at table with such people and why his behaviour provokes censure on the part of the pharisees. The saying does not mean that Jesus for his part excludes the virtuous and the healthy, the Jews that are faithful to the Law. What it does mean is that he feels especially called upon to help those who are regarded as law-breakers by scribes and pharisees, and who therefore no longer fully belong to the community.

Another comment put into the mouth of Jesus occurs within the framework of the controversy about fasting. To the question about why his disciples are not fasting, Jesus replies with the image of the bridegroom (2:19), and then continues: 'But the time will come when the bridegroom will be taken away from them, and on that day they will fast.' After the time of Jesus' presence, the time will come when his absence will be felt, sometimes most painfully. This is an implicit and subtle reference to Jesus' death, which can be understood only by readers who know of it. It is equally typical of the situation in which readers of the book find themselves. To this controversy about fasting, two sayings are added which are both derived from the daily household routine, the mending of an old garment and the keeping of wine in a bag of goatskin. Their common lesson is that the old and the new can no more be accommodated than traditional fasting and the presence of the kingdom in Jesus. The coming of the kingdom of God marks a break in the process of time, it is a kind of watershed between the old and the new. Because of this the tidings proclaimed by Jesus are good *news*.

The narrator has also appended a comment by Jesus to the dispute that follows after his disciples have been seen picking ears of corn on the sabbath: 'The sabbath was made for the sake of man and not man for the sabbath: therefore the son of man is sovereign even over the sabbath' (2:27-28). The first of these two sayings has a sort of parallel in a Jewish text (Mekhilta Exodus 31:13) that may be older than Mark: 'The sabbath has been given for your sake, you have not been given for the sake of the sabbath.' But the first rabbi to whom it is attributed, Rabbi Simon ben Menasha, relates it to situations in which someone is in danger of losing his life. The saying of Jesus, however, points back to the story of the creation. Everything that was made before the sixth day was made for the sake of man, who himself was made on the sixth day. On the seventh day God did not make anything; he rested and blessed that day and made it holy. But, says Jesus, the fact that the rest of the creation was made for man does not mean that man was made for the sake of the sabbath. The sabbath was made for the well-being of man, and this implies that people ought not to be the slaves of the sabbath regulations. To be generous to someone takes priority over keeping the sabbath. From this the second saying follows. The son of man Jesus, who is the soul of generosity, is more qualified than anyone else to weigh these priorities in a concrete situation, to let his disciples pick ears of corn on the sabbath so as to take the edge off their appetite, and to cure a man with a deformed arm on the sabbath, even though he could have lived with this handicap for another day.

These comments add something of an in-depth quality to the portrait of Jesus conveyed by the strictly narrative parts of the text.

Speaking and Silence

The appearance of Jesus is telling in more ways than one. To communicate his message he speaks in every conceivable way: he proclaims and reveals, discusses and instructs, commands and forbids, asks and replies, invites and appeals. But he also speaks through his presence and his actions, so that anyone who meets him can hardly continue on their way unaffected. As a result people speak about Jesus, and already after the first exorcism his fame spreads so fast that he is soon spoken of all over Galilee (1:28), and after a time is even unable to enter or stay in a town without being disturbed (1:45). As Jesus has a message for all Galilee, one would expect him to be happy about his growing popularity because it draws the people towards him, but this proves to be much more ambiguous than the reader realizes.

The very first time a demon says that he knows Jesus and loudly shouts who Jesus is, the latter commands him to be silent (1:25). Here the reader may still think that the only thing Jesus wants is to make him stop screaming, but as is almost immediately apparent, something far more serious is the matter. After the narrator has reported that Jesus casts out numerous evil spirits, he adds that Jesus 'would not let the demons speak, *because they knew who he was*' (1:34). From this one would conclude that the truth about Jesus is not, or not yet, to come to light, at least in that way. But after healing the leper Jesus also insists on silence. He not only urges him to show himself, as was prescribed by the law, to the priest who will make sure that he is cured, but also tells him not to tell anyone anything of what has happened (1:44). The story does not say why the man is not allowed to speak. Is it because Because has touched the leper and has consequently become a source of impurity himself, or perhaps even a danger of contagion for others? Be that as it may, the man exactly others? Be that as it may, the man does exactly the opposite and broadcasts everywhere that he has been cured, and by whom (1:45), with the result that Jesus no longer has any privacy. That the injunction to silence in these cases has a specific reason seems to be confirmed by the fact that elsewhere Jesus does not enjoin silence on people he has cured (e.g 2:1-12; 3:1-6). Only with regard to the demons does the story emphasize that they must

keep to themselves what they know about Jesus' identity: 'The
unclean spirits too, when they saw him, would fall at his feet and
cry aloud, "You are the son of God," but he insisted that they
should not make him known' (3:11-12).

It would seem, therefore, that what readers have known from
the first page of the book, namely that Jesus has been designated
by God as his son, is not to be made public, at least not through
what the demons say about him. For some reason there is
something the matter with Jesus' identity. Naturally the reader
has been made curious about the motive for this secrecy.

5

MUCH WHEAT FROM LITTLE SEED

4:1 – 34

Context and Structure

In contrast to the hurried movements of numerous characters and the quick succession of all sorts of events in the earlier parts of the book, this section is an oasis of peace and quiet. Absolutely nothing happens that directly or indirectly influences the course of the story. The narrator only amplifies Jesus's proclamation. The first sentences relate that Jesus has sat down – apparently alone (4:36) – in the small fishing-boat that at his request in 3:9 has been held in readiness to take him aboard in case the crowd thronging the shore pushes closer. This is the situation depicted at the beginning of the chapter.

After Jesus has told the first parable, the narrator breaks in by withdrawing Jesus, the twelve and other followers from the crowd. When they are alone, Jesus answers their questions about the nature and purpose of parabolic teaching and gives a detailed interpretation of the first parable. About the place and time of this interlude the reader is left in the dark. The story at any rate presumes that after the discourse Jesus is still – or again? –in the boat (4:35-36). Nor can we say with any certainty where this interlude ends. As the original Greek text has 'he said *to them*' both in 4:21 and 4:24, but does not repeat the last two words in 4:26 and 4:30, we had best assume that the narrator ends the interlude with 4:25, and that Jesus in 4:26 proceeds to tell more publicly the many parables by which, according to the final sentences of this section, he usually teaches the people. This may be corroborated by the fact that from 4:26 onwards Jesus returns again to the topic of fruit growing from seed committed to the earth, whereas the preceding verses 4:21-25 are rather about the contrast between dark and light, hiding and revealing. The following representation summarizes this argument:

in a boat
Jesus relates the parable of the seed
to the crowd on the shore

> *in a private interview*
> Jesus, when asked, explains
> the parable of the seed;
> and adds the saying about the lamp
> shedding light on what is in the dark,
> and about the generous measure
> accorded to those who apply
> generous measures themselves

Jesus proceeds with the parable
of the seed that grows by itself,
and the parable of the mustard seed

If this representation is correct, this chapter of parables can be divided as follows:
- *the narrator relates* that Jesus teaches many things by way of parables (4:1-2)
  - ⋆ *Jesus tells* the *first* parable of the seed (4:3-9)
    - ○ *Jesus explains* the parable of the seed to a small circle of followers (4:10-20) adding a few sayings (4:21-25)
  - ⋆ *Jesus tells* the *second* and the *third* parable of the seed (4:26-32)
- *the narrator concludes* that Jesus always taught by way of parables, but explained them to his disciples (4:33-34)

According to this division the chapter has roughly the same circular structure that is found in other parts of the book. And if the view is correct that in such a construction the emphasis lies on the middle part, we shall do well to take it into account when trying to understand the meaning of the chapter.

From Little to Much

Although people may differ about the answer to the question of what should be called a parable and what a parable story, I am of the opinion that the parable of the seed yielding much wheat is both a parable and a parable story, whereas the parables of the seed growing by itself and of the mustard seed are parables but not parable stories. For the sake of convenience I call the other comparisons occurring in this chapter metaphors.

The three parables have much in common. They all relate to agriculture or horticulture and, within this field, to a limited range of activities and processes, specifically the sowing, the germination of the seed and the growth of the seedling into a full-grown plant or shrub, and the reaping of the corn. The nature of the plants is also limited, since they are without exception plants producing food. And the three parables roughly coincide also in their teaching, which could be summarized as follows: things turn out well even when they threaten to go wrong or are beyond control.

The first and the second parable are further connected in that each not only refers to the production of grain but also stresses that, owing to some negative factors, the prospects for that production seem far from certain. In the case of the first parable it is the poor quality of the soil which causes much of the seed to go to waste; and in the case of the second the inability of the farmer to exert any influence on the processes of germination and growth.

The first and the third parable are also connected, because, in both, very little seed is enormously productive. In the first parable the little seed that has fallen into good soil brings forth an abundant crop, and in the third the smallest of seeds grows into the largest of shrubs. Thus the transition from little to much and from small to large forms the central theme in both. A similar theme is present in the second parable: a seed is always small, but it is natural for each tiny seed to develop into an organic and complicated being, which in its turn produces a great quantity of seed.

God's Kingdom

Parables are not told to inform listeners and readers on matters of agriculture and the farmer's fortunes and anxieties. Rather, things which everyone already knows and observes in the world of their own experience are told in order to facilitate the understanding and illuminate the meaning of something else. This is exactly what the narrator says in 4:33.

The specific purpose of the second and third parables is stated explicitly: to elucidate the kingdom of God (4:26 and 4:30). However small and modest it may seem in its beginning, the kingdom of God pushes through and grows irresistibly, like the seed the farmer has sown on his land. This notion may have been so self-evident to Jesus' Jewish listeners that it was superfluous to tell them a parable about it. But after Jesus had been put to death on a cross it was far from evident to his followers. The same applies to followers of Jesus in the days of the composition of Mark, when Christians in several places had suffered persecution or were living in fear of persecution. Just as the farmer is scarcely able to keep himself from wondering why there is no sign of life yet on his land, so those early Christians could not help wondering whether God's kingdom would ever come. It rather looked as though the ungodly powers still had the upper hand.

The other parable dealing explicitly with the kingdom of God is the parable of the mustard seed. Although it is the smallest of all seeds, the mustard seed can in fact produce shrubs with branches that are ten feet in length. The main point of the parable is the contrast between the insignificance of the tiny seed and the size of the shrub – which is so large that birds can settle in its shade. Whether readers are also meant to think of the limited scope of Jesus' work, or rather, what seemed to remain of it after his death, it is difficult to say. In all probability the narrator supposes the listeners on the shore of the lake will have thought of the modest scope of Jesus' work. Galilee was after all only a very small and insignificant part even of the then known world. But from the special emphasis the author lays on Jesus' success at this very point in the book, we may infer that his intended readers were expected to think of what remained of Jesus' work after his death. Living in a metropolis like Rome, Alexandria, or Antioch in Syria, they clearly knew from experience that they were only a negligible minority. But what the parable promises is something else: the birds flocking to find shelter in the shade of the tree are reminiscent of First Testament passages like Daniel 4:9-18, and Ezekiel 17:23 and 31:6, calling to mind the different peoples whose territories will come under the protection and rule of the kingdom of God.

We may rightly wonder whether the parable about the seed of which much is lost, and which nevertheless yields an excellent crop, is to be interpreted along similar lines. As a matter of fact, one of the answers Jesus gives to the question about what he may have meant by it does affirm that this parable also refers to the kingdom of God. But the reader will have noticed that the people on the shore of the lake are not given any clue to the application of the parable. Various interpretations present themselves, as is often the case with parables and metaphors. Some people who read the parable are struck by the fact that the sower scatters the seed about so carelessly: no wonder that much of it gets lost! We should, however, realize that it was customary in Palestine at the time to sow the seed before the field was ploughed. So it is natural that in the parable part of the seed should fall along the path that serves as a short-cut across the field, part in the places where only a thin layer of soil covers the stony ground, and part among the thistles to be ploughed up afterwards. But what the story appears to insist on is the contrast between – on the one hand – the large quantity of seed that bears no fruit and the small quantity that does bear some, and – on the other hand – the small quantity of seed that is productive and the abundance of crop eventually produced.

It has been objected that the parable does not say in so many words that quite a lot of seed is lost. This may be so, but it is unmistakable that the parable intends to give the impression that while three-quarters is wasted, one-quarter bears fruit. Some commentators sharing this view feel that the parable is fatalistic since it represents the loss of seed as the inevitable result of the poor character of the soil, which man is powerless to alter. But such a deterministic belief is quite alien to the parable, and incompatible with its main intention. Besides, the hard-trodden ground of the footpath can be broken up again, and it should not be too difficult to cover the stony ground with good soil and uproot the thistles. But all this is really beside the point, for even if nothing of this kind is done to improve the soil, the parable guarantees that a good harvest will be reaped. Applied to the coming of the kingdom of God, then, the parable might mean that despite much obstruction and many things going wrong, the kingdom of God is bound to come. As readers, however, we had better remember that in Mark the listeners on the shore are kept in complete ignorance of the application of the parable.

The interpretation of the parable *is* made known presently, but only to the twelve and some others as soon as they are alone with Jesus. As readers are intended to overhear this private interview, they are in a special position. For although they do not know how Jesus may have meant the parable to be applied by the hearers on the shore, or whether they have understood it or not, the readers now come to learn what Jesus answers his disciples when they question him about the meaning of the parables. They suddenly begin to realize that the parables may have more than one meaning, a possibility also indicated by the narrator, who closes the parable discourse with the observation that while Jesus told the people parables in order to make them understand what he had to say, he provided his disciples with another or perhaps fuller interpretation when he was alone with them (4:33-34).

The Interpretation

So there is every reason to have a close look at such an interpretation: for example, the one offered of the parable of the seed (4:14-20). The various elements of the parable story reappear in the same order in Jesus' interpretation: the path, the rocky places, the thorns, and finally the good soil. The interpretation is given in a simple and direct way. Each sentence begins somewhat clumsily with the words 'these are . . .' or 'the others are . . .', mostly rendered less clumsily in English translations. This way of explaining things is typical of the book, which uses a similar phrase, 'that is . . .', to introduce explanations of terms supposedly unknown to readers (see e.g. 3:17 and 7:11).

Turning to the interpretation proper, we find that it is based on a double metaphor in which two mutually dependent elements from agriculture – the seed and the soil – are identified with two equally interrelated elements from the communication process – the message or the word and the person to whom it is addressed. The seed is equivalent to the message, the different conditions of the soil to the various ways of listening to it.

The first metaphor is clearly stated but formulated differently from the four metaphors following it. The opening sentence 'the sower sows the word' seems to introduce the metaphors that present the lessons intended by the interpreter. In other words, the basic seed-word metaphor is put first as a foundation for the following, more fully elaborated, metaphors. On the face of it, 'the message' or 'the word' (Greek *logos*), seems to be quite a broad term to use. However, it is most likely meant to refer primarily to the good news proclaimed by Jesus. This may be inferred, firstly, from the fact that in the previous part of the book Jesus is said to proclaim the message (2:2), which in Mark is an expression pregnant with meaning, and, secondly, from the repetition of the same phrase by the narrator at the end of this chapter, which deals with the parables under consideration (4:33). In addition, 'the word' is the technical word in a great number of places in the Second Testament for the Christian message.

Not stated, but positively at work in and and underlying the other metaphors, is the second basic metaphor, the equation of the field or the soil with people's inner selves where words are heard and understood, or to be more precise, the different conditions of the various parts of the soil and the different attitudes of those receiving the word.

From these two basic metaphors, then, the interpreter embarks on the four comparisons that are going to explain the application of the parable. The way in which they are expressed, however, is in some respects rather confusing. In the first (4:15), the initial seed-word metaphor is still used, but in the following three the hearers instead of the word have become the term of comparison. In other places the two elements compared – the spoken word and the scattered seed – have been mixed up. The interpreter speaks, for example, of the sown word that bears no fruit and of people that bear fruit. Yet the intention of the interpretation is clear. Just as in the parable itself, the effect of the word depends both on the extent to which people are prepared to listen and on the external factors that influence them, such as Satan, persecution and riches, the main emphasis here, it seems to me, lies on the different degrees of willingness to listen. This willingness appears to be distinctly graded, whereas there is no clear evidence of such gradation in the case of the external factors. The gradation is as follows:

1. Listen in such a way that what is heard one moment is forgotten the next (4:15)
2. Listen in such a way that what is heard is taken to heart immediately with good will, but without that will being able to withstand persecutions (4:16- 17)
3. Listen in such a way that what is heard is really taken to heart, but does not last once more attractive alternatives present themselves (4:18-20)
4. Listen in such a way that what is heard continues to have a lasting influence on one's conduct (4:20).

That the point at issue is really this difference in degrees of listening is confirmed by the saying closing the interlude: 'Take note of what you hear; the measure you give is the measure you will receive, with something more besides. For the man who has will be given more and the man who has not will forfeit even what he has' (4:24-25). This pronouncement, sometimes wrongly interpreted, does not refer to what material things people possess, but to the extent of their willingness to listen and respond to the good news. The measure of one's listening determines how much one understands of what has been said. Those who listen with their hearts will receive understanding, but those who do not will eventually stop listening altogether. That there is an extra gift refers, as will become clear later, to an understanding which surpasses ordinary understanding.

So it is clear that the first parable, unlike the other two, does not deal with the kingdom of God but with what passes between the speaker and his audience, and with the aspect of listening in particular. Hence the admonitions 'listen' before the parable (4:3) and 'if you have ears to hear' after it (4:9), which in this case have quite a specific meaning. The parable and its interpretation are in a sense the continuation of what began on the first page of Mark. There, in the opening scene, narrator and readers were placed alongside the main character, Jesus; here readers are, as it were, given the opportunity to listen attentively to what is said in and through the story. Seen in the light of its interpretation in 4:14–20, the parable is not meant to comfort preachers or other speakers who meet with little or no response. It is intended, rather, to call for attentive listening, and to point out that there are several degrees of attentiveness.

Finally, attention must be called to a peculiar fact, namely that something is missing from the interpretation. Anyone who puts parable and interpretation side by side and carefully compares the components of each from beginning to end will find that one of the elements has been left unexplained. As it is precisely the character that sets everything in motion, the omission – if we can call it that – is all the more remarkable. If the reader still does not know who is meant, then it will be best to stop reading for a moment and have another look at 4:14–20. There is no mistake about it, the character left undiscussed is the sower himself. Calling attention to this in 1974 Louis Marin, a French specialist in semiotics (the branch of linguistics that deals with the meaning of signs and symbols), argued that such an omission implies automatically that the sower is the teller and interpreter of the parable – Jesus himself. Even more than the proclamation of others, his proclamation is like the sowing of seed, much of which is lost but which nevertheless yields a rich harvest.

Light from the First Testament

Already in the First Testament seed had been used as a metaphor to represent the word of God, as in Isaiah 55:10-11:

As the rain and the snow come down from the heavens
and do not return without watering the earth,
making it yield and giving growth
to provide seed for the sower and bread for the eater,
so the word of my mouth
does not return to me empty,
without carrying out my will
and succeeding in what it was sent to do.

Considered in the light of this, the parable story sounds less artificial than when it is read by itself. But what is more important, the verses from Isaiah may help us to understand more fully what certain elements in the parable mean. There is first of all the intention of the parable. The quotation makes it clear that the parable also refers, at least partly, to the positive effect which the word of the proclamation has on many people, in spite of all appearances to the contrary. Perhaps it is also important that according to the quotation from Isaiah the earth provides seed for the sower. This suggests that there may be a connection between the two parables about seed in this chapter. To put it simply, the seed produced in the first parable is sown again by the farmer in the second. But the significance of Isaiah's words goes beyond this chapter; for apart from providing the seed required for next year's sowing, the crop is used for baking bread for those who need to eat. That is the real and ultimate purpose of sowing. The reader who has learned this from Isaiah is ready to follow Mark when he brings up the subject of eating bread later – and will then remember that there is an inner connection between seed, wheat and bread.

Secret and Riddles

The interpretation of the parable of the seed is preceded and followed by a number of pronouncements in which remarkable things are being said. In reply to the request for an explanation Jesus says: 'To you the secret of the kingdom of God has been given, but to the outsiders everything comes in riddles, so that *they may look and look but see nothing, hear and hear but understand nothing; otherwise they might turn to God and be forgiven.*' The words in italics are a quotation from Isaiah 6:9-10, the use of which here has caused much discussion. The problem was that interpreters felt that the original Greek did not allow translation in any other way that avoided stating that Jesus used parables to prevent people turning to God. It is perhaps due to their preoccupation with this difficult saying that interpreters have paid far less attention to other peculiarities.

So far as I know, it has gone unnoticed that it is highly unusual for the noun 'secret' to be direct object to the verb 'give'. Investigation shows that the combination of these two words does not occur anywhere else in the First and Second Testaments. In the intertestamentary literature I have found only one comparable passage. It is in the apocryphal book of Henoch (circa 100 B.C.):

And after that my grandfather Henoch gave me the teaching of all the secrets in the book of all the parables which had been given to him, and put them together for me in the words of the book of the parables
(Henoch 68:1; Charles, *Apocrypha* II (1913) 232).

If the peculiarity of this combination is overlooked, one commonly interprets Mark as if he said 'to you the secret has been revealed', thereby introducing a stereotyped expression with a quite different meaning. I am convinced that the expression in Mark means what it says, namely that those who are addressed by Jesus here have definitely been given a secret but do not know its content. As with a document enclosed in an envelope, they know that the secret exists, but not what it contains. Are they for this reason in a better position than the outsiders, who are unaware of the existence of a secret? Most certainly! To the outsiders everything comes in riddles, nothing is comprehensible. They do not even know that there is a key to the riddles. But those who have been given a secret know at least that there is a secret and that there are riddles (4:11). And riddles, they know, can be understood if one is in the possession of the key. For the time

being they hear only that the secret refers to the kingdom of God.
A key is not yet provided.

The Secret and the Reader

It is obvious that readers too are now put in a new position.
Having already been confronted with the possibility of different
degrees of listening and understanding, they now have to
consider that there are secret meanings as well, and even that the
parable may contain a riddle needing a solution. In consequence
of what they have read on the first page of Mark, the readers may
know more than the people addressed by Jesus, but it would be an
illusion to think that they know everything there is to know.

There is, however, no reason to suppose that the riddle will
never be solved. On the contrary. That is what the two sayings
that round off the interpretation of the parable in 4:21-22 are
about. 'Does the lamp come in to be put under the bushel or under
the bed? Does it not come in to be put on the lampstand?' It is
worth noticing that the lamp is personified. Readers cannot help
thinking of a person who enlightens them by interpreting a
mysterious narrative and who – through his way of life – sheds
light upon his words. However that may be, when it is dark and
one has a lamp, one is not meant to remain in the dark. What the
first saying expresses by means of a metaphor, the second says in
plain language: 'Nothing is hidden unless it is to be disclosed, and
nothing put under cover unless it is to come into the open.' If
there are a secret and a riddle, there is also the challenge to reveal
the secret and decode the riddle, and we may depend on it that the
disclosure will take place.

It may perhaps seem that by discussing this secret we have
wandered from the parables that speak of what happens during
and after sowing. In fact, the seed ploughed into the soil is
eminently suited to stand for something invisible that is to
become visible, for the secret that is to be disclosed. As long as the
seed is underground it is hidden like a secret of which we know
the existence but not the content. And the appearance of the first
seedlings, their growth into corn or shrubs, the flowering of

plants and the ripe crop of grain or fruit, draw out the same metaphor to illustrate how a secret gradually unfolds as the story goes on and how certain one may be of its ultimate disclosure.

In this context we must consider one more question. Is it possible that the secret discussed in this chapter is somehow related to the secrecy which in the previous part of the book is imposed by Jesus on the cured leper and the demons who know his identity and for that very reason must keep silent? On this question authors differ widely. The answer really supposes that we know what the secret mentioned in 4:11 refers to. If it equally bears on Jesus' identity, then there must be a connection between the two. But since the content of the secret is still obscure, we shall have to postpone answering this question until we come to know more.

The Outsiders

The outsiders referred to in 4:11-12 have to make do with unsolved riddles, and as they do not see and understand anything, they will neither repent nor will their sins be forgiven. It is evident that those addressed by Jesus during the interlude can be regarded as insiders, but it is far from clear who the outsiders are. Quite a few commentators tend to identify the opposition of inside versus outside with the opposition between the Christian congregation and 'the Jews', or 'the old Israel', or whatever they may be called. It is most urgent that the truth of this interpretation should be put to the test.

The simple fact that the twelve were undoubtedly Jews makes it clear how strange and incomprehensible it is to identify the outsiders with 'the Jews' as a whole. To be sure, at least some of the twelve came from Galilee which, because of its mixed population who had lived there for centuries, was looked on with suspicion by Judaean Jews. If, however, there had been a non-Jew in Jesus' company, the pharisees would certainly have pounced on it, but of this there is no evidence whatever in the tradition. So those placed over against the outsiders are – like Jesus – Jews themselves, which shows that one cannot generalize and speak of 'the Jews'. But it would also be too simple to say that the twelve (unlike the outsiders), as representatives of the insiders, not only look and hear but also see and understand. For it is to them that the equally harsh words from Jeremiah 5:21 are applied in Mark 8:17-21: 'You have eyes: can you not see? You have ears: can you not hear?' The reader should always be cautious of oversimplistic notions and identifications.

To support the view that those who are outside could or even should be equated with the Jews, one sometimes appeals to the words from Isaiah quoted in 4:12. They are harsh words indeed. JHWH himself has hardened the heart of his people! Nevertheless, we should realize that neither here nor elsewhere is this the last word. True, we read in Isaiah 6 that the whole land will be laid waste except for one tenth part of it, and that even this will be destroyed so that only one tree-stump remains. But this stock is at the same time a holy seed, and therefore contains the promise of new life (Isaiah 6:13). Where the First Testament speaks of the hardening of Israel, its aim is not to leave Israel for ever to its own fate, but rather to describe its mentality and to remind the prophets of the difficulty of their task (see also, for example, Ezekiel 3:4-9 and Amos 4:6-12).

As further confirmation for the identification of outsiders and Jews one refers to Mark 7:6, which, it is maintained, obviously quotes Isaiah 29:13 with the intention of denouncing the people of Israel: '*This people* pays me lip-service, but their heart is far from me.' But it is perfectly clear from the context that this citation in the quoted words of Jesus is applied exclusively to the pharisees and scribes, and not to 'the Jews'.

It remains to point out that in order to establish the identity of the outsiders, we should not go beyond Mark. If 'outsiders' must be assigned in the book, it would be first of all those who have shut themselves out, like the pharisees and scribes, and those who refuse to enter where Jesus is, like his own relatives. But it is perhaps even more sensible to confine the opposition between insiders and outsiders implied by this chapter to the characters that appear in it. Within the framework of this chapter, then, the outsiders are people who do not want to listen to the word of Jesus or are unwilling to live up to it, while the insiders are those who ask Jesus for an explanation.

One Parable and all the Parables

One final point that needs to be raised concerns the sentence before the interpretation of the parable of the seed, where Jesus says: 'Do you not understand this parable? How then are you to understand all the parables?' (4:13). Two things are, I think, clear. The first is that this parable provides the key to the understanding of all the parables. This is at least true to the extent that the parable in the given interpretation refers to the listening and understanding themselves. If what we have said above is correct, that the reader is put in the picture on the first page of Mark but is only here equipped with the competence he or she needs for real understanding, then this naturally applies to the understanding of the first and of every parable. But there cannot be a complete understanding, for there is still a secret to be disclosed. And it might well be possible that even the first parable is only completely understood by someone who understands the secret or has solved the riddle.

Secondly, Jesus' question in 4:13 creates the impression that perhaps all the parables must have been told before any parable, including the first, can be understood entirely. Accordingly, it would seem that the parables form a coherent whole, of which the different parts illuminate each other. If this is so, we shall have to be patient until the last parable, the parable of the vineyard (12:1-12) has also been told.

The Parable Section as Commentary

Although it does not contribute to the actual development of the story about Jesus, this parable section is nevertheless of the utmost importance. In the earlier part of the book the narrator has shown Jesus' commanding authority among those who listen to his words and witness his deeds. Impressed by this, the reader too cannot but recognize that Jesus deservedly has great authority. What the narrator has Jesus tell and say in this chapter derives from that authority, and so the reader is prepared to let himself be guided in the understanding of the book by the authoritative commentary of Jesus. In the parables of the seed growing by itself and the mustard seed, the commentary explains what the ministry of Jesus means for the coming of the kingdom of God (4:26-32). But it also teaches readers what requirements they must meet in order to come to the real understanding of Jesus' message and possibly of the book itself. It makes clear to them that there are different levels of understanding, and finally points out that if through listening they join the set of people belonging to Jesus, a secret will be confided to them which is to be disclosed later. Whether this is going to take place within the book is an exciting question that cannot be answered yet.

6

GREATER SIGNS, GROWING MISUNDERSTANDING

4:35 – 8:21

Extent and Context

Of no other section of Mark have I so much hesitated to define the limits as this one. One of the reasons is probably the uninviting prospect of having to deal with such a long section in one chapter. For the reasons I gave in chapter 2, and for the following considerations, I have nevertheless decided to discuss it as a whole. Admittedly, the subsection traditionally called 'the section of the loaves' (6:30-8:21) has its own theme and could therefore be treated separately. One would thereby achieve a greater balance in the length of the sections, but on the other hand do injustice to the larger thematic whole which, summarized in the title of this chapter, opens with the storm on the lake and reaches its climax in the bitter reproaches in 8:17-21.

The unity of this section is corroborated by its position within the overall structure of the book. In the section before the parable discourse the narrator has not only introduced readers to Jesus' helpers and adversaries, but also dealt so extensively with the conflict between Jesus and the adversaries that with the latter planning his downfall, the first of the two plots of the story is already drawing to a close. If no time were needed for these plans to materialize, the narrator might have gone on after 3:6, and certainly after 3:30, to tell the story of Jesus' arrest. In the parable section there is already a premonition of a second complication, which is not related to the adversaries but to Jesus' supporters.

Although they have been given the secret of the kingdom of God, they are apparently unable to understand the parable. The present section, then, is largely devoted to this second plot: however well-intentioned they are, Jesus' supporters completely lack the insight expected of them. While the first plot is about what will happen to Jesus, the second relates to what the disciples make of this.

Broad Outline of Events

After the quiet on the lake shore the reader is carried again from event to event at a rate which, as in the first part, is marked by the frequent use of the adverb 'immediately' (Greek *euthus*). In the boat where he has already been sitting, Jesus crosses over with his disciples to the other side of the like. On the way there he calms the storm and prevents their boat from being shipwrecked. He lands in the country of the Gerasenes, where he frees a man from the power of a legion of demons by sending them into a herd of pigs that throw themselves into the lake and are drowned. The Gerasenes will have none of this and implore Jesus to leave their territory. As Jesus is getting into the boat, the cured demoniac wants to go with him, but Jesus orders him to go home and tell his people what has happened to him. After his return to the western shore Jesus heals a woman who has suffered from haemorrhages for twelve years, and tells a girl whom the bystanders believe dead to get up from her bed. Paying a visit to his home town, Nazareth, he encounters only distrust and unbelief, and is rejected. Then he sends the twelve out two by two in order to proclaim his good news, cast out demons and cure the sick. Meanwhile Herod has heard about him and thinks that Jesus is the baptist, whom he has had beheaded. This induces the narrator to tell us in a flashback why and how John was executed.

When the twelve return they are followed by a large crowd of people. As they have nothing to eat and it is impossible to buy anything for them on the spot, Jesus gives five loaves and two fishes to his disciples to distribute among them. The hunger of everyone in the crowd – the men alone number five thousand – is satisfied, and twelve basketfuls of fragments are collected. After this Jesus sends his disciples to the opposite shore while he himself stays behind. But they are wind-bound and cannot make any headway beyond the middle of the lake. Jesus wishes to join them in the night, and when they see him walking on the lake, they think it is a ghost and are terrified. No sooner has he got into the boat than the wind drops just as on the first occasion. When Jesus disembarks at Gennesaret the people recognize him and, as usual, bring the sick, who are cured by touching him. Pharisees and scribes start a debate on the observances connected with ritual cleanliness, and Jesus' reply causes his disciples to question him again about the meaning of what he says. Next, on his journey to Tyre and Sidon, Jesus argues with a pagan woman whose daughter is suffering from demon possession, but complies with her request to deliver the girl from her tormentor. On his return journey Jesus cures a deaf-mute in the Decapolis region. Then a second story of miraculous feeding follows, now with seven loaves for four thousand people and a remainder of seven baskets of fragments. After a short trip on the lake, Jesus disembarks again and resolutely refuses to give the pharisees the sign from heaven they demand. Once more he re-embarks, but the fact that his disciples have forgotten to take bread leads to a somewhat obscure conversation which Jesus ends by reproaching them bitterly for not yet understanding what has happened with the loaves.

Greater Signs

At first sight it may seem that these events merely continue what has already been related in the section of Mark before the parables. This impression is deceptive, however. What is related here is not more of the same, but more in far greater dimensions, for practically all the events in this section surpass the earlier ones both in scale and range. In the first two Jesus operates on the lake shore, but although he has already gone aboard the ship before telling the parables, it is only now that he actually puts to sea, three times in fact. So far he has stayed and worked on one side of the lake, the side which is characterized by the presence of synagogues; now he also goes to the other side, into Gentile territory, thereby considerably extending his range of action. There too he casts out demons, and cures all those who appeal to him for help. Up till now the demons have been individual cases; now Jesus casts our and destroys an entire army of them. And the cures show a climax. The woman who is cured of haemorrhages has been ill for twelve years and has spent her whole fortune on a succession of doctors whose treatments have failed to improve her condition. In stark contrast to this, she is healed by merely touching Jesus' clothes. The little girl of twelve is not just cured of her illness: Jesus snatches her from death. Up till now Jesus has only been rejected by the scribes, pharisees and his next of kin; now a whole town, Nazareth, turns away from him, and a whole region lets him know that they will have none of him. In the previous section Jesus selected and appointed his helpers; now he also sends them out to do what so far he has only done himself. Readers know already that the baptist has been arrested; now they learn that he has been beheaded meanwhile and that his murderer thinks that Jesus is really none other than his victim come to life again. There is also a marked difference in the nature and scope of the signs worked by Jesus. He controls the forces of nature – wind and water – as well as demons and illnesses. And the miraculous feedings are events of unprecedented magnitude, the second of which is probably attended by Gentiles who 'have come from afar'.

One would expect greater signs to cause greater under-standing, but this is definitely not so with Jesus' followers. On the contrary. Already, in the first story, Jesus is asking how it is possible that they still have no faith (4:40). It is moreover extremely ironical that the disciples, having already witnessed one miraculous feeding, should ask on a similar occasion where one can get bread for so many people (8:4)! Nor is this quite all. The fact that they get on the boat again after the second feeding without taking bread with them sustains that irony, as does their misinterpreting Jesus' remark about the leaven of the pharisees and of Herod (8:15-17). And it is perhaps even more ironical that Jesus confronts them with a quotation from the First Testament which has the same message as the one applied in 4:12 to the outsiders who understand nothing and to whom everything comes by way of riddles (8:18). So of Jesus' disciples one may truly say: the greater the signs, the greater their misunderstanding.

Places

The restlessness with which Jesus wanders from place to place in the section before the parable discourse is, if possible, even more striking in this part of the book. We hear no more of a base in Capernaum. A quiet place to retire to is sought twice (6:31 and 46) but found only once (6:46). Although Jesus has been represented more than once before this as travelling throughout Galilee, one gets the impression that the journeys in this part of the gospel are not only more numerous, but also of a different character.

The Boat

Now that they travel by boat, Jesus and his disciples cross the lake several times. Three times a story is told about an incident that occurs during the crossing. And it is certainly not irrelevant that these three stories are closely related. On each occasion something goes wrong, either through a storm, an adverse wind, or through lack of bread. Thus the boat seems to fail first as a shelter from the dangers of the water, then as a means of transport, and finally as a place where people are supposed to meet and understand each other. In the first story the people on board are Jesus and his disciples (4:35-36), in the second, at first only the disciples (6:45-46), and in the third Jesus and his disciples again (8:10). In each of the stories the dramatic focus is upon a very serious breakdown in communication between them, earning the disciples bitter reproaches either from Jesus or the narrator. These moments of crisis in the narrative are related to the critical circumstances in which they occur.

In the boat Jesus is alone with his disciples. In this respect the boat resembles the house where Jesus and his disciples seek refuge from the multitude. But in another respect the boat is the opposite of a house. It is not a place to stay, but a means of travel. Since it must be mobile, a boat is lighter, more fragile, and therefore more vulnerable and less safe than a house of the same size. Its vulnerability is also greater than that of a vehicle, because a boat must carry its passengers safely over the water as well as protect them against it when the wind works up into a gale. The extent to which the disciples are at the mercy of the wind is clearly expressed in the first two stories. In the first their lives are put in jeopardy by a storm; in the second there is such a strong headwind that they cannot make way and need help.

The Opposite Shore

Another new place is the opposite shore of the lake. In fact it is more exact to speak of several opposite shores, although their situation and relation to one another are not always clear. With a lake that is more triangular than circular, the narrator may have the boat sail from any particular point to various opposite shores. Now that the narrator has Jesus and his disciples in the boat, they use it again and again. First for a trip to the country of the Gerasenes and back (4:35; 5:1; 5:21); later in a vain attempt to find a spot without crowds (6:32-34); then, after the first feeding, there is a strange voyage to Bethsaida which ends at Gennesaret (6:45-53); finally, after the second feeding, there is yet another complicated crossing, which brings Jesus and his disciples, after an intermezzo in the region of Dalmanutha (8:10) – a name otherwise fully unknown – eventually to Bethsaida (8:22). With the exception of the first, and perhaps the unknown Dalmanutha, these various shores across the lake are as positive and friendly as the shore where the narrator has Jesus make his first appearance. This is illustrated by the only summary to be found in this section of the book (6:54-56).

It is entirely different in the case of the first place on the other side visited by Jesus, 'the country of the Gerasenes' (5:1), where, according to 5:2, he disembarks alone after crossing the lake in the company of his disciples. The country of the Gerasenes does not lie only geographically opposite the shore where Jesus has been active so far. it is quite different in nearly everything. The pigs reported to be living there indicate the Gentile setting of the story. The scene is laid in barren surroundings, a wasteland of rocks, caves and tombs. The shore seems to be uninhabited, and is therefore, to put it paradoxically, a demons' paradise. Apart from some swineherds there is no one but a man suffering from paranoia, who appears to be in the power of a legion of demons. Like the other demoniacs mentioned in the book he wanders about free, but is said to have been chained up for a time, evidently because he was a danger to himself and others. The reader may see this as an indication of the power demons have in pagan surroundings, and perhaps also of the heartless – pagan? – way in which people on this side of the lake deal with their fellow-men. The struggle between Jesus and the demons leads to negotiations smacking of the absurd. The demons, who are somehow bound to the district, manage to wrest the concession from Jesus that although they must leave the man, they need not leave the district. But this move is only half the battle, because it looks as if the concession has been a kind of stratagem to occasion their destruction.

What happens next is quite the opposite of what the reader has so far been used to. The swineherds take to their heels and report what has happened to the demoniac and what has become of the pigs. And when the people living nearby come and see the man sitting there clothed and in his right mind, they implore Jesus to leave the district. But as the action proceeds a few more contrasts become obvious. While the reader is used to stories about people who are asked by *Jesus* to join him, in this story it is the *man* who asks Jesus if he may go with him. The fact that Jesus turns down his request, sending him home instead, is equally contrary to expectation. And while elsewhere in the book Jesus normally demands secrecy about such events, he does exactly the opposite here; for he instructs the man to make known everywhere what the Lord in his mercy has done for him, with the result that everyone in the Decapolis region is amazed.

With the Decapolis, or the territory of the Ten Towns, we have come to a more extensive pagan region. That is not the only time. In the earlier section of the book Jesus does not travel beyond Galilee. The people living in the regions around Galilee (listed in 3:7-8 as Judaea with the capital Jerusalem, Idumaea, Transjordan, and the neighbourhood of Tyre and Sidon) come to see him, but Jesus does not pay a visit to their territory. In this section, however, Jesus' ministry also extends to the area around Galilee. After visiting the land of the Gerasenes he goes to the territory of Tyre and Sidon (7:24), and from there to the Decapolis (7:31). A lot of ink has been spilt on the itinerary mentioned in 7:31 from Tyre by way of Sidon to the Sea of Galilee through the territory of the Decapolis, as the last bit does not square with what is to be found on maps. But the reader should realize that people in those days used to have geographical representations different from our own, and that it is open to question whether the narrator's topographical knowledge of the places in his book accorded with the facts. The first part of the route is also surprising. Sidon lies to the north of Tyre, so that the journey as it is described in 7:31 follows quite a devious route. But in this case there is no cause for surprise, considering that the First Testament, where the two towns are frequently bracketed together, always has them in the order of Tyre and Sidon, and never the other way round. Why Jesus travels to these parts the text does not say, but the narrator reports that Jesus performs a cure by special request in both regions, after initially objecting to the first precisely because it is requested in a pagan country (7:27). The ensuing game of question and answer between Jesus and the Syrophoenician woman is on the same theme of the position of the Gentiles. It is undoubtedly significant that this theme is in a conversation related to the two feedings, and we will have to elaborate on it later.

The Home Town

As 6:54-56 is a summary rather than a story, the only detailed story set in one particular town or village in this section of the book is that about Jesus' visit to his home town (6:1-6). The town is not mentioned by name, but the reader remembers from the

first page that it is Nazareth. It strikes the reader that Jesus goes to
his home town only relatively late in the book. It seems to me that
this is because readers should have heard that Jesus' fame has
reached Nazareth prior to his visit, and that the inhabitants for
their part should have heard what is being said about the wisdom
of Jesus and the mighty acts he does everywhere (6:2). Among all
the spatial and geographical representations called up by the
book, the two towns Nazareth and Capernaum are clearly one
another's counterparts. In both places Jesus visits and teaches in
the synagogue on the sabbath. In Capernaum Jesus meets with
approval and success because his teaching is immediately
recognized as that of a man of exceptional authority, and his
authority is borne out by the expulsion of a demon. In Nazareth
Jesus is rejected. His compatriots do not find that his word or
person are in any sense exceptional. Quite the contrary. Their
ironical questions show that, in their eyes, his wisdom is all sham
and his miracles just a bag of tricks. Is he not one of them, the son
of the carpenter and his wife? They know his brothers and sisters
by name. Their sarcastic questions sound familiar to Jesus: that is
the way it goes with prophets! Because of their attitude he is not
able to reveal to them, as he could in Capernaum, what powers lie
hidden in him. The only thing he can do is cure a few sick people
by laying his hands upon them, which to the narrator is clearly
something of a lower order, like exorcizing someone. It goes
without saying that the episode about Nazareth is also very
important with respect to the issue of Jesus' identity, which will
be extensively discussed later. All in all, Nazareth could be
described as Jesus' Galilean Jerusalem, a place fraught with
opposition based on supposed knowledge.

Time and Sequence

There are in this section, as in the previous ones, only a few
indications of time. Again mention is made of the sabbath (6:2),
but only, it seems, to provide a background for the teaching in the
synagogue, which in Mark is tied to the sabbath. The first two
stories about the crossing of the lake are set in the dark of the

evening or the night (4:35 and 6:47-48), while the third has to make do without a reference of time. This difference is understandable, for in the first two stories the problems that arise are due to circumstances outside the boat, whereas in the third they are due to the confusion of those on board.

The sequence within this part is perhaps a little arbitrary. In particular, the order in which the various cures are related does not seem to be necessitated by the structure of the story. The same applies to the passage containing the account of the different opinions about the identity of Jesus and the story about the execution of the baptist, both of which might have been placed just as well at another point. To some extent they seem to fill the time between the five events that together determine the chronological order in the section, namely, the three crossings and the two intermediate feedings.

Compared with those in the previous sections, the cures recounted here are more impressive, and as such they represent the first term of the thematic opposition expressed by the title I have given this chapter, the 'greater signs', while the crossings reveal the second, the 'growing misunderstanding'. The accounts of the feedings mark the point of intersection of the two themes. To the unsuspecting crowds, who feast on bread and fish without perhaps knowing, or even guessing, where they came from, it is probably no more than a merry mass meal in the open air. But readers know better, and the disciples ought to know better. In fact, what Jesus does here is an unparalleled sign, if not in kind then in size, which in both cases is stressed by the narrator stating explicitly the number both of those partaking of the meal and the baskets of leftovers; moreover, it is a sign that on account of its material aspects – well-lined bellies and residual superabundance – stays very close to everyday reality.

Jesus' Helpers

In some sections of this chapter Jesus' followers do not play any part at all, or just a walk-on part, while in other places they clearly play the lead. Although appointed by Jesus before this (3:14-15), it is only now that the disciples are actually sent out and receive certain instructions from Jesus as to how to conduct themselves during their mission (6:7-13). When in addition the disciples report later on to Jesus what what they have done and taught (6:30), a present-day reader is reminded of what we would call an apprenticeship, a period of training during which one learns how to do a job by actually doing it under professional supervision. But the traineeship of Jesus' followers who have been promoted to be his helpers does not have the effect that they also understand what Jesus says. On the contrary. When, at the end of a discussion with a group of pharisees and scribes, Jesus replies with a somewhat paradoxical saying, the same situation occurs as after the parable of the seed. As soon as they are alone with Jesus the disciples question him about the saying, so that Jesus asks them, 'Are you as dull as the rest?' (7:17-18). The recurrence of this motif (see 4:40 and 8:17) creates the impression that the narrator finds it extremely important to stress precisely this aspect of their attitude.

Three Times on the Lake

This impression that their lack of understanding is very significant is confirmed by the three stories in which Jesus' twelve confidants cross the lake with him. Like the three warnings of Jesus' execution in the next section, these three stories are the backbone of this part of the book.

In the *first*, the boat is caught in a violent storm at nightfall (4:35-41). Storms are not unusual on the lake. The four fishermen, who are assumed to be on board, have of course weathered many a storm, and should know the ropes. Yet things threaten to get out of hand. The way Jesus is quietly asleep in the stern contrasts sharply with the violence of the storm. Roused by his panic-stricken disciples, Jesus intervenes. He stands up, and addresses the wind and the water so that the storm subsides and there is a dead calm. But the attentive reader who remembers that Jesus has addressed the demon in the synagogue of Capernaum with almost the same words (1:25) realizes that this is no ordinary

storm and that the numerous demons lurking on the other side of
the lake may be behind it. If they know, just like the demon in
1:24, who Jesus is, and that he intends to destroy them, they also
know, of course, that he is on his way towards them and what
will happen if he succeeds in reaching their territory. So, sensing
the menace of impending disaster, they bend the forces of nature
to their will in order to sabotage the crossing and eliminate
Jesus.

But the end of the storm is not the end of the story. Turning to
his disciples Jesus says: 'Why are you such cowards? Have you no
faith even now?' This is a remarkable reproach, and one may well
wonder whether the disciples deserve it, the more so since the
have just before appealed to Jesus for help, which is after all a clear
sign of trust. But again, it is important not to overlook the terms
in which their cry for help is expressed: 'Do you not care that we
perish?' This is a word pregnant with meaning. In Greek it is a
form of the same verb – although this is no longer recognizable in
some translations – as the one used by the demon in the
Capernaum synagogue when he asks Jesus: 'Have you come to
destroy us?' (1:24). And the reader comes across the same (Greek)
verb in 3:6, where the narrator says that Jesus' adversaries are
hatching plans to do away with him. The way the disciples have
put their cry of distress into words is, on further consideration, so
impertinent that Jesus' reproach is not at all inappropriate. They
attribute to Jesus the programme of his adversaries, namely the
destruction of life (cf. 9:22), whereas the entire public ministry of
Jesus shows unmistakably that his sole aim is to restore and save
life (3:4). It should further be noticed that Jesus' question in 4:40 is
part of the only story where he applies his exceptional power for
the benefit of his disciples. It is partly due to this that their lack of
faith precisely at this moment contrasts so strongly with the faith
of the woman who is cured through touching Jesus' clothes (5:34)
and the faith of blind Bartimaeus (10:52), for Jesus says of both
that their faith has saved them.

That the preceding stories reach their culmination in the
account of the first crossing is expressed in the question that the
disciples finally put to themselves: 'Who can this be? Even the
wind and the sea obey him.' Not only the demons that take

possession of human beings, but also the demons that use the forces of nature in order to work mischief, cannot but acknowledge and obey him. It is this that makes the disciples put the crucial question in such plain terms: 'Who is he exactly?'

The *second* story (6:45-51) comes after the first feeding. Just as at the beginning of the first story, the narrator observe that no other people embark with the disciples. As Jesus stays behind as well, the disciples are all by themselves. This time there is no threat of a shipwreck, but a mysterious incident occurs instead. In the dead of night, when the disciples are already well out on the water, the wind is so much against them that they are unable to make any headway. The reader cannot help interpreting the scene as an image of how powerless and disorientated the disciples are without Jesus. Then Jesus comes towards them in the dark, walking on the lake, and intending to pass them by (6:48). This is a most enigmatic piece of information. Does Jesus feign indifference to their predicament so as to defy them? Or does he perhaps intend to overtake and then go before them? The narrator does not say. He draws the reader's attention to something else: the disciples dare not believe their eyes, take Jesus for a ghost, and cry out with fear. Jesus then puts their hearts at rest, and when he climbs into the boat beside them the wind drops and they arrive safely, although – much to the surprise of the reader – not at Bethsaida but at Gennesaret. But before this happens, the narrator underlines the fact that considering their terror after the wind has dropped, the disciples are as blind as ever; for, he adds tellingly, they have learned nothing from the incident of the loaves.

At the *third* crossing the situation is different again (8:13-21). There is no storm and no adverse wind, so outside the boat everything is calm and peaceful. The problems that arise are wholly due to the passengers themselves, who appear to be at cross-purposes on the subject of loaves. Right at the outset the narrator brings to readers' attention the fact that the disciples have forgotten to take bread, so that 'they had no more than one loaf in the boat'. This may seem rather a strange, if not absurd, way of putting it, but it does make readers think, even if they do not know quite what, or on what lines. The ensuing conversation is so full of misunderstandings that the incomprehension of the disciples becomes tangible to the point of being painful. Jesus finally speaks unusually harsh words about the two feedings, calling the disciples blind and deaf outsiders who also are too obstinate to learn anything. An extremely unpleasant anticlimax in the book indeed, the more so since readers, at least if they are reading the book for the first time, cannot for the life of them see what the disciples do not understand and why their behaviour is so blameworthy, and consequently end up feeling embarrassed themselves.

Bread and Fish in Plenty

Between the first three crossings are narrated the two mass feedings (6:34-44 and 8:1-10). We will return to the two stories in another context, but consider them here in the light of the role of the disciples. In the *first* story the disciples notice that an awkward situation has arisen owing to there being such a lot of people together in a lonely place at such a late hour, and they suggest sending them away so that they can buy themselves something to eat in the neighbourhood. But Jesus tells them to give the crowd something to eat themselves. There is real irony in this remark, and it persists until the disciples do in fact hand out the food provided by Jesus. With the same touch of irony the disciples ask Jesus if they are to buy bread for a mass of several thousand with two hundred denarii – the value of as many days' wages for one labourer! Jesus then asks them to go and see how much food there is on hand, and they come back with five loaves and two fish. The disciples are ordered to make the people sit in neatly-arranged groups on the green grass, and after Jesus has said the blessing and broken the loaves and the fish, the disciples distribute the portions among the people, who eat as much as they want and leave quite a lot over.

It is clear that the narrator lays much emphasis on the concern and involvement of the disciples in the event. On further consideration one gets the impression that it is they who are the centre of interest, rather than the crowd, which in no way responds to the meal, either in the first or in the second story. One could go even further than this and maintain that in the narrator's representation the people are perhaps even unaware of having dined so abundantly on so little, for the question of how to satisfy their hunger is only discussed by Jesus and the disciples. That is exactly why it is so amazing that on another similar occasion, when the problem is spotted by Jesus (8:1), the disciples should ask: 'How can anyone provide all these people with bread in this lonely place?' (8:4). It appears that the disciples have no more memory than they have understanding, for memory enables us to see connections, and it is through seeing connections that we are able to strip an incomprehensible event of its enigmatic character.

The Sick and the Suffering

Whether or not the Gerasene paranoid demoniac is regarded as someone who comes to Jesus for healing, there are a few shifts in this section of the book with regard to the sick and the suffering. Whereas in the previous section there are quite a few summary accounts of healing, and the individuals concerned are for the most part men and, as far as we can ascertain, all Jews, the present section has only one summary (6:54-56), and the other stories mainly concern women and people living in Gentile territory.

The last characteristic does not apply, however, to the two cures performed by Jesus on his return from the country of the Gerasenes (5:21-43). The story does not record in which town or villages the cures take place, but from the fact that a synagogue official is involved it is clear that we are again in a Jewish community. The two cures are interwoven to form a single story through the narrator's favourite device of sandwich-construction. The story begins with the synagogue official requesting Jesus to save the life of his dying daughter. On the way to his house Jesus heals a woman, after which the narrator picks up the opening story and relates the cure of the child. Apart from their formal integration, the two stories are thematically connected through all sorts of corresponding and contrasting elements, which for the sake of clarity may be listed as follows:

Similarities

Both sufferers are female
One has been ill for twelve years, the other is twelve years old
They are both healed by a simple touch and
the healing is ascribed to faith in both cases

Contrasts

The sufferer is a woman	The sufferer is a child
The woman is outside in the crowd	The girl lies in bed at home
close behind Jesus	at a distance from Jesus
She can live with her ailment and	She is dying
is under permanent medical treatment	and is past treatment
She herself has faith in Jesus	Her father has faith in Jesus
and turns to him	and turns to him
Jesus does not know this	Jesus goes to the child knowingly
The woman touches Jesus' clothes	Jesus touches the girl
is cured	cures her
in the middle of the crowd	in the seclusion of the house
and is not told to be silent	and enjoins secrecy on those present

That the two stories constitute a certain climax in comparison with the earlier stories of healing has already been mentioned in the section headed 'Greater Signs'. To suggest that the story about the girl is a climax particularly because she is raised from the dead would be saying more than can be substantiated. It is true that the people in the house think that the girl is dead, but Jesus denies it. The story does not say who is right, but the reader is inclined to believe Jesus, who has given evidence before this of knowing things of which other people are ignorant. The relation between trust or faith and the help received, already stressed in the story about the paralytic, is expressly stated in both of these stories, and as a result the faith of the woman and the father is set in contrast with the faithlessness of Jesus' townsmen related in the next incident in the book. The fact that the girl is represented as walking about afterwards belongs to the genre of healing stories, and merely serves to emphasize that the cure has been successful.

The words that follow, 'for she was twelve years old', seem to mean that the girl was old enough to walk, but they may just as well express a desire on the narrator's part to interconnect the two stories even further through making the girl's age equal to the duration of the woman's illness.

Rather surprisingly, the story is rounded off with Jesus' instruction to give the girl something to eat. Is the fact that the girl is able to eat another characteristic feature of the genre to show that she is really cured? Or are the parents perhaps told that their daughter should eat in order to regain her strength? Or does the instruction perhaps form part of some theme we do not yet perceive? No doubt the reader remembers that after her cure Simon's mother-in-law waits upon Jesus and the other people in the house. He will also remember that there have been several reference to eating already: Jesus eating with tax-gatherers and sinners, the disciples picking and eating ears of corn on the sabbath, Jesus being unable to eat bread in a house because of the commotion going on around him. And the reader who has read this entire section in Mark is already acquainted with the two miraculous feedings of the loaves and fish, the discussion about eating with unwashed hands, the dispute with the Syro-phoenician woman about the bread intended for the children and the crumbs left over for the dogs, and finally the puzzling conversation about bread during the last crossing of the lake. Evidently the time for clarification has not yet come, but the attentive reader cannot avoid the impression that 'eating' is a key word which is designed to focus his attention on a matter of special importance.

The third sufferer is a daughter again, although this time of unknown age. This time it is not the father but the mother who does everything in her power to secure the cure of her little daughter (7:24-30). It is more important, however, that the story is set in predominantly Gentile territory and that the child's mother is clearly identified as a hellenist, a Syrophoenician by race. Jesus has tried to conceal his presence, but she is a resourceful enough woman to get through to him with her request. Presumably she is not only a foreigner, but also a member of the upper class. Not without reason she is called a 'hellenist', which in this connection means that she speaks Greek and is consequently an educated woman. This perhaps adds yet another dimension to her already quite racy argument with Jesus. For, although she speaks of crumbs, in times of crop failure the well-to-do were able to pay more for grain than other people, thereby taking the bread out of the mouths of the poorer native population. Be that as it may, her plea to rid her daughter of the demon meets with resistance on Jesus' part. Initially he turns down the request, and he does so in words that sound – there is no point in denying it – unseemly and demeaning; but they merit particular attention for exactly this reason. And those who read Mark in the original Greek would also have their attention drawn to these words by the repetition of certain sound elements. The pronouncement reads as follows: 'Let the children be satisfied first; it is not fair to take the children's bread and throw it to the dogs.' It is possible that the woman's social position as a hellenist of Syrophoenician birth lends a note of reproach to Jesus' response: it is easy enough for you, as it is, but what of the native population? On the other hand, considering that a Jew is talking to a Gentile woman, one cannot avoid the fact that Jews do in fact label Gentiles as dogs on account of their uncleanliness according to ritual (7:1-23), so that meaning can hardly be disregarded by the reader.

Is Jesus represented in Mark as sharing the prejudices about Gentiles held by many other Jews of his time? This possibility cannot be ruled out if one reads only this story. But the reader who has read the first eight chapters of Mark knows that Jesus releases a man from a legion of demons in Gerasa and heals a deaf-mute in the Decapolis without in either case concerning himself about the opposition between Gentiles and Jews. It seems to me, therefore, that the narrator has Jesus speak such unseemly, almost racialist language in order to provoke the adroit reply with which the woman counters his refusal. She agrees with Jesus, but retorts that dogs generally eat the crumbs that fall from the children's table. Jesus now grants the request which at first he refused, adding that he does as she wishes because of what she has said. That the little girl is the first person healed by Jesus from a distance shows a growth in scope that is so typical of the works of Jesus recounted in this chapter. But more importantly, the story also affords dramatic confirmation of the breakthrough to the Gentiles of which the first crossing of the lake marks the beginning. The Jews come first, but this does not mean that the way for the Gentiles is closed.

One final remark is called for. As the story of the Syrophoenician woman stands between the two feedings, it connects the destiny of the Gentiles with that of the Jews in the sense that the needs of God's chosen people are supplied first and most abundantly in the first feeding, and the needs of the Gentiles in the second, that is to say later, and less liberally.

In the case of the last healing, that of the deaf-mute in the Decapolis region (7:31-37), Jesus acts more clearly than elsewhere like someone employing the therapeutic methods of a faith-healer. When requested to lay his hands on the sufferer, he take him aside to heal him in private. Applying a real or symbolic treatment, he concentrates first on his ears, which he opens as it were by putting his finger into them, and next on his tongue, which he moistens with saliva to make it supple again. He then looks up to heaven, sighs deeply, and speaks a word of power in Aramaic: 'Ephphatha'. The narrator explains its meaning: 'Be opened'. The man is cured and can speak again. One would expect that the deaf-mute would immediately be given the opportunity to demonstrate that the treatment has been successful, but the narrator goes on to say that everyone present is forbidden to speak about it. Never is Jesus' injunction to silence more contrary to the result of the therapy than here. Is it any wonder that the people do not keep silent but broadcast everywhere what they have witnessed?

The Adversaries

The adversaries play only a minor role in this part. Their day will come later, when the scenario which is to lead to Jesus' downfall is ready and the time is ripe to put it into effect. Here they only appear in two scenes (7:1-13 and 8:11-13). Following after a summary passage about Jesus' spectacular success among the common people and the account of the great sign of the second feeding, the two scenes remind the reader that the religious leaders, the scribes and the pharisees, are as much opposed to Jesus as ever. From their clashes with Jesus in both scenes the reader can learn something of the grounds on which they object to Jesus, and in this way gain a deeper insight into their motives. The same holds for the reader's understanding of Jesus, who is in a position because of these challenges to emphasize the difference between his position and theirs.

In 7:1 the pharisees are accompanied again by some scribes from Jerusalem. As in the cases of the disciples not fasting and picking corn on the sabbath, they blame Jesus, this time for allowing his disciples to eat bread without first washing their hands. They ask him: 'Why do your disciples not conform to the ancient tradition, but eat their food with defiled hands?'

For the benefit of readers unacquainted with the background of this question, the narrator gives a short explanation. This information is also useful for the present-day reader, who might think that the washing is just a matter of hygiene. But as the narrator points out, it is more than that. The 'cleanliness' intended by this measure has to do with the desire mentioned earlier, namely to observe the Torah as fully as possible, including the rules that had to be kept by the priests when assisting at the sacrificial rites in the temple. The rules of ceremonial cleansing were closely associated with food and meals. They probably marked Jewish society in the days of Jesus even more strongly than the rules about sabbath observance, although there were also the voices of rabbis who put such practices in true perspective by insisting on the greater importance of inward purity. In his reply to the scribe and pharisees, Jesus first relativizes the second part of their objection by quoting Isaiah 29:13, which denounces the hypocrisy of sham religion devoid of inner conviction, and then refutes the first part with the last line of the same quotation: 'they teach the commandments of men'. His indictment against them is that they neglect the commandment of God and only worry about the traditions of men. It seems to me that this is a very important pronouncement, because it concentrates precisely on what the scribes themselves regard as their proper task: to put into practice the written Torah, in continuity with their predecessors, and bring it up to date. Although this ongoing process is meant to safeguard the observance of the written Torah, which is after all the law of Moses, its consequence is that new and often highly detailed precepts and prohibitions are added. Together with the written Torah these additions, sometimes called 'the fence around the Torah', constitute the complete Torah.

In Mark's account Jesus then elaborates the last point, saying that by giving priority to the traditions of men the scribes and pharisees do in fact act against the written Torah. To support his charge Jesus cites two commandments from the law of Moses, which are both about the respect due to one's father and mother, and which, Jesus continues, are nullified through the lawful application of a trick. Anyone who declares that his property is 'corban' (the narrator explains that by this it becomes a sort of temple property) is no longer obliged to help his parents when they are in distress. Thus Jesus is represented as being at loggerheads with scribes and pharisees precisely on the two issues that are typical of them and on which there was a broad consensus among the Jews of the day. Although Jesus, in Mark's representation, is a Jew like other Jews, sharing most of their views and practices, he is at the same time made to appear as a dissident who cannot be incorporated with the rabbis or scribes of his day.

To wind up the discussion, Jesus passes to the related question of the impurity of certain foods. After an exhortation to listen carefully he continues somewhat mysteriously: nothing that goes into a man from outside can make him unclean. This cryptic saying sounds like a riddle, and when the disciples question him about it he gives the following explanation. What goes from the outside to the inside is food, which enters through the mouth into the stomach and so passes out into the drain. What goes from the inside to the outside is the actions that people perform. They spring from the heart. And the evil actions that come from there and for which each person is individually responsible: it is they that make someone unclean. Finally, as if to remove the last doubts the reader may still have about the consequence of Jesus' words, the narrator states roundly: 'Thus he declared all foods clean' (7:19).

We meet the pharisees again in Dalmanutha, where Jesus and his disciples have gone after the second feeding. The pharisees ask Jesus to give them a sign from heaven to prove the validity of his claims. Do they have in mind a sign different from the many signs worked by Jesus himself on earth? There is no indication that the pharisees have any knowledge of the fact that four thousand people have just had a copious meal on seven loaves and a few fish. However that may be, Jesus' reply is quite clear: to the people of this generation neither Jesus nor God shall give any sign to legitimize Jesus. His proclamation that the kingdom of God has come and that this requires a change of heart needs no validation. Besides, such signs are not so unambiguously clear as the pharisees think, as can be seen from 13:22. He who intends to delay changing his conduct until he sees the son of man coming on the clouds – the only really unmistakable sign that shall be given (13:26) – condemns himself.

The Execution of the Baptist

Some commentators are of the opinion that the main reason why the story about Herod's execution of the baptist occurs in this part of the book is to fill the time between the mission of the twelve in 6:7-13 and their reporting back to Jesus in 6:30. To understand that there is more to it than that, it is necessary to look back to 3:6, the first of the two places where the Herodians – sometimes translated as 'partisans of Herod' – are mentioned. In 3:6 the narrator records, as the reader will remember, that after witnessing the cure of the man with the withered arm, the pharisees leave the synagogue and begin to plot with the Herodians, discussing how they may destroy Jesus. The second reference occurs later in the book, when the authorities in Jerusalem realize that the parable about the cruel and murderous wine-growers is aimed directly against them, and subsequently attempt to have Jesus arrested. To this purpose they send a number of pharisees and Herodians to Jesus in order to elicit an incriminating statement from him that should occasion his arrest (12:13). The reader is in the dark as to whom exactly the term 'Herodians' refers. As far as I know it had not been used before, nor was it used in the days when Mark was written, which leads me to suspect that the author of Mark invented it himself. If this is so, it is natural to connect it with Herod, and regard the Herodians as his agents.

Herod himself is mentioned twice in this section, in 6:14-29 and 8:15. In 8:15 his name is linked with that of the pharisees. After the second feeding and the discussion with the pharisees in Dalmanutha, Jesus says to his disciples when they have re-embarked: 'Beware, be on your guard against the leaven of the pharisees and the leaven of Herod.' That this cryptic remark throws the disciples into confusion is in no way surprising. Even if they understand the metaphor of the leaven, which is possibly used here as a symbol for an imperceptible but irresistibly-spreading evil influence, they cannot know why Jesus names Herod in this connection. Judging from the book there is no reason to assume that the disciples knew what the readers know, namely that Herod was involved in the execution of the baptist and that the pharisees, in alliance with that same Herod, are plotting Jesus' elimination.

The story of John's execution follows naturally on the rumours about Jesus' identity and Herod's own view about Jesus (6:14-15). The story makes it perfectly clear to readers what happens to those falling into the hands of Herod and his accomplices. Even if Herod is well-disposed to someone, as in the case of John, that person will still come to grief. At this point two things deserve particular attention. First, by telling the story about John's execution after the rumours about Jesus' identity, the narrator puts readers in a position that is contrary to that of Herod, who claims that Jesus is none other than the baptist, whom he beheaded, raised from the dead. Even if they have read no further than this chapter, readers know that this is absolutely untrue. Besides, they realize that the murder of the forerunner foreshadows the violent death of Jesus.

The second point concerns the wording of Herod's view. Informed readers know that it is impossible for Herod to have actually thought that anyone had been 'raised from the dead', simply because Jews believed exclusively in the resurrection of dead at the end of time, either in a universal resurrection or the resurrection of the righteous alone. So readers are faced with the question of why the narrator puts the phrase into Herod's mouth. Is it perhaps meant to be an early hint to readers that far from being the last word, the seemingly inescapable murder of Jesus will be followed by what Herod mistakenly thinks of John, namely that he has risen from the dead? Accordingly, readers would already be prepared for Jesus' own announcement, made three times in the next section of the book, that three days after his death he will rise again. It would, moreover, underline the fact that the two plots in the life-story of Jesus – the scheming of his adversaries to kill him and the misunderstanding of his disciples – are reflected in the story about John, who is executed by a Herod who does not understand him (6:20).

There are several similarities between the story of John's execution and other stories of the same kind, such as those about the prophet who upbraids the king – think of Nathan in the case of David, or Elijah in that of Ahab (2 Samuel 12 and 1 Kings 21) – and the king who gradually begins to feel sympathy for the wise man or the prophet, his prisoner, as the procurator Felix does for Paul (Acts 24). But in Mark it is of far greater importance that what is related about John anticipates what will be related about Jesus. In the circumstances there is nothing strange about the fact that John is 'seized' and 'chained' (6:17), but it is remarkable that exactly the same words to describe what happens are used of Jesus (cf. 6:17 and 14:44-49; 6:17 and 15:1). That Herod feels respect for John and tries to protect him has its counterpart in Pilate's amazement that Jesus does not answer charges brought against him, and in his attempt to release him (15:3-11). The pressure applied by Herodias through her daughter corresponds to the pressure of the chief priests who stir up the multitude (15:11). The meal at which the head of John is brought in like a dish upon a platter seems a bizarre perversion of the last supper, at which Jesus equates the two main dishes of bread and wine with his own broken body and shed blood (14:22-24). Finally, the fact that John's disciples come and take his body and lay it in a tomb contrasts sharply with the burial of Jesus, who is not buried by his disciples but by an outsider (15:45-46).

Told in this way and at this particular point, this flashback about the execution of the baptist not only connects the beginning of the book with the end; it also prefigures the fate of Jesus in that of John. Thus it brings home to readers that the consultations between the pharisees and the Herodians – of whose outcome they are not yet informed – have set going a process that is irreversible unless Jesus takes flight or ceases his activities.

The Crowd

In this part of the book the crowd plays a more important part than in the preceding sections, where it is portrayed mainly as Jesus' audience when he speaks in the open air, and as a responsive witness of his healing power. We are reminded of this by one of the later scenes, in which Jesus calls the listening crowd his new family, made up of those who do the will of God.

In this section the narrator continues the play of changing Jesus' discussion partners that started in the parable chapter. Sometimes Jesus succeeds in withdrawing from the multitude (4:36; 5:37; 6:45; 7:17; 7:33; 8:9); at other times his attempts are less successful (6:32-33; 7:24). In some cases the crowd is merely present without Jesus paying any attention to it (5:24-34); on other occasions he expressly takes its fate to heart (6:34). An example of the latter is when his attempt to seek privacy is frustrated by the very crowd he hopes to leave behind by sailing to the other side of the lake (6:31-33). As he disembarks and finds them waiting there, he is overcome with compassion because 'they were like sheep without a shepherd', as the text explains with an implicit quotation from the First Testament. And this pity induces him to teach the multitude at such length that it is evening before anybody realizes.

With this incident we have come again to the mass meal, which is twice laid on for the multitude in a place where it is practically impossible to get food. We have already discussed the two stories in relation to the important part the disciples play in them. And it is perhaps right that we have spoken of their role first, for I am inclined to believe that this is the aspect stressed most in Mark. On the other hand, the importance of the two mass meals for the role of the crowd should not be underestimated. They are the only two works Jesus performs for the crowd's benefit, for the point of the two stories is not that Jesus is out to multiply loaves – as I think is wrongly suggested by the term 'the miraculous multiplication of the loaves' – but that Jesus is concerned about the hungry multitudes. By that I do not mean that one does justice to the story if one assumes, as is sometimes suggested, that through some influence associated with Jesus, the people who happen to have bread share it with those who have not. Such a representation would not only mutilate the underlying meaning of Mark's whole narrative, but also reduce the two events to the triviality of a day-tripper's misfortune who has forgotten to take a packed lunch.

Even if we ignore for a moment the roots these stories have in the First Testament, they obviously mean to relate extraordinary events. What we have here is nothing less than a meal that is improvised by Jesus in an emergency, and at which he, acting as host, divides – and then has his disciples distribute – a little bread and a little fish into such portions that there is more than enough for everybody. if one is not compelled to use the normal Greek expression for eating, *fagō artous*, which literally means 'eat loaves', or if one considers the two events to be connected with Jesus' last meal, the question arises as to why mention is also made of the eating of fish; the more so because in the second story the fish seem to have been added as an afterthought (8:7). It seems to me there is a simple explanation for this. Bread without anything to go with it is only a frugal meal, and that would be the opposite of the kind of meal suggested by both stories. That in the narrator's view the two meals are depicted as an anticipation of the messianic banquet, or, as I myself have thought and written, of the last supper, I no longer consider very likely. But this is not to deny there exists a certain affinity in phrasing between these two stories and the account of Jesus' last paschal meal, which, however, has other causes, as I hope will become clear later.

It is most improbable that the numbers in both stories are meant to provide information about how many eaters are actually present and how many baskets are in fact collected on each occasion. So it is natural to suppose that the given numbers have a symbolic meaning. Thus the twelve baskets have been associated with the twelve apostles and the five baskets with the five deacons who are the subject of Acts 6. Yet, such an interpretation is difficult to demonstrate. That the numbers in the first account differ from those in the second follows from the fact that the narrator clearly wishes to tell two distinct stories. The proportions between the numbers, however, probably serve to indicate that the first feeding is more abundant than the second, as a brief summary shows:

The First Meal	*The Second Meal*
5 loaves	7 loaves
5000 men	4000 people
12 baskets with fragments	7 baskets with fragments

With more baskets left over from fewer loaves, and more eaters, the first meal is clearly the more abundant of the two.

There is yet another difference that seems to have some relevance. In the second story the narrator has Jesus say of the hungry people that 'some of them have come from afar'. 'From afar' is, both in rabbinic writings and in some places in the Second Testament (Act 2:39 and Ephesians 2:11-22), a term that is applied to the Gentiles generally. It may have the same meaning here, especially if we remember the place of origin of Jesus' listeners mentioned in 3:7-8. In that case the second meal is said to be attended also by Gentiles, probably those who have already come to Jesus before: a conclusion that is consonant with the growing prominence given to them in this section.

What strikes the reader most, especially after reading the preceding stories of healing and exorcism, is that in neither of the two stories of feeding do the crowd seem to have the slightest suspicion of the extraordinary happening they are taking part in. Nor is there anyone else who expresses surprise about the event. Apparently the narrator leaves that to the reader, who on this occasion is also allowed to witness far more than the four and the five thousand who enjoy the meal of loaves and fishes, or those among them who collect the baskets full of broken pieces afterwards.

Perspectives from the First Testament

In quite a number of places in this section passages from the First Testament provide a background that may add new perspectives to the story.

The first example of this is the account of the *first crossing of the lake* by Jesus with his disciples (4:35-41). To this story, already rich and meaningful in itself, one or more dimensions are added if the reader understands it in the light of its First Testament context. For, as a reader acquainted with the First Testament knows, Jesus is not the first prophet to sleep quietly through a violent storm that threatens to wreck the ship and endanger the lives of those on board. His predecessor is Jonah, who is the subject of a short but complete book of the First Testament. There are, furthermore, some terms in Mark's story that can only be traced back to the book of Jonah, so that the reader who notices these similarities – which of course is only possible if he reads both stories in Greek – is referred from one to the other. It appears, then, that in certain important aspects Jesus is represented as the direct opposite of Jonah. The latter is a recalcitrant prophet who evades his divine mission by boarding a ship where he is later found fast asleep during a storm, totally unaware of the menace of an impending shipwreck, but, when woken up, confesses that he is a disobedient prophet, and is finally thrown into the sea to break God's curse and quiet the storm.

In contrast to Jonah, Jesus is the obedient prophet who, so far from evading his mission, takes it upon himself to sail to the Gentiles, and when roused from sleep during the storm is not thrown overboard, but through his presence and his word stills the storm and saves his disciples from a certain death by drowning. After Jonah has arrived in Nineveh – and this marks another difference with Jesus – he only carries out his mission so long as he can announce the destruction of pagan Nineveh, but resentfully withdraws from it as soon as JHWH decides to spare the city because the Ninevites have repented of their wickedness. Jonah's programme is one of doom, death and destruction, that of Jesus one of salvation, life and renewal (although on one occasion he will announce destruction too, but only of the temple). Finally it is intriguing that the disciples' cry in distress, 'Master, do you not care that we perish?' sounds like a variation of the first half of the prayer said by the sailors before they throw Jonah overboard: 'O Lord, do not let us perish at the price of this man's life; do not charge us with the death of an innocent man' (Jonah 1:14).

The similarities and differences between the two stories may be summarized as follows:

Similarities

prophet in Israel
sent to Gentiles abroad
gone aboard a ship
a dangerous storm, imminent shipwreck
asleep
roused from sleep

Differences

Jonah	*Jesus*
disobedient	obedient
evades his mission	true to his mission
thrown overboard so that ship is saved	saves ship through his activity
only willing to announce punishment and death	announces salvation and life

If readers of Mark are actually being persecuted or are living in constant fear of persecution – as the first generation of readers probably were – then they are reminded of other passages from the First Testament evoked by Mark's story. Several psalms, Psalm 44 for instance, are spoken by people in danger of being killed in persecutions who begin to doubt if JHWH is still on their side: 'Bestir thyself, Lord; why dost thou sleep? Awake, do not reject us for ever. Why dost thou hide thy face, heedless of our misery and our sufferings? (Ps 44:23-24). These are feelings typical of people who are persecuted and find it difficult not to experience their suffering as a sign of the absence of the one who has promised to protect them. So readers in this situation readily understand the words spoken by the disciples when they wake Jesus: 'Master, do you not care that we perish?' as expressing their own sense of desolation. But Jesus' reply makes it clear that such feelings are a sign of unbelief and lack of confidence.

A second example is the story of the *demoniac* in the country of the *Gerasenes* (5:1-20). In general intention as well as in a number of details, the story bears a remarkable resemblance to Isaiah 65:1-5.

> I was there to be sought by a people who did not ask,
> to be found by men who did not seek me.
> I said, 'Here am I, here am I',
> to a nation that did not invoke me by name.
> I spread out my hands all day
> appealing to an unruly people
> who went their evil way,
> following their own devices,
> a people who provoked me
> continually to my face,
> offering sacrifice in gardens, burning incense on brick altars,
> crouching among graves, spending nights in caves,
> eating swine's flesh, their cauldrons full of a tainted brew.
> 'Stay where you are,' they cry,
> 'do not dare touch me; or I might make you unclean.'

This passage is the beginning of an oracle in which JHWH's announcement that he will punish those who serve idols is placed in the context of his promise to extend the gift of salvation to all, even to those who do not seek him. It is precisely the universal character of the gift of salvation, which is here offered specifically to those who worship idols, live among graves and in caves, that received clear expression in Jesus' crossing to the country of the Gerasenes.

And for the cure of the deaf-mute which Jesus also performs in Gentile territory (7:31-35), the reader is referred to Isaiah 35:3-6.

Strengthen the feeble arms,
steady the tottering knees;
say to the anxious, Be strong and fear not,
See, your God comes with vengeance,
with dread retribution he comes to save you.
Then shall blind men's eyes be opened,
and the ears of the deaf unstopped.
Then shall the lame man leap like a deer,
and the tongue of the dumb shout aloud.

In these words of Isaiah nearly all the healings of Jesus are mentioned. Against this background they are to be seen as the signs of the new age: which for Isaiah himself, his audience and first readers is the time when YHWH will lead the exiles from Babylon back to Palestine, and for the readers of Mark is the time of God's kingdom which has come in Jesus.

This section of Mark also contains a number of stories and details that remind the reader of the *Elijah-Elisha cycle*. Thus, on account of subject-matter and certain details, the reader can easily establish a connection between the raising to life of the sons of the widow at Zarephath (1 Kings 17:17-24) and the woman at Shunem (2 Kings 4:18-37) and the healing stories of the daughter of Jairus and the Syrophoenician woman. Through the perversion at Herod's court and the role of Herodias the execution of the baptist is reminiscent of what happens to Elijah at the court of Ahab and Jezebel (1 Kings 18-19). And it is noteworthy that Elijah and Elisha are both said to have already worked a miraculous feeding (1 Kings 17:7-16 and 2 Kings 4:42-44). All this strengthens the impression that Mark means to emphasize the close likeness between the doings of John and Jesus on the one hand and those of the 'prophetic duo' Elijah and Elisha on the other.

'Who Can This Be?'

That is the question with which the first story of this section ends (4:41). As it arises from what Jesus says and does, it is all the more confusing to the reader that people are sometimes allowed to speak about his identity and sometimes not. Thus it is remarkable that so far, the twelve have never been told explicitly to keep silent about what they see and hear. Also the injunction to silence in 5:43 concerning the healing of Jairus' daughter is not specifically or exclusively directed to the disciples. It also applies to the child's parents, who, together with them, have witnessed what has happened in their house (5:40). In certain cases Jesus does not demand silence from anyone, as in the stories about the woman with haemorrhages (5:34), the two feedings (6:35-44 and 8:1-10), the healings at Gennesaret (6:55-56) and the healing of the daughter of the Syrophoenician woman (7:30). After healing the deaf-mute, on the other hand, Jesus expressly forbids people to speak about it, but the narrator observes at this point that the command has a contrary effect. And from this additional comment we may infer that in his view this is typical of many more cases, or even the usual state of affairs: 'Jesus forbade them to tell anyone; but the more he forbade them, the more they published it. Their astonishment knew no bounds: "All that he does, he does well" . . .' (7:36-37).

But what really baffles the reader is that after Jesus has freed the Gerasene demoniac from a legion of demons, he sends the man home with the express command to tell his people in the Decapolis what has happened to him. Is this because it occurs in a story where, as we have already said, the world is apparently turned upside down? Or could the opinion that the command to secrecy applies particularly to Jewish regions be correct? But if this were so, it is most extraordinary that it is the healing of the deaf-mute in the Decapolis in particular that should be followed by such a command.

It is in any case indisputable that the reader is thrown into confusion by these incoherent elements in the story, and is faced with a choice between two explanations. The first is that the narrator has been rather careless and inconsistent on this point. The second is that it is perhaps part of his strategy to wilfully confuse the reader, like the artist who draws pictures in such a way that the hidden figure or the differences between the two at first sight identical pictures are almost untraceable. Which of the two explanations is correct, it is as yet difficult to say.

Meanwhile the answer to the question 'Who can this be?' still remains open, at least for the disciples who have asked it. It is different for the reader, who has several answers put before him by other people (6:14-16). Some take Jesus for John the baptist come to life again; others think that he is Elijah, or one of the prophets – the likes of whom, according to some First Testament passages, such as Psalm 74:9, have not been seen for a long time. The reader has known from the first page of the book that these are only hints and guesses, which are incomplete and in part quite wrong. As to Jesus being John or a prophet, the reader remembers that Jesus has been baptized by John and may – like Elisha from Elijah – have received something of his spirit from him. But the reader also remembers that the spirit of God has come upon him and that this is the creative force behind what Jesus does. Accordingly he is more than a member of one of the brotherhoods of prophets (in Hebrew *ben nabi*, literally 'prophet's son', as in Amos 7:14). So far Jesus has referred to himself twice as 'son of man', a word that on the one hand simply meant 'a human being', and in the Aramaic of the time was used as a modest way of referring to oneself, something like 'poor little me' in English, but on the other hand was full of mysterious associations. The voice from heaven has called Jesus revealingly 'my son'. This is one of the names that appears also to be known to the demons who shout it at him when they sense the menace of imminent disaster (3:11; 5:7). The reader knows for certain that Jesus is not the baptist, and is equally sure that he is not just one of the prophets. He might be Elijah, because a great many things he does are reminiscent of the things that were formerly done by the prophetic duo Elijah-Elisha. But the reader remembers also that on the first page of the book it is John, and not Jesus, who is depicted as Elijah come back, and that John defers to Jesus as one greater and mightier than himself. All in all, the reader may well begin to feel a little like the outsider to whom everything happens in riddles.

A Corner of the Veil

Yet there is reason to suppose that a corner of the veil is perhaps lifted in this part of the story for the benefit of readers. Two things seem to indicate this possibility. The first is that the reproving words of Jesus during the third crossing of the lake, 'Do you *still* not understand?' (8:17-20) also concern and affect readers. Apparently, over and above what they think they understand, there is something they do not. The second indication may be even more important. When overhearing the violent argument at the third crossing, readers realize that besides the advantage given to them on the first page, they are here given a second advantage over the disciples. Their misunderstanding in 8:14-21 concerns the enigmatic pronouncement 'Beware, be on your guard against the leaven of the pharisees and the leaven of Herod' (8:15). Having read the story about the execution of the baptist, readers know that this saying refers to the liquidation of Jesus which is being plotted by the pharisees and Herodians. This advantage in knowledge, however, is by no means sufficient to unveil the secret surrounding the identity of Jesus.

Do the words of Jesus contain perhaps yet another clue? It is obvious that what the disciples and, for the time being, readers as well, do not comprehend has somehow to do with what Jesus says about the miraculous feedings. But the question is, with which element of them? The disciples think it has to do with the loaves they have forgotten to take with them, but that is exactly what Jesus rejects. What other elements can be considered? Perhaps the numbers: *five* loaves for *five thousand* people with a residue of *twelve* baskets the first time and *seven* loaves for *four thousand* people and *seven* baskets of leftovers the second time? There has of course been much speculation about these numbers, but to someone who has not grown up with numerology it all sounds rather far-fetched and improbable. Meanwhile readers notice that the disciples, who at the second feeding have forgotten all about the first, afterwards suddenly appear to remember the second as well as the first (8:19-21). But it is clear that this recollection does not in any way help them understand what Jesus means. Readers also notice that not a single word is mentioned about the fish, which can only mean that the emphasis comes in fact to lie on the loaves. But Jesus' question about how much was left after everyone had eaten their fill leads the attention away from the few loaves available at the beginning to the many baskets full of broken pieces left over at the end. So it seems that the loaves cannot be remembered until they have been broken, and likewise that the stories of the feedings with bread can only be understood through the abundance of broken bread that remains afterwards.

Do these elements not remind readers of the parable of the seed yielding an abundant crop? And does not the situation itself, in which Jesus tries to make his disciples see what the two feedings really mean, lead a reader back to the situation where Jesus, after telling the parable of the seed, explicitly says to his disciples that they are given the secret of the kingdom? It would seem, therefore, that the stories of feeding and the subsequent discussion at the third crossing of the lake take up the threads of a continuous story which cannot be properly understood unless the parable of the seed and the miraculous feedings are brought into relation with one another. Through the recurrence of these themes the text directs readers to interpret the book, which is read front to back, in the opposite direction: that is, from back to front.

Reading the stories of feeding and the parables of Mark 4 in this way, one cannot but be struck by several common characteristics which reveal something like a layer of secondary meanings. There is, in the first place, the connection between seed, wheat and bread: the seed is normally sown for the production of the wheat from which the bread is baked. In everyday language one might say that in an upper layer of the book the parable chapter produces the wheat needed for the baking of the loaves that will be distributed at the two feedings. Perhaps it is also relevant in this connection that there are both two parables about seed producing wheat (4:3-8 and 4:26-29) and two stories of feeding. What is significant, at any rate, is an aspect which the first of these parables has in common with the two stories relating the mass meals. In both cases there is a dramatic contrast between very little and very much. In the parable story a large quantity of the seed falls in the wrong places and comes to nothing, and only a little falls into good soil; but this small quantity yields an abundant crop which is many times larger than the sowing-seed. In the two instances of miraculous feeding there are just a few loaves available for masses of people, but this small amount can feed all of them and still remain as broken pieces in quantities many times larger than the number of loaves on hand at the beginning of the distribution.

Whether readers have now discovered the key that enables them to gain access to the secret, it is still too early to say. They will have to wait and see if they are on the right track. Provisionally, some evidence in confirmation of this is to be found in the fact that in earlier sections of Mark – sometimes at unexpected moments – mention has been made of the eating of ears of corn (2:23-26), of loaves (3:30; 7:2 where some translations omit 'loaves', which is grammatically correct, and 7:27), or of giving something to eat (5:43). The development of the narrative will show whether this thread is continued throughout the book, and if so, whether it really concerns the secret of Jesus' identity.

The Continuation of the Story

One of the themes carried further in this part of the book is that of the growing misunderstanding of the disciples, especially the twelve. This appears from the narrator's own comments and those which he puts into the mouth of Jesus. The most important of these is no doubt the comment with which he concludes his account of the second crossing: '. . . for they had not understood the incident of the loaves; their minds were closed' (6:52). With these words he not only repeats in his own voice the comment implied in the question that Jesus puts to the disciples when they wake him during the storm at the first crossing, 'Have you not faith even now?' (4:41), but also anticipates the elaborate reproaches Jesus heaps upon them at the third crossing, when he rebukes them for their hardened hearts, their blind eyes and deaf ears, beginning and ending with the words: 'Do you *still* not understand?' (8:17-21). To these we should perhaps add the comment the narrator has Jesus make in Nazareth, where he meets only with the parochial distrust of his compatriots: 'A prophet will always be held in honour except in his home town, and among his kinsmen and family' (6:4). For the members of his new family understand him no more than his townsmen and relatives.

With this the second plot of the story becomes clearly visible.

The first plot, which is concerned with the complications arising from the opposition of the scribes and pharisees, raises a number of questions, at least in the mind of the reader who does not know the ending of the story. Will their plans to eliminate him induce Jesus to change his conduct, resign himself to what seems to be his destiny, or will he fearlessly go on doing what he has done so far? The reader is also in suspense about the question of whether Jesus' adversaries will manage to carry out their plans, and if they do, what will then become of the kingdom of God that is supposed to have begun with him? The second plot concerns the understanding and acceptance of Jesus. Those who are nearest to him, who follow him and act as his helpers, fail to understand him. The ensuing complications make the reader expect that Jesus will do everything possible to make them perceive exactly what the secret of his life and work is, and how that will affect their lives as well. But the crucial question is whether Jesus, whose efforts to make his followers see things his way have so far been without avail, will be more successful later, and how this will influence the development of the story.

7

THE WAY

8:22 – 10:52

Context and Structure

The place of this section in the overall structure of Mark has
already been discussed in chapter 2. We must now consider its
position within the sequence of events that make up the narrative
of the book.

Although Jesus' ministry in Galilee has been very successful on
the whole, it has met with two serious setbacks. The first is that
Jesus' adversaries, who are joined by common interests with the
religious leaders in Jerusalem, are plotting to put him out of the
way, and the second is that his disciples and helpers do not
understand what he says and does. Especially after 8:22-10:52, the
reader cannot help but realize that far from being isolated
incidents, the cases in which the disciples misunderstand Jesus
are, no less than the mortal hatred of his enemies, such an organic
part of the story that the narrative structure of the book can be
described in terms of these two plots. If the first comes to light in
the opening chapters and finally dominates the last chapters of the
book, the second becomes visible in chapters 4 to 8 and comes to a
head in 8:22-10:52. Thus, framed on either side by the hostility of
Jesus' adversaries, the misunderstanding of Jesus by his disciples
takes up the two central sections of the book.

	chapters
(A1) Jesus' adversaries are intent on his execution	1 – 3

122

    (B1) The disciples do not understand what Jesus   4 – 8
        says and does
    (B2) Jesus fails to get his disciples to   8 – 10
        understand him
  (A2) Jesus' adversaries succeed in carrying   11-15
    out their plans

In both cases it is Jesus who tastes defeat. He does not succeed in making his disciples understand him, but his enemies are successful in their plan to put an end to his life. Since Jesus' continued attempts to be understood in this section of Mark founder on the obtuseness of his disciples, the story does not really progress. At the end of chapter 10 they are as imperceptive as in 8:21. The reader should not infer, however, that this part is less important than the other parts of the book. On the contrary, it is not unusual, in stories of many different kinds, that the narrator, before relating the final resolution of the conflict, declares what the story means to himself, to the reader, or both. As we shall see later, the central section does in fact tell readers how and why the events described in the book are so important for them. Accordingly, it is not surprising that although this section does not contain a discourse, it does relate words rather than deeds of Jesus.

    Naturally, these sayings of Jesus are not equally important. That there is a certain hierarchy between them appears plain from the fact that one thematic unit is repeated three times. These three blocks are clearly the backbone of the composition. They each begin with what is usually called the 'prediction of the passion' (8:31; 9:31; 10:33-34), really a glib and inadequate term to use, because Jesus speaks in fact about his execution and his resurrection. The triad shows how important the narrator thinks this announcement is for his readers, an importance which is emphasized by the fact that each is followed by pronouncements about the conduct of people who wish to follow Jesus (8:34-9:1; 9:33-48; 10:35-45). And the narrator makes it perfectly clear that these sayings not only concern the disciples but have a wider context as well. In 8:34 the narrator explicitly brings in the crowd, with the result that the next saying is directed to the disciples as well as to the multitude. And the pronouncements in 8:34-38 and 9:35-49 in particular are formulated in such broad terms that Jesus seems to address himself directly to the reader.

Finally, as far as the structure of this section is concerned, it is of the utmost importance that what Jesus says here is embedded between the only two stories telling the cure of a blind man (8:22-26 and 10:46-52). They form the frame around this part of the text, thus providing it with the familiar sandwich-construction. We will deal with these two stories later.

Main Outline of Events

As the present section largely consists of saying of Jesus, the storyline is quite thin, and the few things that do happen are unimportant for the continuation of the story. The dramatic development can be described as follows.

Jesus cures a blind man in Bethsaida, and from there proceeds with his disciples to Caesarea Philippi, which is situated to the north of Galilee. Here a question asked by Jesus gives rise to a lengthy debate on his identity, and for the first time Jesus speaks about the execution that awaits him, and his resurrection. Peter rejects his teaching and is severely reprimanded. Then Jesus makes it clear to the disciples as well as to the crowd that his followers must realize that they will fare no better than he himself. Six days later he takes Peter, James and John with him and leads them up a high mountain. There they see him transfigured and dressed in unusually white clothes, and conversing with Elijah and Moses. A voice from heaven addresses them saying, 'This is my dear son. Listen to him'. Coming down the mountain, Jesus warns them to tell no one what they have seen until he has risen from the dead. Meanwhile, the other disciples have failed to free a boy from the power of an evil spirit.

After Jesus himself has cast out the demon, he continues on his way into Galilee, avoiding the crowds as much as possible so as to be able to devote himself entirely to the instruction of his disciples. He speaks about his violent death and his resurrection for the second time, but although the disciples do not understand what he says, they dare not ask him. When they start talking about which of them is the greatest, Jesus intervenes to point out that he who wants to be the first must make himself last of all and servant of all. He then speaks to them about marital fidelity and how people ought to behave in view of the kingdom of God. After this someone comes up to Jesus to ask the way to eternal life. But when Jesus advises him to abandon his riches and follow him, he fails to rise to the challenge and slinks off. It is an occasion for the disciples to remind Jesus that they have left everything for his sake, upon which Jesus promises them that they have not done so in vain. Jesus then speaks for the third time, and more fully than before, about his execution and resurrection. When the disciples quarrel again about precedence Jesus makes it clear to them how absurd the question is in the light of his own position. Meanwhile they have reached Jericho, and on leaving the town Jesus cures another blind man, a beggar, who then follows him.

Places

This section of Mark begins in Bethsaida (8:22). Outside this village Jesus cures the first blind man, be it with difficulty and in stages, and commands once more some kind of secrecy. The place lies on the Sea of Galilee (6:45). For that reason the story could be reckoned to belong to the previous section, but it is wiser to regard it as a transitional story. All the other movements relate to the route that starts in the environs of Caesarea Philippi and leads to Jericho. The latter is nearer to Jerusalem than any of the places so far mentioned in Mark, although it does not lie in the immediate vicinity of the capital.

Caesarea Philippi was named after Caesar Augustus, the first Roman emperor, and its builder Philip, whose wife Herod married (6:17). In this region Jesus is beyond the reach of his enemies. He need only stay here to be safe from them. Does the narrator locate Peter's profession that Jesus is the messiah in the neighbourhood of Caesarea because, being a city of emperors and kings, it may easily conjure up the thought of another king for Israel? Or does he place this part of the text here – as far away from

Jerusalem as possible, and outside Galilee – mainly because of Jesus' announcement of his execution, in order to make it plain to his readers that in going open-eyed towards his judges and executioners, Jesus remains unfalteringly loyal to his mission, which is, notwithstanding all opposition, to help and save people, announce God's kingdom, and call his listeners to a new way of life?

The mountain which Jesus then ascends with three of his disciples has no name in Mark. To give it a name would be mere guesswork and a mistake as well. For it is it not only an arbitrary mountain in or outside Galilee, but also the mountain in the wilderness of Sinai which Moses climbed to speak with God (Exodus 19), and where, after six days, he heard God's voice out of the cloud (Exodus 24:15-16), and the mount Horeb as well, where Elijah was permitted to perceive God in the whisper of a breeze (1 Kings 19:9-13). There is a certain analogy between ascending and descending the mountain on the one hand and entering and leaving the house in Capernaum on the other (9:33). In both cases Jesus retires with a smaller group so that a separation is effected between that group and the multitude. There is also a difference between the mountain and the house, which is not so much the difference between outside and inside as that between being nearer and less near to God.

From the top of the mountain we return again to the everyday world of the plain (9:14-27), the place where, so to speak, everyone is: Jesus, the three disciples mentioned, the other disciples, the crowd, the scribes, a father with his son, who shows symptoms of epilepsy, and a demon, who is present in the boy.

If the first announcement of Jesus' execution is set outside Galilee, the narrator has Jesus pronounce the second inside Galilee. Jesus does not stay there, but journeys through it as unobtrusively as possible (9:30-31), to arrive once again at Capernaum and the house mentioned in earlier chapters (9:33). From Capernaum he travels to Judaea, still on the other side of the river Jordan (10:1) – which according to our maps is hardly feasible, but need not be so to the narrator – and from there to Jerusalem (10:32). Somewhere along the last part of the route to Jericho the third announcement is set. It is the most detailed and

most explicit of the three, and, for that matter, of all the forecasts
that occur in the book, and like the first and the second, is
pronounced on the way (10:33-34). Thus Jesus comes with his
companions to within a day's journey from Jerusalem, namely, to
Jericho, which at the end of the section he enters and leaves again,
now also accompanied by Bartimaeus after Jesus has cured him of
his blindness (10:46 and 52).

More important than the places lying on or connected by the
route from Caesarea to Jericho is the way itself and where it
ultimately leads to: Jerusalem. It strikes the reader that both the
question about who Jesus is (8:27-29) and the three
announcements of his passion and resurrection are situated 'on the
way' (8:27; 9:30; 10:32). 'The way' is hardly the place where Jesus
can keep his whereabouts secret (9:30-31), but the narrator must
have thought it more important to stress the similarity between
the theme of the message Jesus communicates to his disciples and
the place where he teaches them: the way. The message is about
Jesus' way of life and the way of life of whoever wishes to follow
him. The way taken by Jesus and the disciples is at the same time a
way of learning, first and foremost for those who together with
Jesus are on the way to Jerusalem, but no doubt also for readers,
who through the words of Mark are able to join them.

Indications of Time and Sequence

As in the preceding sections, there are only a few indications of
time apart from the sequence of events. Yet I would like to make
two further observations. The first refers to the less frequent use
of 'immediately' in this and the following sections, the second to a
curious indication of time which crops up in the course of this
one.

The adverb 'immediately' (Greek *euthus*), which quickens the
pace of the story in the earlier sections so much, occurs far less
frequently in the remainder of the book. Although the word does
not disappear entirely, the difference in frequency – no less than
almost forty times in the first half of the book, compared with
only ten times in the second – is quite remarkable. It would seem,

therefore, that from this point onwards Jesus' ministry is under
less pressure and strain. This is not surprising because the
problem that confronts Jesus now, the disciples' misunderstanding, cannot be solved overnight. It is a delicate matter
which, as appears from this chapter, needs time to develop and is
one to which Jesus must return repeatedly.

The second observation relates to the unexpected indication of
time 'six days later' at the beginning of the account of the
transfiguration on the mountain (9:2). Up to now the reader has
not found such a specific indication of time in the book, nor will
he find one again for some time. Only when Jesus arrives in
Jerusalem are events supplied with a date, and the story tells us
from day to day and, between his condemnation and execution,
even from one part of the day to the next, what happens to Jesus.
This makes the question of why the indication just mentioned is
used at this particular point all the more intriguing. On the
supposition that this part of the book exists independently, the
unexpected occurrence of 'six days later' could indicate a
somewhat careless incorporation of pre-given text. But such an
explanation would be a stop-gap solution that should not satisfy
the reader, who feels that this detail can be understood from
within the text as it stands. To this end he should recall the First
Testament background evoked by the story of the transfiguration
already referred to above: 'So Moses went up the mountain and a
cloud covered it. The glory of JHWH rested upon Mount Sinai,
and the cloud covered the mountain for six days; on the seventh
day he called to Moses out of the cloud' (Exodus 24:15-16).
Through the phrase 'six days later', together with the words 'the
mountain' and 'the cloud', the scene of the transfiguration comes
to belong to the succession of memorable events that have taken
place at Sinai. Mount Sinai is of great importance for the lives of
both Moses and Elijah. As Moses comes down the mountain he
finds the people dancing round the golden bull-calf (Exodus 32),
the outstanding example of their incomprehension and unfaithfulness. And it is to Sinai or Horeb, as it is also called, that Elijah
flees to be safe from Queen Jezebel's threat to kill him (1 Kings
19). What the reader will be told about Jesus in the rest of the book
is apparently not without precedent.

The sequence of events is not relevant to the development of the story. Yet a few things about the three announcements of Jesus' execution and resurrection merit our particular attention. The first important point to note is that they form an ascending series which, starting from indirect speech in the first and changing to direct speech in the second, leads up to the climax in the third, the most detailed and elaborate of the three. The second point is that the three announcements serve at least partly as an answer to the question of who Jesus is (8:27-29). Thus they replace the title 'messiah' used by Peter with the words 'son of man', and summarize what people generally, but particularly the temple authorities, will do to Jesus – kill him – and what God will do for him – raise him from the dead.

Finally we should call attention to a most remarkable contrast. After Peter has replied 'You are the messiah ' to Jesus' question 'Who do you say I am?', the narrator observes that Jesus gives the disciples strict orders not to tell anyone about him (8:31), which, incidentally, is the first time in the book that Jesus enjoins secrecy on them. The first warning of Jesus' execution and resurrection, on the other hand, is followed by the narrator's comment: 'He spoke about it plainly' (8:32). These two statements follow one another so closely that even a reader who has a very short memory is sure to connect them. That Jesus is called the messiah is apparently not to be made known; that he will die a humiliating death but be raised by God from the dead seems to be something that everyone is allowed to know.

Of the utmost importance is the place of the cures of the two blind men in the story. The cure at Bethsaida needs considerable effort on the part of Jesus (8:22-26). He employs an elaborate therapy and, as in the case of the deaf-mute, uses saliva with which he moistens the blind man's eyes, and finally lays his hands upon them. But the effect is not satisfactory. The blind man can now see vague shapes and knows that they must be people moving about, but he says that they look like trees. Further treatment is necessary. So Jesus lays his hands upon him once more, and now the man can see everything clearly and is cured completely. The cure reinforces the reader's impression that Jesus is also successful in a very difficult case. He has therefore every reason to be optimistic, for if Jesus is able to cope with such an awkward situation – be it only at the second attempt – then he will also manage to remove the blindfold from the eyes of his disciples (8:17-21); if need be, likewise with a repeated explanation. Yet this expectation is not fulfilled. After Jesus has twice told his disciples what will happen to him, the narrator says: 'But they did not understand what he said, and were afraid to ask' (9:32). Even a third attempt by Jesus has no effect. What Jesus succeeds in doing in the case of the blind man of Bethsaida, he is unable to do in the case of his disciples.

The second story, which relates the cure of blind Bartimaeus (10:46-52), nevertheless creates a tiny but important opening. The difficulties Jesus encounters this time are entirely due to the crowd, who try to shut the man up when he shouts that Jesus is the son of David, and calls on him to cure him. Fortunately they do not succeed, so that Jesus can cure him, or rather, can explain that his own faith has cured him (10:52). The blind man's faith stands in sharp contrast to the unbelief of the disciples. Accordingly the narrator rounds off the story about Bartimaeus with the words: 'And at once he recovered his sight and followed him on the way'. So there is at least one person who, so far from going after Jesus as a blind man, follows him as someone who sees.

Bartimaeus of Jericho is an outsider, the first in a row of curious passers-by, such as the widow who drops her money into the alms box (12:41-44), the woman who anoints Jesus (14:3-9), the man who carries the jar of water into the house where Jesus is to eat his passover supper (14:13), the boy who escapes arrest by leaving his clothes in the hands of the soldiers who try to seize him (14:51-52), Simon from Cyrene who helps Jesus to carry the cross (15:21), and Joseph of Arimathaea who takes care of his burial (15:43-46). Perhaps readers would rather identify themselves with these figures than with the disciples?

Supporters

The leading role in this section is played by the disciples. In the earlier chapters there are quite a few episodes in which they are not mentioned (for example, the three stories about the appearances of Jesus in the synagogues of Capernaum and Nazareth, several healing stories such as those of the leper, the paralytic and the deaf-mute, and the exorcisms in the country of the Gerasenes and the territory of Tyre and Sidon), but that is exceptional in this section. In fact, the only story that does not mention them is the one about the blind man at Bethsaida. On all other occasions the disciples are with Jesus, who gives all his time and attention to them, even when, on the face of it, the story is about other people.

A case in point is the story about the man who cannot follow Jesus because he is unable to abandon his wealth. It is told by Mark mainly for the sake of the episode about the disciples that comes after it (10:17-31). It is a story about a vocation that fails in spite of the fact that the man in question, according to his own words, has observed the commandments of the Torah since his youth, for which Jesus loves him (a high tribute indeed seeing he is the only one of whom the narrator says that!). This is an extremely favourable starting-point. When, despite this, he decides not to follow Jesus, it is because in another respect his position is far from favourable: he loves his many possessions too much to sell them and give the money to the poor. Jesus now turns to his disciples and, clearly for their sake, remarks how difficult it is for a rich man to enter into the kingdom of God. When they appear to be amazed at this, Jesus does not weaken his words, but instead heightens their effect by comparing the rich man's predicament to that of a camel trying to pass through the eye of a needle. To a question expressing their dismay, Jesus replies that what is impossible for man is not impossible for God. Peter then points out to him that he and the other disciples have left everything to become his followers. Enumerating the people and things they have given up for his sake – family (only the wife is not mentioned), home, and business – Jesus tells him that they will be generously rewarded. One of the things the reader may think of in this connection is security within the new family of Jesus. But in contrast to the disciples in the story, the reader realizes that this new-found security cannot be complete, for in the circumstances it is precisely the new family of Jesus that is exposed to persecution. Having opened with the question about how to win eternal life, the story concludes with Jesus' promise of it.

Three of the four disciples called first by Jesus, Peter, James and John, have a special place in the book. In the preceding section Jesus allows no one except these three to accompany him to the house of Jairus and witness the cure of his daughter. In this section they are the only ones privileged to be present at Jesus' transfiguration on the mountain. But the fact that Jesus chooses them rather than the others does not ensure that they display any greater insight into his life and work, or understand any better what to follow him really means. The way in which they react to what they see and hear on the mountain, and to what Jesus tells them on the way down, only gives evidence of their lack of understanding. In addition to this, the narrator both begins and ends this section with incidents of similar significance.

It opens with Peter's refusal to accept Jesus' passion (8:32-34) and closes with James and John asking Jesus to give them the places of honour in his kingdom (10:35-40). On both occasions Jesus sternly reprimands his disciples for misunderstanding him so crudely. The second incident ends, moreover, in a conflict between the brothers and the other disciples, which gives Jesus cause to explain to them that the way of the world where the rulers of nations lord it over their subjects is not the way of the kingdom of God, where people live in the service of one another. And before continuing on his way to Jerusalem, he ends by pointing out to them once again that they cannot be his disciples unless they follow in his footsteps: 'For even the son of man did not come to be served but to serve, and to surrender his life as a ransom for many' (10:41-45).

Adversaries, Sufferers, Demons, and the Crowd

Apart from the two blind men, who, as we noted earlier, are more than just ordinary sufferers seeking healing, in the sense that they perform a thematic function in the book, the sick and the suffering, as well as the adversaries, make only one or two entrances in this section of Mark. This is due to the situation: Jesus wishes to be alone with his disciples as much as possible. Yet all the char-

acters just mentioned come together in the scene that follows after
Jesus' transfiguration (9:14-29): the crowd, the scribes, who are
wrapped up in a debate with the disciples who have not been on
the mountain with Jesus, a father with his son who appears to be
suffering from epileptic fits, and a demon who, protesting loudly
and throwing his victim into violent convulsions, eventually
leaves the boy at Jesus' command. Surrounded by the sympathetic crowd but critically observed by the scribes, Jesus, the
disciples, and the father with his son, enact a scene which is a
perfect illustration of the varied themes converging in this
section. Jesus' reproach of unbelief, and, as if to belie this, the
belief of the father who cries out, 'I have faith, help me where faith
falls short'; the disciples who do not succeed in healing the boy
and Jesus who does; the boy who, like Jairus' daughter, is thought
to be dead and is precisely then taken by the hand and raised by
Jesus; all these elements form a pattern of interrelated meanings.

In essence this pattern can be described as a double contrast: the
contrast between the disciples who cannot cure the boy and Jesus
who can, and that between, on the one hand, the father who,
although he thinks his faith is deficient, really believes, and on
the other the disciples who, although they have been with Jesus
for so long, do not. In this connection it is noteworthy that,
unlike traditional wonder stories or a story like that about Elisha
with his servant Gehazi in 2 Kings 4:29-37, this scene is not meant
to highlight the power of the wonder-workers by laying special
emphasis on the futile attempts of others who are obviously
incapable of working a miracle. Its purpose is exactly the
opposite, namely, to emphasize as strongly as possible how
powerless the disciples are. The same point is made again at the
end of the scene, when the disciples ask Jesus why they could not
cope with the boy's illness (9:28). Admittedly, as is clear from his
words, 'What an unbelieving and perverse generation! How long
shall I be with you? How long must I endure you?', Jesus is not
only exasperated by the unbelief of his disciples, but also by that
of the whole living generation. But in the preceding section the
disciples have so consistently been cast as unbelievers (4:41; 6:52;
7:18; 8:17-21) that it is almost impossible for the reader not to see
them as the prototypes of unbelief.

The crowds and the adversaries appear also in 10:1-2, the beginning of an episode in which the latter try to upset Jesus by putting the question to him about whether a man is allowed to divorce his wife. With a reference to the first book of the Torah Jesus answers with a negative. A surprising detail of his response is that he rejects the so-called note of dismissal, of which Deuteronomy 24:1-3 speaks (though without either enforcing or approving it), because Moses made this arrangement as a concession to people's obduracy. In Mark Jesus' reply, which is perfectly clear to the reader, is again reason for the disciples, as soon as they are indoors, to question Jesus. Jesus complies with their request, and, shifting from the matter of divorce to that of remarriage, explains why the latter is to be condemned. Perhaps this is meant to underline that the disciples do not even comprehend what is obvious to readers, and apparently persist in their attitude of not understanding anything. The story does not tell us whether they understand Jesus' further explanation. We should perhaps conclude from this that what Jesus says here is of greater importance to readers than to the disciples, or that their misunderstanding specifically concerns the question of Jesus' identity.

Present and Future

What is in any case of special relevance to readers of Mark is the theme of persecution, which, as it is connected with the theme of the way and the journey to Jerusalem, is a principal element in the central section of the book. The picture Jesus gives of himself in the three announcements of his execution and resurrection is that of one who is persecuted and killed for his perseverance and loyalty by his adversaries, but restored to life by God. At the same time Jesus makes it quite clear that the perseverance and loyalty of his followers may well have similar consequences, for whenever he speaks of his own passion he also mentions the potential sufferings of anyone who wishes to follow him.

After recording the first announcement and the ensuing discussion with Peter, the text says explicitly that Jesus addressed the crowd as well as the disciples (8:34), so that the words that follow extend beyond the disciples. This applies first of all to the saying that anyone who wishes to follow him must 'leave self behind' (8:34). It follows that the book does not set self-renunciation against self-determination, self-development or even selfishness, but against the renunciation of Jesus. That is the choice which someone standing before a judge or executioner is forced to make under penalty of torture or even death, and it is to this that Jesus' demand that each follower of his must be prepared to take up his cross refers. The first readers of Mark could not see this saying as a metaphor standing for the acceptance of all sorts of tribulations or for self-castigation. They knew that Jesus had been put to death on a cross and that others had suffered crucifixion for the sake of Jesus or for political reasons at the order of the Roman authorities, and so they realized that the same might also happen to themselves. In front of a judge or an executioner is is possible to save one's life by renouncing Jesus. But anyone who does so loses his life in the kingdom of God. Paradoxically, anyone who remains true till death loses his life to save it.

The second announcement is also followed by a discussion (9:33-41). This time the issue is which of the disciples is the greatest, and if someone who is not a follower of Jesus is allowed to cast out demons. The passage that comes after the discussion is practically incomprehensible to present-day readers. There is first a very severe judgement on those who induce people believing in Jesus to defect from him (9:42): they will be punished so harshly that it would be better for them to be thrown into the sea with a millstone round their neck. This judgement does not concern everyone who incites believers to wrong-doing, but refers specifically to judges who persuade Christians to abjure Jesus. Then there follows a triple pronouncement about hand, foot or eye which a believer had better cut off or tear out than allow them to be the cause of his loss of faith. Eusebius writes in his Church History that Origen, a great scholar and theologian who lived in the third century, preferred to go through life castrated on the basis of these sayings. No doubt a grievous mistake. The verb used here (Greek *skandalizō*) clearly reflects a context of persecution (9:42; 9:43-47; see also 4:17). Besides, the reader acquainted with the First Testament knows that in 2 Maccabees 7 the cutting off of hands and feet, the tearing out of the tongue, and the stripping of the skin are named as tortures to which the seven Maccabean brothers were submitted. Jesus' words are not concerned with preventive self-mutilation. They are, rather, a moving plea not to give in to torture but stand firm even in danger of death.

The third announcement is again followed by a discussion (10:35-40). The subject is discipleship again, but now considered in the light of the request about who will be granted the places of honour in the kingdom of God. Referring to his passion, Jesus asks James and John if they can drink the cup that he shall drink. The discussion ends with a reference to the son of man who does not wish to command service from others but is ready to render it to them, and is even willing to face suffering and death for their sake.

The Identity of Jesus, the Son of Man

With that last reference to the son of man we return to the question about Jesus' identity, which has been brought up explicitly at the beginning of this section (8:28). The replies in circulation have already been mentioned in the previous section (6:14-15), but are here repeated in almost the same words. This is an indication that the narrator considers this information of special importance for his readers, even though it is based on a misunderstanding, or perhaps exactly for that reason. Wrong answers keep the reader in suspense and make him wonder what the correct answer may be. Is perhaps Peter's reply 'You are the messiah' (8:30) the right answer? The narrator expresses no opinion on this, but he does say that Jesus charges the disciples to keep it from anyone else (8:31). This is, as we have said before, the first time in the book that they are enjoined to silence. The injunction seems to be similar to those imposed on the demons when they shout certain names at Jesus. This does not imply, however, the Jesus disclaims the designation attributed to him by Peter. Since 'messiah' is one of the two names by which the narrator refers to Jesus in the title of the book, the reader cannot iɪ ɪagine that. The injunction may even indicate that the name is in fact quite appropriate. After all, according to the narrator the demons too are commanded to silence precisely because they know who Jesus is (1:34).

Immediately after this injunction Jesus speaks for the first time – and openly! – about his execution and resurrection, and thereby calls himself 'the son of man' (8:31), as he will do in the following two announcements. How is the reader to understand this expression? In the light of Daniel 7:13, where it signifies a figure like a man on whom power and sovereignty are conferred (an image of persecuted Israel that obtains satisfaction and is restored to honour)? Or rather in the light of Ezekiel, where on almost every page God addresses the prophet as son of man? Is it a self-designation attesting to a sense of modesty, or rather one of elevation and dignity? As yet the book does not give a clear answer to these questions, although the expression has so far been used only in connection with powers not associated with ordinary human beings (2:10 and 2:18). Is the self-designation 'son of man' perhaps meant to correct or complement Peter's reply 'You are the messiah', about which the disciples are not allowed to speak to anyone? That is quite possible.

Another term that attracts the reader's attention is the verb 'must'. Who determines that the son of man must undergo great sufferings, be put to death, and rise after three days? No doubt God, as is clear from 8:33. Not that he is out for blood. Only if the chief priests and scribes carry through their plan to kill Jesus does God demand of the son of man that he be prepared to accept a violent death.

This is part of Jesus' teaching against which Peter fiercely protests (8:32). Even readers who have noticed that the necessity expressed by 'must' not only concerns the execution but also the resurrection of Jesus may find themselves in sympathy with Peter and approve of his opposition. But in that case the uncommonly harsh words directed against Peter, 'away with you, satan', apply also to them. Instead of following Jesus, Peter tries to stop him. It appears that he is no longer intent on the way of God but on what is important to man (8:33). Can we not infer from this that the title 'messiah', as it is used and subsequently interpreted by Peter,

is, if not false, at least inadequate, and must be supplemented with
'son of man' and 'son of God'? Both of these occur in the passages
that follow: 'son of man' as the name belonging on the one hand
to the execution and resurrection, and on the other to the future
coming of the son of man in the glory of his father (8:38); 'son of
God' as the name recommended by the heavenly voice, which
now addressed Peter, James and John too, advising them to listen
to Jesus (9:7).

The story of the transfiguration on the mountain (9:1-13) is a
high point in what the book says about Jesus, but a low point in
what it says about the disciples. It presents Jesus as belonging to
yet another time and place than the times and places in which the
story of the book is set. On the mountain Jesus becomes visible as
a superterrestrial figure who belongs to the future time when the
son of man comes in the glory of his father. Elijah and Moses –
named in this unusual order – are talking with him. And here in
the middle of the book the voice from heaven makes itself heard
again, this time to address the three disciples Jesus has asked to
accompany him.

But with regard to the attitude of the disciples the story is at a
low point indeed. Although Jesus shows himself to them in
another form, they do not understand him any better. Peter's
proposal to build three shelters on the mountain in order to
prolong their stay there meets with no response from Jesus but is
described as most inappropriate by the narrator. After the event
Jesus impresses on them not to tell anyone what they have seen
until he has risen from the dead – the only time in the book that a
time limit is set to the injunction. According to the narrator the
disciples observe this warning, but he adds the comment that they
discuss among themselves what 'rising from the dead' may mean.
Curiously enough, he does not say that at the first mention of
Jesus' resurrection, in 8:31. The reader who asks himself why it is
said only now, after the story of the transfiguration, cannot but
conclude that the three must have witnessed some anticipated
revelation of Jesus' resurrection and the coming of the son of man
at the end time, which according to the beginning of the book has
been ushered in by the prophet Elijah (9:11-13). Whether the three
disciples have understood anything of this mysterious manifest-

ation the story does not say, but the reader knows from the prelude that this Elijah come back is none other than John the baptist.

Owing to their special experience, these three disciples at least have caught up with the reader, who no longer has an advantage over them. This does not imply, however, that they now understand who Jesus really is, and what fateful implications his life will have for them also. On the contrary, in 9:32 the narrator reports again that they do not understand what Jesus says and are even afraid to ask him. And through their request for the best places in his kingdom James and John betray similar incomprehension. By contrast with the disciples, readers understand that the words 'messiah' and 'son of God', which have been communicated to them as names of Jesus in the prelude of the book, cannot give a true picture of Jesus' identity unless they are combined with 'son of man' to include the aspect of the messiah's suffering. The central section of the book has, moreover, made it clear to the reader that a lot more is required of him or her than the ability to use the right titles for Jesus. Those who wish to change from a reader into a follower must go the way of Jesus and follow it right to the end, however bitter and painful the end may be.

Another Corner of the Veil

In the preceding section of Mark the veil covering the secret given to the disciples and the readers has been slightly raised so as to enable readers to see the pattern *seed – wheat – bread – eating* and the contrast *little – much* continued in the signs of the loaves. Is there additional information in this section that may contribute to a further unveiling of the secret? Assuming the secret to concern Jesus' identity, readers realize that the present section of the book has told them a lot. The murder of the son of man as well as his resurrection have been discussed at length, and although the cross on which Jesus will be executed has not yet been mentioned, Jesus' followers have learned that they too, if necessary, must be prepared to stake their lives and carry their cross to the place of execution. But about the secret of the seed and what the implications are of Jesus' breaking the few loaves in such a way that they yield plenty for the masses to eat, there is nothing in this part of Mark.

Yet maybe there is, but in a negative way. For on closer consideration, it is remarkable that this section makes no mention whatsoever of loaves and eating, whereas it does refer to drinking. Verse 9:41 speaks of giving someone a cup of water to drink because he belongs to Christ, and verses 10:30–39 speak of drinking the cup of Jesus, which must have to do with his execution. Does that say something? On rereading the book, it strikes the reader that up to 8:22 Mark, unlike Matthew and Luke, refers exclusively to eating, and not once to drinking. Then, in the central part, there is not a single reference to eating, but several to drinking from a cup. Should we perhaps think here of a strategic device used by the narrator who, in this subtle way, prepares the way for a new section which is to refer to both eating and drinking? We cannot answer this question until we have read the rest of the book.

The Continuation of the Story

While the book has progressed in the sense that it has given readers a lot of valuable information, the story has not progressed at all. This is because this section is devoted to Jesus' attempts to free the disciples from their blindness. The cure of the blind man at Bethsaida raises the expectation that Jesus will also succeed in opening the eyes of his disciples, be it perhaps only in two or three stages. However, despite Jesus' efforts and what three of them see on the high mountain, the disciples remain as blind as before. This section concludes with the story of the blind beggar from Jericho, whose attitude stands in dramatic contrast to the disciples' lack of insight. Through his faith Bartimaeus recovers his sight and follows Jesus on the road to Jerusalem.

The book, on the other hand, has made considerable progress. The narrator has conveyed to his readers that they have to see Jesus not only as messiah and son of God, but also as son of man; that they have to accept his execution and resurrection as two necessary stages in Jesus' life, and, most importantly, that this understanding implies the readiness to follow Jesus on his way.

8

FINAL TRIAL OF STRENGTH
11:1 – 13:2

Context and Structure

At the beginning of this section the narrator takes the characters, and consequently the readers, by way of Bethphage and Bethany to Jerusalem and the temple. This change of location brings with it a change of theme, for this part of Mark concerns Jesus' attitude towards the temple and the temple authorities in Jerusalem. What will eventually happen in Jerusalem, readers have heard three times from Jesus himself in the previous section. In view of the authority that they have learned to attach to Jesus' words, they have no reason to doubt that these pronouncements will come true. In that sense readers' expectations are entirely in keeping with what the book is in fact going to tell them. However, Jesus is not arrested immediately and is, at least for a while, free to move about in the vicinity of the city and the precincts of the temple.

The section can be divided as follows to reveal its sandwich-construction:

- Jesus arrives in the temple and observes the scene (11:1-11)
  * Discussion about Jesus' appearance in the temple (11:12-33)
  ○ The parable of the murderous winegrowers (12:1-12)
  * Discussions about a number of issues (12:13-40)
- Jesus observes the people in the temple and leaves (12:41-13:2)

Within this section a smaller part (11:12-21) appears to have been submitted to the same technique. This is where the so-called cleansing of the temple is sandwiched between the cursing and the withering of the fig tree:

* Jesus pronounces the fig tree barren (11:12-14)
* Jesus chases the merchants and money-changers from the temple (11:15-19)
* The disciples find the fig tree withered. (11:20-21)

Main Outline of the Story

Before entering Jerusalem Jesus sends two disciples to a village nearby to borrow a colt. Cheered by his supporters, he then rides back into the city and visits the temple. He observes everything happening there, but together with the twelve, leaves Jerusalem again at nightfall to spend the night at Bethany. Next morning he returns to the city. On the way there he curses a fig tree that has leaves but no fruit. The moment he arrives in the temple he begins driving out the merchants and money-changers trading there. Again Jesus and the twelve spend the night outside Jerusalem. When passing the fig tree next morning they see it is completely withered. This causes Jesus to speak about the power of trustful prayer. In the temple Jesus is troubled by the chief priests, scribes and elders, who ask him by what authority he acts as he does. A fierce argument follows. Jesus replies by telling a story about a proprietor of a vineyard who is treated shamefully by his tenants and reacts by destroying them. To this he adds the saying that the stone which the builders rejected has become the cornerstone. Several groups of opponents try and tempt Jesus to speak out on vexed questions such as the liability to pay taxes to Caesar and the resurrection of the dead, and one of the scribes asks him which is the most important of all the commandments. Jesus in his turn questions them about the identity of the messiah, attacks the behaviour and way of life of the scribes, and praises a poor widow who gives her last penny for the temple. Finally, he leaves the temple buildings and when one of the disciple shows himself impressed by their imposing greatness and splendour, Jesus announces that they will be completely destroyed.

Times and Places

In this section of the book the story begins to show a remarkable unity of times and places. That is not surprising, because from now on everything takes place in Jerusalem or its immediate surroundings, and within a period of only a few days, three of which are named (11:11; 11:12-19 and 11:20). As no other day is mentioned after 11:20, and the counting of days is continued only in 14:1, the reader may assume that this part of the story takes no more than a few days.

All movements, without exception, are restricted to the temple and the village of Bethany just outside Jerusalem. In this part of the book Jerusalem seems to consist only of the temple buildings. The chapter opens by bridging the distance between Jericho and Bethany. As soon as Jesus arrives at Bethany he arranges his journey to and arrival in Jerusalem. After entering the city he visits the temple, looks at the whole scene, and as it is quite late, returns with the twelve to Bethany, to go back to Jerusalem early next morning (11:1-11). This is to be the regular procedure of the days before Jesus' arrest. Every morning he goes to the temple and every morning returns to Bethany. That is typical of the situation in which he finds himself. A city with gates that are closed at night is usually a safer place than an open village nearby. But in a case where the municipal authorities are hatching a plot against a person's life the closed city becomes a trap (thus also in Acts 9:23-25). The section ends with Jesus leaving the temple and announcing its destruction (13:1-2). Since Jesus goes from the temple to the Mount of Olives, where he sits down facing the temple (13:3), the reader is reminded of Ezekiel 8-11, where the prophet sees the glory of JHWH leaving the temple and Jerusalem through the east gate and resting to the east of the city, before Jerusalem and the temple are committed to the flames.

The Disciples

In this section of the book Jesus' supporters and helpers play only a minor role. In quite a few episodes they are not even mentioned, although the story implies that they accompany Jesus whenever he goes to Bethany or the temple. In only two places are they more than mere listeners. In the first, Jesus instructs two of them to find a colt for him (11:1-7). It is remarkable that Jesus foresees and predicts to the smallest detail what will occur. That this happens immediately after Jesus has arrived in the surroundings of Jerusalem convinces the reader that his announcement of what will happen to him there is not based on conjecture either, but on real knowledge of his future.

Comparable to this is the role the disciples play in the incident of the fig tree (11:12-21). When they are with Jesus on their way from Bethany to Jerusalem on the second day, Jesus feels hungry, and, seeing in the distance a fig tree full of leaves, he goes to pick a few figs. Not finding any, he expresses the wish that no one may ever eat fruit from it again. When they pass the tree next day it appears to be withered to the roots. Verse 11:14 says explicitly that the disciples hear Jesus utter that curse, and in 11:21 Peter is said to remember it and subsequently draw Jesus' attention to the fact that the tree has actually withered. This story surpasses the first by far, in that it is not really about the foreknowledge of Jesus, but rather about the efficacy of his word. Thus, both the disciples and the readers are reminded once more to what extent Jesus can really be called a man of authority. Yet, in the sentences that follow, Jesus makes it quite clear that to accomplish such a deed – and another that is still more impressive – lies within the power of anyone who trusts in God completely and really believes that what he says will happen (11:23), and that therefore trustful prayer will never remain without effect (11:24).

The Fig Tree and the Temple

On his way to Jerusalem Jesus has devoted himself entirely to the instruction of the disciples. Now that he has reached the end of his journey he focuses all his attention on his adversaries. Although he is on enemy soil, Jesus does not mince his words, nor does he avoid his opponents. So not unexpectedly, things build up to a final trial of strength between Jesus and his adversaries, all of whom he meets once more in this section.

After the narrator has told us that the chief priests and scribes are afraid of Jesus because of the strong hold he has over the crowd (11:18), he relates that the chief priests, scribes and elders approach Jesus to question his authority (11:27). In their presence Jesus tells the parable of the vicious winegrowers, and probably as a reaction to this a number of pharisees and Herodians are sent to trap him with a question (12:13). On the same occasion, or shortly after, the Sadducees take issue with Jesus on the matter of the resurrection (12:18), and a scribe who, somehow contrary to the reader's expectation, turns out to be a sympathetic discussion partner, asks Jesus which commandment ought to come first (12:28). As the scribes, chief priests and elders are strongly connected in Mark with the Jerusalem of the temple, and are also present as a group at Jesus' arrest, trial and execution, I shall for the sake of convenience call them the temple authorities.

It is with these temple authorities that the story of the fig tree is concerned. For it is the narrator himself who makes it clear to the reader that this story is not only about the fig tree. He does so in two ways. First, by putting this story as a frame on either side of the account of Jesus' cleansing of the temple, as a result of which the fate of the withered tree is connected with that of the temple. Secondly, by inserting into the story of the fig tree the remarkable sentence 'for it was not the season for figs' (11:13), which tells the reader that Jesus has really no reason to blame this particular fig tree for being unfruitful because at this time of the year all fig trees have leaves but no fruit. So the story is not about the fig tree that will never again bear fruit, but about the temple, or perhaps, rather, about what it stands for, the existing religious order, which according to Jesus is now doomed to sterility. Accordingly the fig tree that produces leaves but no fruit is an image of the temple itself. For although it was really meant to be a house of prayer, not only for Israel but for all the nations, it does not bring forth the fruit expected of it, but instead yields profit to merchants and money-changers who cheat people out of their money.

It may seem strange to us that a tree is used as a metaphor for a building or institution, but as we can see from Jeremiah 1:10 and 1 Corinthians 3:6-17, as well as from Mark 12:1-11, planting and building belong together as the two primary activities by which, according to the biblical authors, man secures his future (see Deuteronomy 20:5-6 and Luke 17:28). The integration of the stories of the fig tree and the cleansing of the temple is meant to suggest that, even apart from the temple authorities' intention to eliminate Jesus, the temple and the order represented by it are thoroughly perverted. That is a very severe judgement indeed. But the narrator and the one through whom Jesus has pronounced this judgement are not alone in this. They are preceded by Jeremiah and Ezekiel, and in Jesus' time by the Samaritans, Essenes, and other dissident Jews, who passed the same judgement and often put it in even harsher words.

Within the framework of the story about the fig tree and the temple, the text explicitly says that on hearing Jesus' devastating criticism the chief priests and scribes seek ways of securing his execution but decide to postpone their plans for fear of the crowd, who are very impressed with the teaching of Jesus (11:18). And so all the enemies of Jesus join forces to do away with him: pharisees and Herodians (3:6 and 12:13), chief priests, scribes and elders (11:27).

Representatives of the latter group come to Jesus as he is walking in the temple and try to trap him with a challenge to tell them what authority he has for his actions (11:28). Jesus replies with a counter-question, asking them if the baptism of John came from God or from men. This puts the questioners in a dilemma. If they say that it was an act of God, then Jesus will no doubt ask them why they went to John to be baptized by him (as, according to 1:15, all the people of Jerusalem did) but did not believe his words. Which of John's words is the reader to think of in this connection? His exhortation to repentance? In that case the temple authorities did receive John's baptism of repentance but without really changing their lives. However, John's exhortation to repentance is mentioned only implicitly and casually in 1:4, whereas the reference to the one who comes after him is stated explicitly and in direct speech in 1:7-8. In other words, the reader is meant to think that the temple authorities attached no credence to what John said about Jesus. So if they answered that the baptism of John came from God, their reply would not be consistent with their rejection and their intention to silence him.

On the other hand – so the temple authorities argue among themselves in the story – the alternative answer, that John's baptism was not from God, is bound to antagonize public opinion, which with Jesus' popularity among the common people will make it even more difficult for them to carry out their plans. So for reasons of strategy they decide to give no reply.

By relating this discussion and the deliberations of the temple authorities, the narrator refers readers to the prelude of Mark, and thus enables them to gain a deeper insight into the origin and extent of Jesus' authority. All his actions and words are connected with John and go back to the spirit of God's descent on him after he had accepted baptism at John's hand. Jesus has the right to act the way he does because of what the voice from heaven said to him. He, more than the authorities, is more at home in the temple, because God has called him his dear son.

The Son Put to Death and the Stone Rejected

After he has repelled their attack Jesus at once takes the initiative by telling his opponents the parables of the greedy, murderous winegrowers (12:1-9) and the discarded stone (12:10-11). The first is a parable story, a story within the story of the book, told by the main character. Jesus tells the two parables to the temple authorities, but naturally the reader can overhear them. If one listens carefully to the quite distinct voices of the author and Jesus, one will discern a notable parallel between them which is important for the understanding of both stories. Just as the author has led his readers into the temple, so Jesus takes his listeners – and thereby the author the readers – into the vineyard. For there, inside the enclosure, the narrator places his listeners. What they see in the vineyard is very similar to what the reader has found in the temple: a group of aggressive men who apparently think nothing of killing someone and are actually planning a murder, and over against them the only son of the owner of the temple or the proprietor of the vineyard. The timing is as important as the place and the people involved. The author takes his readers to the temple at the time the authorities are planning to kill Jesus. This

matches the moment in the parable when the tenants see the last
servant, recognize him as the landlord's son and heir, and decide
to murder him. The structural connection between the parable
story and this particular part of the narrative is represented in the
following figure, in which the similarities show how the two
stories reflect each other.

the level of the listeners and the readers

	SON	TENANTS
JESUS	*TEMPLE AUTHORITIES* VINEYARDS	MURDEROUS PLANS
TEMPLE	*MURDEROUS PLANS*	

But the parable of the vineyard is not only a reflection of what is
happening in the temple at the moment. In the temple Jesus
speaks also about what still awaits him in Jerusalem, namely that
the temple authorities, who continue a long tradition of torturing
and killing prophets, will eventually also kill Jesus – in the parable
story the dear son of the absentee owner of the vineyard. Here, in
the veiled and yet revealing terms of a story, Jesus tells the temple
authorities exactly the same as he has told his disciples in the three
announcements of his execution. As to the time of the event,
readers of the book are in a different position to that of the temple
authorities listening to the parable. True, they have decided to kill
Jesus, and would probably have seized him already, had not their
fear of the people held them back (11:18 and 12:12). The murder
of Jesus is still in the future for them. It is different for readers,

who, of course, read the book after the murder of Jesus has taken place.

But there is something else. The parable story is followed by Jesus asking his listeners what the owner of the vineyard will do. Naturally the reader, too, will consciously or unconsciously give a tentative answer to this question, and can check whether their answer agrees with that of Jesus himself: The owner of the vineyard will come and destroy those tenants and entrust the vineyard to others. Whether this may be taken to reflect the actual, concrete facts as much as the parable itself is not clear. But the answer certainly implies a threat which reminds the reader of the fate of the barren fig tree.

The second parable is not a story but a quotation from the First Testament, which expresses in a metaphor the aspect of Jesus' announcements that is not to be found in the parable story. With the same confidence with which rabbinical exegesis plays with scriptural passages, the narrator has Jesus pick words from the same psalm that was sung to him as he entered Jerusalem. Psalm 11. It is a song of praise thanking JHWH for deliverance from hardship and enemy oppression. The stone which the builders rejected has been chosen by JHWH to become the cornerstone for a new building (Psalm 118:22-23). The temple authorities possibly think that Jesus is speaking of replacing the existing temple by a new building, as some witnesses will allege at his trial (14:58). To the reader, however, it is clear the the metaphor of the stone rejected by the builders but turned into the cornerstone by God refers to Jesus' resurrection from the dead.

It is noteworthy that in contrast to what is repeatedly the case with the disciples, Jesus' adversaries have no trouble at all understanding the parable without further explanation. The narrator underlines that they recognize that the parable is aimed at them, and consequently, despite their anxiety about the attitude of the public, want to arrest Jesus. Are we to infer from this that the story has unintentionally a contrary effect? If it is meant as a counter-attack, perhaps it has. But is it a counter-attack? It may well be a last attempt on the part of Jesus to open the eyes of his enemies to the implications of their intention to eliminate him, for there is a possibility that they may still come to their senses and stop what they are going to do. In that case the attempt has been in vain. It is not clear whether the temple authorities understand whom they intend to execute. Probably they do. It is true that the narrator says only that they understand that the parable is directed against them, and not that they also realize what the execution of Jesus really means. But if they recognize themselves in the murderous tenants, they must recognize Jesus in the son of the owner. In that case the effect of the parable is rather that they know now who their victim is, or thinks he is, but nevertheless decide to go through with their plan and keep the inheritance to themselves.

In Discussion with Pharisees, Herodians and Sadducees

After the two parables come a number of discussions with other groups of adversaries involved in this trial of strength with Jesus. Instructed by the temple authorities a number of *pharisees* (who, as we know, object to any association with Gentiles and people like tax-gatherers who are in close contact with them) and *Herodians* try to get Jesus into trouble by asking him if it is right to pay tribute to the Roman emperor. Pointing at the image and inscription on a Roman coin Jesus turns the tables on them, saying that one should give God and Caesar what is due to each (12:13-17).

The second group is that of the *Sadducees*, who also trouble Jesus with a question that is the expression of their own ideas, and are duly introduced by the narrator as those who are confident that there is no resurrection (12:18-27). They cite the case of a woman who in conformity with the levirate law (Deuteronomy 25:5) married seven brothers in a row who, like the seven husbands of Sarah in Tobit 6, all died. By asking whose wife she will be when the dead rise again, they try to show Jesus how absurd it is to believe in the resurrection. Since Jesus has repeatedly announced his own resurrection, this question is more exciting to the reader than the first one about paying tribute to Caesar. And if the Sadducees are right, the resurrection of Jesus is equally uncertain. In the first part of his answer Jesus brushes their case aside, because it rests on a grossly material representation of the resurrection, and in the second part refers to Exodus 3:6 to emphasize that the God of Abraham, Isaac and Jacob is not the God of the dead, but of the living. It is clear that God's programme is one of life, while that of the Sadducees is one of death, just as Jesus represents a programme of salvation, while his adversaries generally represent a programme of destruction.

When the next person to come forward is a *scribe* (12:28-34), readers half expect that he will ask Jesus another apparently innocent question. But they should know better, for there is nowhere else in Mark where an individual scribe or pharisee appears, or is as much as mentioned. The man does not try to upset Jesus by putting him to the test. Instead, there is an exchange of ideas rather than a discussion, a willingness to learn rather than argue. They both agree on the first commandment, love the Lord your God with all your strength, which is also the opening words of the *Shema*, the daily prayer of every Jew. To this Jesus adds a second commandment, that of the love of one's fellow human beings, saying that there is no other commandment greater than these. The scribe goes along with Jesus, summarizes his words, and concludes that these commandments are much more important than any burnt offerings or sacrifices. Jesus closes the encounter with the observation that he is not far from the kingdom of God. To the reader the scribe is not in the first place the exception that proves the rule; he rather shows a perspective that is open to everyone, even if they belong to the adversaries' camp.

However, the next two passages are directed against the scribes again. Referring to Psalm 110:1 Jesus asks whether the messiah, of whom the scribes say that he is the son of David, should not be called the lord or master of David rather than his son (12:35-37). Jesus speaks of the messiah in rather abstract terms, but knowing that the narrator considers Jesus to be the messiah the reader is intrigued by this saying. In Mark Jesus does not reject the names 'son of David' and 'messiah', or even those shouted at him by the demons, but neither does he declare that they are appropriate to himself. The narrator, on the other hand, presents Jesus as messiah and son of God in the title of the book, and, significantly enough, observes that the demons shouting names at Jesus know him (1:24; 1:34; 3:11). The reader cannot avoid the impression that many names are suitable for Jesus, but that any one name by itself is inadequate to express who he is.

The discussions in the temple end with a sharp attack on the scribes, who, according to Jesus, make a show of long prayers, parade the streets in striking robes, and take the places of honour, but instead of protecting the weak, as is the duty of everyone, abuse their position by swindling the most vulnerable.

The end of the section brings the writing-off of the temple. When Jesus leaves the temple he does so in more senses than one (13:1-2). To the disciple pointing out to him the majesty of the temple buildings Jesus says that not one single stone will be left on another. This reminds the reader of the story of the fig tree which is withered from the roots and appears to be stone-dead. What has happened to the tree is also a diagnosis of the condition of the temple authorities, who meanwhile have started to plan Jesus' liquidation (11:18 and 12:1-9). From what Jesus has said the reader knows that these plans will succeed, and recognizes in them the temple authorities' programme of ruin and destruction. On account of these plans the temple establishment has served its turn, and, according to Jesus, both the temple authorities and the temple will be destroyed. Burnt offerings and sacrifices, together with the rules of ceremonial purity connected with them, will come to an end. The love of God and one's neighbour will receive unequalled and unchallenged priority. As the narrator has Jesus enter Jerusalem and the temple at the beginning of the section, so he has him leaving the city and the temple again at the end. With Jesus' words concerning the destiny of the temple the story of the fig tree is brought to its logical conclusion.

The Identity of Jesus and the First Testament

The blind beggar Bartimaeus twice addresses Jesus as 'son of David' at the end of the previous section (10:47-48), but it seems that the reader does not realize the importance of this name until he hears it again, or one very similar to it, from the lips of the crowd in the account of Jesus' entry into Jerusalem at the beginning of this one. The quotation from Psalm 118:26 speaks of 'the coming kingdom of our father David'. And in 12:35 Jesus himself asks how the scribes can say that the messiah is (the) son of David. This question seems to imply reserve rather than agreement, which is understandable, because in texts from the same period like the so-called Psalms of Solomon the name is associated with things that are incompatible with the image the narrator wishes to evoke of Jesus. The messiah, who is there referred to as 'the son of David', will not only free Jerusalem from the power of foreign tyrants and redistribute the whole country among the twelve tribes. He will also purge the city and the country of the heathen and make it a holy land where no injustice is to be found. He will then bring the pagan nations under his yoke and rule them with a rod of iron (especially Psalms of Solomon 17:21-33). This representation of the messiah appears to be more in line with the dreams of the pharisees than with the ministry of Jesus. On the other hand, the name provides a connection with the figure of David, whose person and image have certainly served as a model for the presentation of Jesus in Mark. David is a man after God's heart (1 Samuel 13:14), and through being anointed king becomes, like King Saul before him (1 Samuel 10:5-6 and 10-12), a prophet as well (1 Samuel 16:13; 2 Samuel 23:1-2; Mark 12:36); he is moreover, able to drive the demon out of Saul through the way he plays the harp for him (1 Samuel 16:23). He speaks and acts in the strength of God's spirit. So on account of a number of features in Mark's portrait of Jesus the reader can recognize in this descendant of David (Romans 1:3 and 2 Timothy 2:8) a definite likeness to David, but feels on the other hand that he should view the name 'son of David' with all due reserve.

In this connection we must speak again of the parables of the winegrowers and the cornerstone. The first places Jesus among the men who were sent with a message to Israel and paid for it with their lives, like the prophet Zechariah (2 Chronicles 24:20-22), the prophets Jezebel had put to death (1 Kings 19:10), Uriah (Jeremiah 26:23), and perhaps those massacred by Manasseh (2 Kings 21:15), one of whose victims according to Jewish tradition was Isaiah. Jesus' position at the end of the line of

prophets is unique, because he is not sent as a servant but as the
son. The second parable gives a further application of the first in
that it says that although he has been rejected by the builders,
Jesus has been turned into the cornerstone or keystone by God.
Besides, if the first readers of Mark knew Hebrew, they were
probably quick to perceive the similarity suggested between *ben*
(son) and *eben* (stone) and therefore the relation between the two
parables. Whether the *cornerstone* is meant to make the reader
think of a new temple, the narrator does not say. On the other
hand, there is no doubt that the builders who discard and throw
away the stone represent the temple authorities. If readers take the
stone to mean the *corner*stone, then they understand that with
Jesus a new beginning is made. If readers think rather of *key*stone,
then this will call up Jesus' elevation through his resurrection.

   Thus names and images are joined together to form a colourful
mosaic of meanings. The murdered son of God is son of David
and the cornerstone or keystone as well. But despite these new
clues the aspect of Jesus' identity that was unknown before has not
really been revealed to the reader.

Another Corner of the Veil?

Yet, in a sense another corner of the veil has been lifted. Now that
they have all been told the parables can be understood in relation
with one another, as 4:13 requires. It seems certain that there is a
correlation between them, as the following summary of the similarities and contrasts between the only two parable stories in the
whole book (4:3-8 and 12:1-9) shows.

Similarities

placed at about the same distance from the beginning and end of
the book
the only two parable stories in Mark
referring to agriculture and horticulture
concerned with the production of food
reflect what happens to Jesus

Contrasts

situated in 'Galilee' section	situated in 'Jerusalem' section
distance from the beginning	distance from the end
major emphasis on sowing time	major emphasis on harvest time
production of corn	production of grapes
for the purpose of eating	for the purpose of drinking
stress on the outside	stress on the inside
turns out well	turns out badly
meaning not understood	meaning understood
by supporters	by adversaries
is about Jesus' word	is about Jesus' body
is explained	is not explained

The two parable stories are not only two related metaphors for what the book tells us about Jesus – his success in Galilee as well as his failure in Jerusalem – but together with the stories of the two miraculous feedings they also form the beginnings of a network of related secondary meanings, of which the proper reference still remains in the dark. If in the first half of the book the little seed falling into good soil produces a lot of corn and only a few loaves satisfy the hunger of large crowds, in the second half the parable story of the winegrowers provides the grapes which produce the wine people can drink with their food. Up till now this has not been discussed. But attentive readers remember that eating is regularly mentioned in the first half of the book, even in places where there seems to be little reason for it (3:20; 5:43; 6:31), and drinking is not, whereas in the second half, up to chapter 14, it is not eating but drinking that is mentioned (9:41; 10:38–39). Thus, certain word are being tied together to form a string of inter-related meanings, in which the field has to do with the vineyard, the wheat with grapes, and eating with drinking. After eating and bread have played such an important part in the first half of the book, the reader now waits for the wine. And what the son has suffered at the hands of the tenants of the vineyard makes the reader expect that the wine will somehow be connected with what will happen to Jesus in Jerusalem. But that too requires some further explanation.

Continuation of the Story

After the relative calm in the preceding central section devoted to
'the way', the pace of the story quickens again as soon as Jesus
arrives in Jerusalem. Through a parable story he shows his
adversaries the nature and the consequences of the murder they
are planning. The narrator says explicitly that they realize that the
story is directed against them, but he does not say whether they
realized who their victim really is. It is clear that they would
rather kill Jesus straightaway, but mainly because they feel uneasy
about the reaction of the public the decide to wait. Meanwhile,
from the side of those who feel threatened by Jesus, the opposition against him grows. Besides the pharisees and Herodians
the chief priests, the scribes and elders, the spiritual leaders
attached to the temple of Jerusalem, start consulting one another
about how to put an end to Jesus' actions and influence. That
should be easier in Jerusalem than in Galilee. On the other hand,
the time is not so propitious. Among the crowds coming up to the
capital for the paschal celebrations there are bound to be many
who have seen and heard Jesus before and whose sympathies lie
with him and his cause. As a result public opinion is an uncertain
factor. So, with the passover festival drawing near, the tension
increases. The authorities realize that if they fail to silence Jesus
now it will be much more difficult to do so later after he has gone
back to Galilee.

9

LOOKING AHEAD

13:3-37

Context and Structure

In this second great discourse of Jesus Mark's story comes to a standstill. That was also the case in the part devoted to the first great discourse, the parable section, where the plot resulting from the resolution of Jesus' adversaries to kill him was not carried forward by any event or discussion related there. But in that section of Mark the second plot of the story, namely the misunderstanding of Jesus by his disciples, became visible. Here the resolution of both plots is suspended, so that it is no exaggeration to say that as far as the development of the story is concerned this section has no function. For that reason, and because it contains elements that are quite foreign and perhaps even unpalatable to present-day readers, Jesus' apocalyptic discourse is often felt to be a strange and even disturbing element in the book. If it was left out, no one would miss it.

However, if readers actually skipped it, they would undoubtedly do great injustice to the narrator, who wishes to convey a message as well as tell a story. It is for this reason that, abandoning his role as a narrator for a moment, the writer sometimes addresses his listeners or readers directly in order to explain something or draw their attention to something. It can hardly be an accident that the writer addresses his readers explicitly only once in Mark in this chapter (13:14). Without abandoning his role as a narrator, he has yet another way to control the meaning of his story: whenever he sees fit he can quote the words of an authoritative character, for example of the one whose voice is heard from heaven. The present section is an excellent example of this. Next to the voice from heaven no other voice has greater authority than that of Jesus. And a comparison with the parable section, where the narrator himself repeatedly comes to the fore with 'and he said (to them)' shows us that nowhere in the book does he have Jesus speak so long and so continuously as in this particular section, which is therefore of special importance as a commentary on what the book tells us about Jesus.

This commentary concerns the relevance of the story to the time following the period described in the book. This is a very important matter because it is the time of the readers themselves. If a narrator wishes to bring the time of his readers into a story, he can only do so by means of a limited number of literary techniques, since the verb forms employed by the proper narrative text – e.g. the past and the historical present – do not refer to the time of the narrator or his listeners. The narrator may evoke that time, for example, by inserting his own remarks about it in the story. If, however, he does not wish to give up his role as a narrator, he may bring the time of the readers into the story by having a character speak about it, which to that character is, of course, the future. This is what Mark does in this chapter. He has Jesus look ahead and speak about what is to happen later. The reader recognizes this since the narrator has Jesus use the future tense twenty-seven times and a form of the imperative no less than twenty-one times.

The division of the discourse about what will happen from the time of Jesus down to the end time follows the pattern that the reader has learned to expect from earlier sections. Without any great difficulty and without in any way forcing the structure, the reader can again identify the presence of a multiple sandwich-construction, which can be set out as follows.

(A1) The time before the coming of the son of man (13:5-23)
    (a1) many will be misled (13:5-6)
        (b1) news of wars and natural disasters (13:7-8)
            (c) *there will be persecutions* (13:9-13)
        (b2) the sign of the desecration of the holy place (13:14-20)
    (a2) pseudo-messiahs will cause errors (13:21-23)

(B) The coming of the son of man (13:24-27)
    (d1) cosmological catastrophes (13:24-25)
      (e) *they will see the son of man coming* (13:26)
    (d2) the gathering of the elect (13:27)

(A2) The sign of the coming (13:28-37)
    (f1) the parable of the fig tree : understanding the signs (13:28-29)
      (g) *no man nor son of man knows the exact hour* (13:30-32)
    (f2) the parable of the door-keeper : staying awake (13:33-37)

The Location

The discourse is delivered on the Mount of Olives, where Jesus has sat down, like a judge who 'sits' to administer justice or a professor who take a university 'chair' to teach. Although this section of Mark is part of the narrative cluster situated in and near Jerusalem, the Mount of Olives, like Bethany, lies outside the city and, what is even more important in this connection, opposite the temple, as the story explicitly reports. This is more than a record of Jesus' geographical location. It defines the position of Jesus, who has turned against the perverted temple establishment, and after leaving the temple perseveres in his attitude towards it. The Mount of Olives is a place pregnant with meaning for readers who are familiar with the First Testament. In Ezekiel 11:23 it is the place where the glory of JHWH retires from degenerate Jerusalem. According to Zechariah 14:4 it is where JHWH will pass judgement on Jerusalem. Moreover, in his *Jewish War*, which appeared about A.D.75, Flavius Josephus mentions the belief that the messiah will appear on the Mount of Olives before commencing the liberation of Jerusalem from the Romans. Since the narrator has chosen to locate Jesus' discourse about the future and the end time on the Mount of Olives, it is quite clear to the reader that this place gives a distinct colour both to the words Jesus speaks here and to his final departure from the temple.

Disciples and Readers

Jesus' disciples are mentioned only once, and then not even all disciples or the twelve. Although his discourse is in fact concerned with what will happen to all human beings, to the earth they live on and the cosmos surrounding it, Jesus speaks exclusively to four of the disciples, Peter, James, John and Andrew. They have asked him when the destruction of the temple will take place and what sign will announce that the end time has come. Their question is reminiscent of the scribes asking Jesus in 8:11 for a sign from heaven, but evidently has a wholly different purpose, particularly because it does not require Jesus to establish his identity. It may seem strange that the disciples connect the destruction of the temple to the end time. But if the first readers are already acquainted with the – to them very recent – destruction of the temple, the combination of the two elements is really quite understandable. For in the situation created by the destruction of the temple the question becomes urgent if that event – for all Jews and Christians of Jewish origin an extremely traumatic experience – marks the beginning of the end time, and if things will now take their course in accordance with the well-known scenarios depicted in current apocalyptic books.

That those to whom Jesus addresses himself are so few becomes understandable when the reader realizes Jesus is here disclosing the end of the current order of existence. Secrecy and a small esoteric audience are standard characteristics of such revelations in the apocalyptic literature that has come down to us from that time. That his audience consists of these four may be connected with the fact that at the start of the book they are mentioned as the first disciples of Jesus. The order of the names fits in with the fact that the three disciples mentioned first form a privileged group in other places and that the same order is also found in the list of apostles given in 3:16-19.

The tiny size of the group of listeners is at odds with the fact that much of what Jesus says here bears on others as well and, not infrequently, on many and even on all. The narrator goes beyond the representation of the very limited audience in two ways. He does it first of all through the closing sentence of the whole discourse in 13:37: 'And what I say to you, I say to everyone.' Thus, against the small group of four the vast, even infinitely large, multitude of 'all' is set as those for whom Jesus' words are meant. Through their place right at the end these words probably refer to every piece of advice given before, that is, to the whole discourse. Secondly, the narrator inserts, and that within the middle of a sentence spoken by Jesus, the words 'let the reader understand' (13:14). Some interpreters think this is meant as a hint for someone reading the text to an audience or congregation. But although the word concerned (Greek *anaginōskō*) has this meaning in some places, there are other places in Mark where it can only mean 'to read' (2:25; 12:10 and 12:26). If this is also the case here, the narrator has Jesus speak directly to whoever reads out, listens to or reads the text for themselves, and moreover, both adheres to and breaks through the convention of representing revelations as directed to a limited audience, so that readers find they are addressed more directly in this discourse than in the words of Jesus reported elsewhere in the book.

Other characters – like demons, adversaries, and people seeking healing – do not occur at all in the narrative text of this chapter, although they may be said to have their counterparts within the spoken text of Jesus: pseudo-messiahs who work great signs, princes and judges who call Jesus' followers to account, and pregnant and nursing women.

The Time of The Reader

The difference in time between the utterances of Jesus, the writing of the book, and the reading of it, on the one hand, and the interpolation addressed to the reader in 13:14, on the other, gives us every reason to presume that the narrator wishes to warn the readers through this section of a situation that already exists or may arise at any moment.

In the first part (A1) the characteristics of that time are clearly described. It is a time mainly characterized by *persecutions*. These are mentioned in detail and also placed in the centre of the first part (13:9-13). The passage brings together and reinforces text signals that are scattered throughout the earlier parts of the book (4:17; 4:37; 8:34-9:1; 9:42-48; 10:30). One of these (8:34-9:1) combines the persecutions, the coming of the son of man, and the announcement that this will happen before the generation then living has passed away in the same order, as can be seen from the following outline.

persecutions	8:34–37	13:9–13
the coming of the son of man	8:38	13:26
before the living generation has passed away	9:1	13:30

If Jesus says in 8:34–37 that his followers should be prepared to give up their lives rather than renounce his name when taken to court for their beliefs, in 13:9–13 this situation is made more explicit. The judges are specifically mentioned and appear to be Jews as well as Gentiles. Their victims stand before them not only to answer the charge that they have proclaimed and, in spite of threats, have gone on proclaiming the good news of Jesus, but also to do so again in their presence. Thus, before the son of man comes the good news will have been proclaimed to all Gentile nations, as it has been determined (13:9–10). Whoever is hauled before such a court need not worry about how to find the right words. The holy spirit will give them to him (13:11). And whoever loses his life will be saved because he has endured to the end (8:35–37; 13:12–13).

If the question of when these things will happen is left unanswered in the central passage of the first part of Jesus' reply (13:9–13), the situation is different in the passage surrounding it (a1, b1, b2, and a2). The first two (a1 and b1) mention all sorts of horrors which create the impression that they immediately precede and mark the beginning of the end time, although in fact they do not. First, the very frequent and successful appearances of people who proclaim *false doctrines* and pretend to be the messiah or even pose as Jesus himself come back to earth. Second, *wars* and terrifying rumours of war. And, finally, *natural disasters* in various places. It is inevitable that these events will happen, but they are not directly related to the end. They are the beginning of the birth-pangs of the end time and the time of the messiah, but the end itself may yet be far distant. Persecutions will also begin in that period, for it is the readers themselves who are warned not to be taken in by false doctrines, not to panic, and to be on their guard against judges and those who bring charges against them and plot their death.

The warning becomes even more urgent in the two passages that follow the central part about the persecutions (b2 and a2). The people who are in Judaea must flee at once, and not go back into the house to fetch any of their belongings or even a cloak. The signal for the flight is a highly mysterious sign: when they see the *disastrous abomination* set up in a place where it ought not to be at all. This mysteriousness is all the more remarkable since the signal for the flight seems also to be the sign for which the four disciples have asked at the beginning of the chapter (13:4). Besides, the narrator's advice that the reader should do his utmost to understand what is said here suggests that the mysteriousness is intentional. In times of persecutions it may be necessary to communicate in guarded terms and even in secret language which cannot be understood by enemies.

What can the term refer to? The curious combination *disastrous abomination* or *abomination of desolation* also occurs in the book of Daniel (9:27; 11:31; 12:11), where it refers to the altar of Zeus set up by Antiochus IV in the temple of Jerusalem at the time of the great persecution of 167–164 B.C. This act profaned and therefore destroyed the temple, not as a building but as a sanctuary. It seems that the reader must look for an answer along these lines. Accordingly, authors who presume that Mark is based on an earlier document think of the statue that the emperor Caligula intended to erect in the temple as a symbol of the victory of the imperial cult. As a result of his death in A.D.41 this proposal was not carried out, but knowledge of the intention was enough in itself to cause great unrest in the country. But it is obvious that Mark cannot be referring his readers to that event. To the readers of Mark the erection of the altar by Antiochus and the intended sacrilege of the temple by Caligula belong to the past, even if the latter event occurred only a few decades before the first reading of Mark. From the fact that the narrator calls on the reader to make sure that he understands what is written here, we had perhaps best infer that he deliberately has Jesus announce an obscure and ambiguous signal.

The question arises, in fact, whether the sign under consideration is meant for the readers at all. Unless they are inhabitants of Judaea the necessity to flee does not apply to them, and more or

less the same is true of the advice to escape at once: if one happens
to be on the roof, down the outside stairs without going into the
house, and if one is in the field, directly to the mountains without
first going home. Also the hope that it may not happen in winter
is perhaps connected with Judaea, for the water of the Jordan is
known to rise to such a level that it is impossible for people to
cross the river safely. It would seem, however, that the passage is
understood best if we take it to refer to a wartime situation in
which the temple is first profaned – for example by a general
intruding into the Holy of Holies – and then destroyed. Besides,
the expression *disastrous abomination* will certainly remind the
reader of Jesus' announcement that of the fine buildings of the
temple not one stone will be left upon another, and of the question
of the disciples when this will happen.

Finally, 13:20 says clearly that the time of the persecutions and
the flight referred to *has been* shortened, so that the event in
question – whatever it may be precisely – is likely to have already
happened. Accordingly, in the next part of the discourse Jesus
holds out to his listeners the short-term prospect of the coming of
the son of man. That would also mean that the good news must
have been proclaimed before then to all nations (3:10). Although
this cannot be true for all the nations existing at this period, it may
be true for the nations in the then known western world, comprising Italy, Greece, Asia Minor, the Near East, Egypt, North
Africa and Spain; in other words, the countries around the Mediterranean and the neighbouring areas.

As to the readers who do not live in Judaea – the group to which
the first readers probably belonged – they can only take note of
the appeal made in 13:15-17. But the passage may also have a
certain effect for these readers. It seems to me that the mysteriousness of the signal creates a sense of uncertainty which
anticipates the condition of not knowing and the necessity of
being continuously on the lookout so strongly emphasized in the
third part of the discourse (13:28-37, referred to as A2 above).

The Coming of the Son of Man

Jesus has spoken of 'the son of man' before. In the first two places, in 2:10 and 2:28, he has used the term in such a way that it does not necessarily refer to himself. But from 8:31 onwards he has used it regularly within the framework of the announcements of his execution and resurrection, so that the reader has come to understand that the son of man is none other than Jesus himself. In 8:38 he speaks for the first time about a coming of the son of man in the future. This is brought up again in 13:26. It may be useful to point out that the Greek term (*ho huios tou anthrōpou*) sounds so un-Greek that a Greek does not know what to make of it unless he knows it already from Daniel, Ezekiel or the apocalyptic books. The fact that in 8:38 Jesus first uses the pronouns 'me' and 'my' ('if anyone is ashamed of *me* and *my* words'), and then 'the son of man' and 'he' ('the *son of man* will be ashamed of him when *he* comes'), may have caused some confusion in the mind of the reader about the identity of the son of man. But now that the term has been mentioned so often in connection with the execution and resurrection of Jesus, there can be no doubt that it applies to Jesus himself.

After the cosmic disasters have taken place everyone will see Jesus as the son of man coming in the clouds with great power and glory (13:26). Although the prophet Daniel is not referred to by name, Jesus' words announcing this coming are taken from Daniel 7:13, where they refer to the Jewish people who, after severe persecutions, will be vindicated by JHWH, given the place of honour and invested with the power to rule over the nations of the world. It is not improbable that in the days of Mark these word were already associated with the messiah in Jewish circles, but then of course with the messiah from the house of David, whose coming was still expected. And although in Aramaic one can use the term '(the) son of man' (*bar nasj* or *bar nasja*) to refer to oneself for reasons of modesty, it is unprecedented in a Jewish milieu that someone, even if he has messianic pretensions, should announce himself as *a* or *the* messianic son of man. Yet it is undeniable that Jesus is referring to himself when he speaks of the son of man who has the right to forgive sins and is sovereign over the sabbath, and who in the short term will be executed and rise after three days, and in the long term will come with power and glory. That Jesus is still to come as the son of man presupposes on the one hand that he will first have shared the fate of persecuted Israel referred to by Daniel, and on the other that after this he will have been raised from the dead. The cosmological catastrophes and the assembling of the chosen by God's messengers, who here become the messengers of the son of man Jesus, belong to the conventional representations of the apocalyptic framework within which Jesus announces this coming in 13:24-26. But what Mark has Jesus say of himself within this traditional framework is not only unconventional but also contrary to prevailing Jewish conviction and belief.

The Date of the Coming and the Fulfilment

The question of when the fulfilment will take place and by what signs that point in time may be calculated has always been a matter of the greatest interest in apocalyptic everywhere. Hence the question of the four disciples in 13:4. The answer is given through two parables, of which the first, the parable of the fig tree, exemplifies the course of things in nature: when its shoots appear and are breaking into leaf, summer is coming. In the same way, there is a kind of intrinsic connection between the events mentioned and the end. When those events are happening, the end is near. But the reader may well ask how he is to understand the precise nature of that connection. Persecutions, wars, and disasters are always happening somewhere, and that Jesus' followers are misled is no rare event either. The only specific event mentioned, the disastrous abomination set up in a place where it ought not to be, is too vague and ambiguous to help him any further. All this reduces the importance of the connection between the events that are to announce the coming of the son of man and the coming itself. The connection is weakened even further by the second parable: as little as the door-keeper knows on what day and at what hour of the day or night the master of the house is coming home, so little do we know when the son of man Jesus will come again; that it is why it is necessary to remain continuously watchful.

The contrast expressed by the two parables is reflected in a contradiction between the two sayings inserted between them, in 13:30-33. On the one hand Jesus says that the end will arrive before the generation then living has passed away. And the reader remembers that prior to this he has said something similar with regard to the definitive and public breakthrough of God's kingdom (9:11). But on the other hand, Jesus states most emphatically that as for the day or hour no one knows, not even the heavenly messengers, nor the son, but only the father. Son of God or son of man, Jesus does not have this knowledge either. It seems to me that the least we can say of the inconsistency between the two pronouncements is that the reader gets confused. If Jesus, in whatever capacity, does not know the day or the hour, what value can then be attached to his knowledge of the term set for his contemporaries? Does he himself not give us to understand that it is no more than a guess or perhaps only a wish, and that this knowledge is of a different nature and value than, for example, his foreknowledge of the way two of his disciples will find the colt on which he rides into Jerusalem (11:1-6)? Or could it be that the very ignorance of the day and hour of the end entails that every generation has to reckon with the possibility of being the last? Be that as it may, what is really important in this chapter is not primarily the information about what is going to happen and when, but the repeated exhortation to be continuously on the alert (13:5; 13:9; 13:23; 13:33) and watchful (13:33; 13:37) because the moment of the coming of the son of man remains unknown and will be unexpected to everyone (13:32; 13:33; 13:35; 13:36).

Jesus and His Followers

This section of Mark shows that on at least two important points there is continuity between what happens to Jesus and to his followers. Like Jesus, they will be exposed to persecutions. The verb 'deliver up' (Greek *paradidōmi)* with a person as direct object refers strictly speaking to that person's arrest, but in a wider sense it covers the unjust and arbitrary treatment he receives at the hands of those who have him in their power. The word is used with reference to John the baptist (1:14), Jesus (e.g. in chapter 14), and his followers (13:9; 13:12), so that they are joined together by what happens to each of them. The same applies to their being summoned to appear before governors and kings in order to bear witness before them (13:9). The second point concerns the exact moment of the coming of the son of man. Of this the son of man and son of God Jesus is, and will be, just as ignorant as his followers (13:32; 13:33-34), so that in this respect too they are in exactly the same position.

The Adversaries

Although none of Jesus' adversaries figure as characters in this part of the text, their counterparts appear in the discourse of Jesus, where in accordance with the shifting of the scene they are given various names but invariably embody the forces of evil. This applies to pseudo-messiahs, by whom many will be led astray (13:6; 13:21), and who could be regarded as the very image of the scribes and pharisees. The governors and kings of 13:9 treat the followers of Jesus in the same way as the chief priests and Pilate treat Jesus. The relatives who turn against members of their own family and hand them over to the executioners (13:12) act in a way that is comparable both to the rejection of Jesus by his next of kin and his fellow townsmen and to the part played by the crowd pressing Pilate for Jesus' execution.

The Fulfilment and the First Testament

Nowhere is it so obvious as here that it is difficult and questionable to discuss Mark without taking into account that the narrator and his first readers were acquainted with the text of the First Testament and the apocalyptic books. In other places later readers can usually understand most of what the narrator wishes to say with his own story even if they lack such knowledge. That is hardly the case in this section, where a twentieth-century reader enters a conceptual universe determined by literary conventions and dramatic presentations so foreign to his own cultural background that he cannot but look at it with puzzled wonder. It becomes more accessible, however, when he realizes that it gives expression to the First Testament concept of the day of JHWH, in the Greek translation of the bible called 'the day of the Lord' (*hē hēmera tou Kuriou*). Initially it is the day Israel looks forward to and on which it expects to be delivered from its oppressors. Through the influence of the prophets its meaning is extended to include the punishment of Israel's enemies. Again through prophetic influence Israel gradually comes to understand that salvation and punishment are not necessarily administered in accordance with the distinction between the Jews and other nations. Thus the day of JHWH becomes more and more the day of judgement as we know it from the later prophets, who describe it as an event of cosmic dimensions.

In the last few centuries before Jesus, interest in the day of JHWH greatly increased as a result of the persecution of Israel under Antiochus IV. It was in those days of distress, too, that the book of Daniel originated, which is a truly apocalyptic work. In the later, apocryphal books of this nature, the events of the day of JHWH were even laid down in detailed scenarios. In some of these there is also a part assigned to a 'son of man', but it is probable that we have to do here with Christian additions to originally Jewish texts.

What Jesus announces in this section of Mark is more or less similar in content and tone to the usual apocalyptic scenarios except for two very important differences: it is impossible to know and calculate the time of the end, and the one who will come to judge (8:38) is Jesus himself. The second point in particular is extremely relevant to the question of Jesus' identity. Mark speaks nowhere about a pre-existence of Jesus, and it would seem that he does not presuppose it either. But the book speaks the more clearly about what, for want of a better term, I would like to call the post-existence of Jesus. Of this the narrator gives several instances. In this part of Mark it is the tortured, executed and risen Jesus cast for the part of the judge who, according to the scenario of the end time, is due to come in the clouds with great power and majesty to conduct the final judgement, indict and punish the unrepentant, acquit and bring together the just.

10

ELIMINATION
14:1 – 15:39

Context and Structure

Already at quite an early stage of Jesus' ministry the pharisees and accomplices of Herod have agreed to eliminate Jesus. This section relates to the final result of their cooperation, which in terms of the story means the climax of the first plot. How Jesus is actually silenced will not come as a surprise to the reader. After all, Jesus himself has repeatedly announced what will eventually happen to him. And whenever he has foretold short-term events his predictions have come true. The climax takes place in two stages: in the first, which is related in this chapter, Jesus' adversaries carry out their plan to eliminate him; in the second Jesus rises from the dead. Of the first phase a detailed description is given in the third announcement (10:33-34): 1. the handing over to the chief priests and scribes; 2. the death sentence; 3. the handing over to the pagans; 4. the mockery and spitting; 5. the flogging; 6. the execution. To the second phase the announcements never devote more than a few words: the resurrection three days later. The story itself reflects the same difference in that it devotes about ten times as much space to the arrest, trial and execution as it does to the resurrection.

This section of Mark appears in its natural biographical and chronological position: at the end. Its structure is also straightforward: the betrayal by Judas, the arrest, the interrogation and sentence of the high council, the handing over to Pilate, the assessment of the punishment by the governor, the flogging, the mockery, the leading away to the place of execution, the cruci-

fixion, death and burial are told in the order in which events of
this nature usually take place. Within the whole course of events
in Jerusalem the passover meal could have taken place earlier, not
later, but it is of course tied to one day. It is therefore unnecessary
to find a special reason behind the narrator's deviation from using
the sandwich-construction. The book relates events in their
natural, biographical order. This order is so obvious and self-
evident that after the chronological survey given above there is no
need to discuss the main line of the story in this chapter.

Yet it is interesting to note that even in a chapter where the
events are mainly told in chronological order, the narrator uses at
least four sandwich-constructions to connect or contrast certain
themes, or heighten their dramatic effect. At the beginning of the
subsection, the anointing of Jesus at Bethany (14:3-8) anticipates
his burial, which is related at the end (15:42-46). The anointing at
Bethany itself is preceded and followed by interim information
on the progress of the plans that are to lead to Jesus' death (14:1-2
and 14:10-11). The central part on bread and wine is flanked on
one side by the announcement of the betrayal by one of the twelve
(14:18-21) and on the other by the announcement of the flight of
the others and of Peter's denial (14:27-31). The interrogation of
Jesus is preceded by the information that Peter has entered the
house of the high priest (14:54) and is followed by the account of
Peter's denial of Jesus (14:66-72).

Times and Places

As we have said before, the narrator generally makes only a
sparing use of indications of time, but employs them much more
abundantly in this chapter. From the following chronological
survey it also appears that these indications become more specific
towards the end, so that the time on the last day is almost
measured by the hour.

14:1	two days before the passover and the feast of unleavened bread
14:12	the first day of unleavened bread

14:17	the evening
14:68	at cockcrow
15:1	the morning
15:25	the third hour
15:33	the sixth hour
15:34	the ninth hour

But the period in which these events take place is also significant. Jesus' arrest and execution are placed at the time of the jewish *pesach* festival. This is important for the story in various ways. In the first place because Jerusalem is crowded with pilgrims who have come to the capital to celebrate the passover. The paschal lambs could not be slaughtered anywhere but in the temple, so that the opening rite of the feast, which consists of the eating of the lamb with unleavened bread and bitter herbs, and the drinking of the wine, could only take place in Jerusalem. Among other things, the passover feast recalls and celebrates the deliverance out of Egypt, and was therefore, especially in days of oppression and foreign occupation, liable to stir up messianic expectations, which might easily spark off riots or subversive activities against Rome. So, for fear of rousing the masses they may be unable to control, which might lead to the miscarriage of their plans to eliminate Jesus, or even to a bloody intervention by the Roman troops, Jesus' adversaries decide not to seize and kill him during the festival.

But the setting of Jesus' execution on the feast of the passover is also important at a deeper level. It shows the irony of Jesus' end, for the feast also commemorates the occasion when JHWH killed all the first-born of Egypt but spared those of the children of Israel, as he had earlier spared Abraham's son on the same mountain where later the temple would be built and the paschal lambs would be slaughtered (Genesis 22 and 2 Chronicles 13). On this same night the son of God is not spared but arrested and sentenced to death by the leaders of that same Israel. The contrasts that the feast of the passover and the temple mountain call up in the mind of the reader give the story an exceedingly unpleasant flavour.

The places involved are also described in some detail. Only

now, at the beginning of this section, is the reader told that since Jesus started visiting Jerusalem he has stayed in the house of Simon the leper at Bethany (14:3). That he has his disciples look in Jerusalem for a place to celebrate the passover meal is quite normal, as is the ease with which they acquire a large upper room. It is very intriguing, however, that after the meal Jesus does not return to Bethany but goes to the Mount of Olives. In a garden called Gethsemane, out in the open and far from the city crowds, Jesus prepares himself for the things to come. The accessibility of the place heightens Jesus' vulnerability, which is especially highlighted in this part of the story. His determination to seek out a place that is perfectly suitable for his enemies, who shun publicity and commotion of any kind, contrasts strongly with the agony he later falls into in the garden.

Until the moment of his arrest Jesus has gone his own way. After his arrest the adversaries' servants first take him to the place where the chief priests have assembled for a meeting of the high council, and then, next morning, to Pilate, who seems to interrogate him out of doors in a place where the crowd is free to enter. Only after the verdict do the soldiers take Jesus into the praetorium, from where he is brought to Golgotha to be executed on the cross. In describing these movements in such detail the narrator gives the impression that he attaches great importance to a careful setting of the story. Besides, the character of these movements gives the story a certain duality. In the first half Jesus determines his own movements and the story too is thought to be or to take place where Jesus is. The adversaries are thought to be somewhere else (14:11 and 14:43). In the second half everything happens in places where the adversaries are in charge, and the disciples are elsewhere. In the middle the story of Jesus' arrest and condemnation brings Jesus himself, one of the disciples and the adversaries to one and the same place.

The Adversaries

This is the part of Mark devoted to the adversaries, a group that usually consists of the chief priests, scribes and elders, even in situations where not all three of them are named. The pharisees are no longer mentioned. At the beginning of the section the adversaries are said to be looking for a way to seize Jesus by some trick and have him put to death, and at the end they stand around the crucified Jesus to mock him and attend his execution. The end shows the fact that, and the way in which, they have realized the plan devised at the beginning. In addition, the story in between relates that a disciple of Jesus, the last one on the list of the twelve, offers to deliver Jesus to them, while another disciple, the first of the twelve, refuses to acknowledge that he has anything to do with him. Unlike the disciples in the second half of the section, the adversaries are continuously present, as they were in the first half. It is not that the reader witnesses their activity on the stage of the book, but they are so busy backstage that he cannot help hearing them.

The first thing the reader hears is that they would like to take advantage of Jesus' presence in Jerusalem, but are afraid of a disturbance among the people and therefore decide to seize him by stratagem and wait until after the feast. They seem to take it for granted that the celebrating crowds are so favourably disposed towards Jesus that they will resist a public arrest. The narrator returns to the subject after the anointing at Bethany. After this incident Judas Iscariot goes to the temple authorities to offer to deliver Jesus to them. The text does not say whether he asks to be paid for this, but with the preceding story laying so much stress on costly ointment, wastefulness and money, the reader gets that impression, especially when he reads that the chief priests actually promise to give money to Judas, who subsequently starts looking for a suitable opportunity to hand Jesus over to them. Here again the reader appears to be a step ahead of the disciples, who are as yet unaware that one of them will turn Jesus over to the enemy. The twelve are confronted with this when Judas is celebrating the passover meal with them. The continued presence of Judas in their midst makes it impossible for the reader to forget the adversaries. The narrator does not tell us when Judas goes away to carry out his promise. But even if Judas is no longer present when Jesus announces on the way to the Mount of Olives that all the disciples will desert him, the reader senses the pervasive presence of the adversaries in this episode as well. For when Jesus, with a quotation from the prophet Zechariah, goes on to say that the shepherd will be struck down (Zechariah 13:7), the servants and soldiers who strike and maltreat him do so by order of members of the high council.

But it is not until the arrest in the garden that the adversaries really have Jesus in their power. In the orchard Jesus has already announced their coming. After Judas has indicated who is to be arrested, the accomplices of the temple authorities apprehend him. The incident of the high priest's servant, who loses an ear when one of Jesus' party draws his sword, is dealt with in a matter-of-fact way in Mark without the narrator paying any more attention to it. After a protest from Jesus against the unwarranted display of power on the part of his adversaries, the prisoner is led off to the high priest.

Trial and Crucifixion

Framed impressively between the treason of Judas on one side and the abjuration of Peter on the other, the story relating the interrogation of Jesus and his condemnation by the high priest and the members of the high council – whose names remain unknown to the reader – forms a climax within this chapter. The narrator states in no uncertain terms that before the beginning of the interrogation Jesus' death has already been decided on. It is only a matter of finding witnesses who will make such incriminating statements against Jesus that he can be sentenced to death. But their accusations do not agree, after which false witnesses appear who declare that they have heard Jesus say: 'I will pull down this temple made with human hands, and in three days I will build another, not made with hands.' They are false witnesses, since Jesus has spoken only to his disciples about the destruction of the temple and his resurrection after three days, and in entirely different terms. What Jesus has said to the adversaries about the stone that is to be turned into the cornerstone by God is too indistinct and enigmatic to serve as witnesses' testimony. They have not heard him say so themselves, so they can only bring forward hearsay evidence. And, Mark continues, even on this point their evidence does not agree. But he does not tell the reader what the difference is. Yet although their testimony is formally false, the reader knows very well that materially these witnesses are not altogether wrong. According to Jesus the temple buildings will be razed to the ground, and the temple ordinance will have to make way for an order of which the centre is no longer the temple, a building or a set of rules and instructions, but the risen Jesus, a person of flesh and blood, who expresses what according to God is the destiny of men and the world. Jesus has never said or suggested that he himself would demolish the temple, yet when the high priest questions him about the statements made by these witnesses Jesus remains silent.

The high priest realizes that it will be impossible to secure Jesus' condemnation in this way, so he decides to take the initiative himself and ask Jesus straight out: 'Are you the messiah, the son of the Blessed One?' Only now does Jesus break his silence to state emphatically: 'I am, and you will see the son of man seated at the right hand of God and coming with the clouds of heaven.' To the reader it is clear that Jesus here casts aside all mysteriousness and speaks without any reservations. He recognizes the three names that are of the greatest importance in the book. 'Messiah' is the name given to him by those who after all are closest to him (8:29) and also the one adopted by the narrator in the title of the book (1:1). 'Son of the Blessed One' is an otherwise unknown Jewish-sounding variation of the name called twice from heaven (1:11 and 9:7), and this name, too, the narrator has adopted in the title by adding to 'messiah' the designation 'son of God'. 'Son of man' is the name which is used only by Jesus and by no one else in the book, and which is here surrounded by clear references to Psalm 110:1 and Daniel 7:13.

This moment is of exceptional importance for the story. Jesus affirms that he is the one whose identity is attributed to him by the high priest, although he knows full well, according to the narrator, what the consequences of his statement will be. At the same time he says that the roles will be reversed. Jesus stands before the high council as a defendant on the brink of being sentenced and punished. But when the son of man takes his place on the right hand of God and comes with the clouds of heaven, he will judge those who now sentence him. Just as in 8:38 and 13:26, the reader is referred to a future that is to begin after Jesus' elimination and to be concluded with the coming of the son of man, who as a judge will put things right.

The high priest's reaction in the story is different from that of the reader. Where the latter interprets Jesus' reply as a revelation of the truth about Jesus, the high priest considers it outrageously arrogant, describing it as the worst form of lying: blasphemy. Accordingly, this is the charge brought against Jesus and the ground for the death sentence which the members of the high council immediately and unanimously pronounce. The fact that a number of those present spit on Jesus, blindfold and strike him, pestering him to demonstrate his gift of prophecy by telling them who has hit him, turns at least some of the judges into torturers, making them lose what credibility they have in the eyes of the reader.

Of these adversaries the reader will meet the chief priests and the scribes once again on the second last page of the book, when, hanging on the cross between two robbers, Jesus is exposed to the mockery of the passers-by, the chief priests and the scribes, and even of the two men who are crucified with him. The reader is not told what the latter say to Jesus. The passers-by speak directly to the crucified Jesus, telling him with a reference to the accusation made at the trial that he who thinks himself able to destroy the temple and rebuild it in three days should try and come down from the cross and save himself. Clearly, the implication is that it is easier to come down from the cross than to demolish and rebuild the temple. The reader knows, of course, that the fact that Jesus does not come down from the cross does not mean that the temple will remain standing.

The chief priests and scribes do not speak to Jesus; they talk among themselves. The narrator has them call Jesus scornfully 'messiah, king of Israel', which is the Jewish version of 'king of the Jews'. They, too, sneeringly challenge Jesus to come down from the cross, but in two respects their mockery surpasses that of the passers-by. If they see him come down from the cross, they say, then they will believe. Whether this remark, coming from their lips, should be understood ironically, is a difficult question to answer. But in Mark there is no question of there being such a connection between seeing and believing. After all, the numerous signs Jesus has worked so far have not resulted in faith. This goes not only for Jesus' adversaries but even for his followers. And the few times Jesus has praised someone for his or her faith, it is with reference to trust that precedes a healing. The second element touches a central theme of the book even more clearly. The chief priests and scribes also say: 'He saves others, but he cannot save himself.' As to the first part, it is not only correct but also gives a short summary of Jesus' programme of life as opposed to those of the demons and Jesus' adversaries. But the second part . . . According to the narrator these people may not know any better. But readers do. On the one hand they have heard about Jesus conquering and destroying an entire legion of demons. And that is a lot more than a company of a hundred soldiers. And on the other hand they remember that Jesus has said that someone whose ultimate goal it is to save *himself* will lose his true life (8:34-35). Jesus could come down from the cross if he wanted to, but he does not want to because the chief priests and scribes would not change their attitude, and he himself would have to conform to their views and practices and abandon the path through life which God has outlined for him.

Pilate and his Soldiers

The members of the high council clearly have the initiative, and the Roman procurator Pilate – the narrator mentions his name but not his function – is persuaded against his will to approve and confirm the punishment they have already imposed on Jesus. His question about whether Jesus is the king of the Jews makes the reader suspect that in Mark's representation the chief priests have not mentioned the all-important allegation of blasphemy but have seized upon the names 'messiah' and 'son of the Blessed One' to deliver Jesus as one who claims to be the messiah and is therefore a threat to the Roman peace and state. Jesus' reply is evasive. And other charges and more questions yield nothing but a stubborn silence. To overcome the deadlock Pilate takes up the question from the crowd asking him to grant amnesty to a prisoner, which is a usual favour at the festival season. Realizing that it is the chief priests that wish to settle an account with Jesus he asks the crowd if they would like him to release 'the king of the Jews'. But the chief priests put pressure on them to demand the release of a certain Barabbas, a man who killed someone during an insurrection. The reader who knows that 'bar' means son (10:46) and 'abba' father (14:36) realizes that taken in the fullest sense of these words the name 'bar-abbas' is due only to Jesus. This gives the story a double meaning, to which I shall return later.

What calls for immediate attention is the surprising and completely unexpected change in the attitude of the crowd, who so far have only shown sympathy for Jesus. In the preceding chapters it has been emphasized no less than three times (11:18; 11:32; 12:12) that the adversaries are rightly afraid of the reactions of the crowd lest it discovers that they are plotting to eliminate Jesus. The change is not only unexpected but also complete. Instead of being a hindrance to the murder of Jesus, the crowd is now an effective aid. In fact, now that they have begun to ask for the customary favour of having a prisoner released to them, and Pilate supposedly is a man inclined to leave to others the decision about who is to be granted amnesty, the multitude suddenly occupies a key position in the story of Jesus' life. It is the chief priests who persuade the crowd to ask Pilate that he should release Barabbas and twice demand that he should crucify Jesus. In this way the crowd is changed from an obstacle into an instrument. Their shout to crucify Jesus, and the same shout repeated to answer Pilate's rhetorical question, from which it is clear that he is unable to see the prisoner guilty of the charges levelled against him, induce Pilate to conclude that his plan has fallen through. He releases Barabbas and orders Jesus to be flogged and crucified.

It is not without reason that these two actions are named together in the closing sentence (15:15). It is not only that the guilty party is set free and the innocent person put to death. The story also shows that the chief priests have the multitude ask for the release of Barabbas because they wish to prevent Jesus escaping execution. Thus, Jesus is put to death in the place of someone else, so that his death is a vicarious execution. Since the name Barabbas says something that is true of every man, namely that he is the son of a father, it has a similar function to 'Everyman' in medieval morality plays, giving the vicarious execution an application that goes beyond the one character that bears that name.

The soldiers not only flog Jesus but also make a mockery of him. Pilate has asked Jesus seriously if he considers himself the king of the Jews, an important question in occupied Jewish territory. Before taking Jesus to the place of execution the soldiers make him a mock king, although Jesus has given no evidence of regarding himself as the king of the Jews. They alternate the purple cloak, the saluting and the kneeling with physical torture: they place a crown of thorns on his head and strike on it with a cane. After the torture Pilate's soldiers also carry out the execution, which is likewise related soberly and concisely.

But although the soldiers are accomplices of the adversaries, one of these, the centurion, is brought forward by the narrator as the one who is the first to say something about Jesus that is nearer to the truth than any other pronouncement by a human being in Mark. The temple authorities have said that they would believe Jesus if they first saw him come down from the cross. This man sees the same as the temple authorities, namely, that Jesus does not descend from the cross. But he also sees the expression of unlimited loyalty in this dying stranger, and precisely on that ground exclaims that this man was really God's son. This is certainly not a full confession of the Christian faith, as the reader realizes when he thinks of the title of the book. A full confession does not concern the Jesus who was, but the Jesus who is, and what he inspires people to do through what he started.

The Supporters

This chapter ends in tragedy not only for Jesus but also for his supporters. True, they do not get killed, but they are disloyal to Jesus. The desert him because they are afraid of possible actions on the part of Jesus' adversaries. The story clearly builds up to a climax: it begins with incomprehension and ends with treason, seeking safety in flight and the renunciation of Jesus.

The anointing in the house of Simon the leper ends, as other incidents before it, in a discussion which shows complete incomprehension of what is going on. It centres on the cost of the balm, three hundred denarii representing a small annual salary, which according to some of those present could have been spent better on the poor. Although this recommendation fully corresponds with what Jesus himself has said elsewhere in the book (10:21), it entirely overlooks the fact that the Jerusalem authorities are getting ready to kill him soon. It is true that the characters do not know what the narrator has just told the reader about this (14:1-2), but if the twelve are present, which may be presumed from 11:11, it goes without saying that they must remember what Jesus has predicted several times on the way to Jerusalem. Accordingly, the present misunderstanding compounds their failure to understand these earlier predictions. Those who protest against the waste are reprimanded; the woman, on the other hand, is praised in a way not found elsewhere in the book. Wherever in the world the good news is proclaimed, what she has done will be told in order to keep the memory of her alive. So important is right understanding and acting upon it. That this is said exclusively of a woman should make the reader think, especially because at the beginning of the last section of the book as well, women are the only ones who stand firm at Jesus' cross. In passing the narrator gives the reader to understand what 'good news' (Greek *euaggelion*, transcribed into 'evangel', now obsolete, and derivatives like 'evangelist') really is. Three words here are of capital importance: proclaim, story, and memory. 'Good news' is not yet a book about Jesus, for that does not exist yet. What exists is that which is proclaimed about Jesus' death and resurrection in the form of a story, a story which, moreover, retains the memory of what he himself has said and done before his death and resurrection.

Together at the Passover Meal

The preparation for and the partaking of the passover meal are limited to Jesus and the twelve. It was quite normal for the inhabitants of Jerusalem to accommodate pilgrims who had come to Jerusalem as a family or a group of friends, numbering some ten or twelve people, to celebrate the passover feast. Just as with the donkey in 11:2-6, Jesus tells two of his disciples in detail what they will find when they go to Jerusalem to prepare for passover and make arrangements for a room to be ready for them. The sign directing the two to the particular upper room concerned – a man carrying a jar of water – is intriguing. It is conspicuous and unusual enough to serve as a sign, for water is normally fetched from the well by women. Men carry other liquids like wine, but they do so in skins, not in jars. The sign is intriguing to the reader because numerous other signs might have been chosen. In other words, is it significant that this particular sign is given? And what could its meaning be? Perhaps the water brought into the house is to be used for the hand-washing before the meal, and is thus meant to suggest that the disciples, who on other occasions eat without washing their hands (7:2), do wash their hands before this special meal? But this can only be conjectural. Be that as it may, after 11:2-6 the reader is not surprised that the two disciples should find everything exactly the way Jesus has foretold.

Contrary to expectation, the passover meal itself is not really described at all, but only hinted at. The narrator relates, however two special incidents. The first is the foretelling of treason by one of the twelve. This is entirely in keeping with the other predictions by Jesus which are so strongly associated with his last few days in Jerusalem. Attentive readers will undoubtedly remember that although Jesus has predicted his murder several times, he has not said before that someone from his own circle will betray him. If readers already know, it is because the narrator has told them so at the end of the list of the twelve, in 3:19. On account of that information readers are sure to have thought spontaneously of Judas when in 9:31 and 10:33 Jesus announced the way he would be handed over to the temple authorities (Greek *paradidōmi*), but so far it has not yet been stated in unequivocal terms that he is going to be given up to the enemy by one of them. Pressed to disclose the identity of the traitor, Jesus confines himself to a mysterious and obscure reply, telling them in fact no more than before, namely, that it is one of the table-companions. So readers still have an advantage over the characters, while on the other hand the information given fills the gap in the announcements about the events of the last week. Jesus' foreknowledge gives the impression that by anticipating what is to happen to him he has his future in his own hands to some extent.

The second incident, which also takes place during the passover meal, is no less mysterious. The ritual signs enacted at the passover meal with the unleavened loaves and the wine are either supplemented or replaced – the story keeps the reader guessing which of the two exactly is the case – by a new sign. The broken bread, Jesus says, refers to his body, the cup of wine that has been drunk to his shed blood, which seals a new covenant for the benefit of many people. Only in combination with the shed blood does it appear that the body referred to is likewise that of the murdered Jesus. Thus Jesus makes clear through a sign what so far he has announced only with words. Readers do not learn whether the twelve have understood this sign. Neither do they read here that Jesus tells them to repeat later what he himself has just done. The incident concludes with Jesus' promise not to drink wine again until the day he drinks new wine in the kingdom of God brought to its consummation in heaven. That Jesus refers to wine as 'the fruit of the vine' draws readers' attention to connections that will be discussed in another section of this chapter.

In the Garden of Gethsemane

After closing the passover meal with the usual song of praise, Jesus sets out into the night with the twelve for the Mount of Olives. Again he elaborates on his earlier announcements, warning the twelve that the traitor will not be the only one to fail him. Without exception every one of the twelve will desert him. At the same time Jesus announces that the murdered shepherd will, after his resurrection, go before them again into Galilee. But these words seem to fall on deaf ears within the book. Peter is the first to contradict Jesus, but reacts only to what he has said about their desertion. Here, if he ever does, he speaks only for himself.

Even if the others desert Jesus, he shall not. Turning to Peter, Jesus says that he will desert him before the end of the new day – according to Jewish chronology the day begins at sunset – even before the cock has crowed the second time – according to Greek and Roman chronology the moment of sunrise. He will not only desert but also disown Jesus, and not just once but up to three times. Whatever Peter may remember about Jesus' predictions coming true, it is not of much help to him now. But he seems to have taken to heart the lesson Jesus has taught in 8:34-38 and 9:42-47 because he finishes by saying that he would rather die than disown Jesus. And the other ten agree with him. Naturally the reader cannot help wondering if the eleven, warned as they have been, will remain loyal to Jesus when he is killed.

The answer is not long in coming. Like a number of Jesus' previous predictions, this one too comes true very soon. In Gethsemane it becomes clear what people's words are worth. Mark's reply to that question leaves no room for doubt: nothing at all. To begin with there are the three who have seen and heard more of Jesus, for example on the mountain, than the others. Jesus takes them with him further than the other disciples. Again something is revealed to them that is kept from the others: Jesus is, so he tells them, terrified, and like anyone in fear of death he does not wish to be alone. He asks the three to wait at a short distance from him and stay awake with him. Readers, and they alone, are informed by the narrator of what Jesus prays now that the hour of his elimination is imminent, namely, that he may be spared this cup, an image for torture and deadly bloodshed. Jesus adds immediately, however, that he is prepared to do what God expects him to do, but that does not lessen his fears. Just as a voice twice calls Jesus 'son' in the book, so Jesus addresses God with *abba*, which has more or less the same emotional value as our 'dad(dy)'. To his prayer there is no response from heaven. God is silent.

And three times over Jesus turns to the three that are near to him for support, but here too his appeal falls on deaf ears. Twice he finds them asleep. The reader remembers that Jesus too was asleep when his disciples were in their death agony, but that when woken up he supported and rescued them (4:35-41). Each time

Jesus leaves them the three disciples fall asleep, so that they are even unable to stand by Jesus in his death agony. Finding the three asleep the third time Jesus tells them ironically that they may go on sleeping now if they wish. The hour has come. Anyone who remembers the words of Peter and the others mentioned above will find it almost impossible not to think of them as so much hot air. That is certainly what they prove to be. Betrayed by one of them, Jesus is deserted by the other eleven, who, after a rather grotesque attempt to do something heroic with a sword, take to their heels. Neither Jesus nor the narrator pays any attention to the ear that is cut off. It is a detail which strikes readers as somewhat grotesque. Besides, they know from the book that the possession of ears does not guarantee that people really hear and understand (4:11-12 and 8:18). The eleven who escape – of Judas readers hear no more in Mark – are no better off with their two ears than the chief priest's servant who has to make do with one.

There is only one person, an anonymous young man, who tries to follow the accomplices of the temple authorities with their detainee. But when they get hold of the linen cloth wrapped around him, he too take to his heels. That he is said to have nothing on make some commentators think of a catechumen who on Easter night descends naked into the baptism-pit. Others suspect that the author of the book himself appears on the stage for a moment through the character of this young man, just as Hitchcock used to pop up in his own films. Be that as it may, readers understand that impulsiveness and good will are not enough if one really wishes to defy Jesus' adversaries and choose the side of the persecuted.

Peter

But with this the story of the twelve is not finished. The prediction about Peter has not come true yet. Initially he flees just like the others. But he who with his brother Andrew was called first and was nicknamed rock (*Petros*) by Jesus seems to hold out longest. When Jesus is taken before the council for the nocturnal trial in the palace of the high priest, Peter appears to have followed the group at a safer distance than the young man mentioned above, and to have entered the palace without hindrance. He has mingled with the crowd of people warming themselves at a fire in the inner court where he can follow what will happen to Jesus without being noticed himself. Although pleasantly surprised to find Peter here, the reader cannot help remembering what Jesus said when Peter promised that he would always be loyal to him. The narrator does not try the reader's patience for long. What happens to Jesus and Peter – perhaps simultaneously – is told in two successive stories, of which the first records Jesus' interrogation and the second the awkward situation into which Peter has got himself. Although there is probably only the light from the fire and Peter is not a public figure, he is recognized by a maidservant as one of the men of Jesus' party, and she tells him so. Peter plays the innocent and retires to the porch, from where it will be easier for him to seek safety in flight. When the girl spots him again she also tells the bystanders. Again Peter denies it. But noticing he is a Galilean the bystanders confirm the girl's opinion. Peter denies it for the third time, now cursing and swearing he does not know 'this man you speak of'. The reader is shocked at Peter's denial. He has not only renounced Jesus but has cursed him as well, and in using the description 'this man you speak of' he puts the greatest possible distance between himself and Jesus. Immediately after these words the cock crows the second time. This reminds the reader of the appalling ease with which Peter has turned away from Jesus: he has renounced him three times within the short space of time it takes for a cock to crow twice. On hearing the cock crow Peter remembers the words of Jesus as well as his own solemn oath. He has renounced Jesus even without his life being at stake in any way. When Peter becomes aware of what he has done he bursts into tears. With Peter making his exit Jesus' disciples depart from the story for good.

The Crowd and the Individual

Now that the crowd has been mentioned for the last time the reader realizes that there is a tension between the crowd and specific individuals. That same tension makes itself felt in some earlier sections of the book, but less conspicuously. There the reader repeatedly meets, beside the crowd individuals with whom Jesus concerns himself. The crowd usually reacts positively to the healing. The reader is first confronted with an unfriendly crowd in the story about Bartimaeus (10:46-52). When Bartimaeus calls out to Jesus to help him, many from the crowd try to silence him until Jesus himself tells them to go and fetch him. The more the crowd turns away from Jesus, the greater the number of individuals who without belonging to either supporters or adversaries adopt a positive attitude towards Jesus. In one of the earlier sections of the book it was blind Bartimaeus who, after his healing, sees Jesus and follows him on the way. In this section it is the woman who anoints Jesus, the young man who follows him after the twelve have fled, Simon from Cyrene who at least part of the way carries the cross for Jesus, and the centurion who sees him die. In the next it will be Joseph of Arimathea who buries Jesus in a tomb which somehow or other belongs to him. Without exception they are people who act in the right way where Jesus' supporters fail. Do not they rather than the disciples play the role readers of the book might wish to imitate?

On the Cross

When Jesus dies on the cross the only people left besides the centurion are a group of bystanders. This strikes readers because they expect both the crowd and the adversaries to be present at the place of execution, the former to watch the execution and the latter to make certain that Jesus is finally eliminated. Neither the crowd nor the adversaries are mentioned again. In the meantime it has become too dark to see anything. The challenging remark of the temple authorities that they would like to see Jesus come down from the cross is followed by a three hours' darkness which covers the whole country or even the whole earth, depriving everyone of their view. A reader trying to imagine this can only think of a total eclipse of the sun like the one predicted to take place on the last day in 13:24.

When that darkness is over at the ninth hour Jesus calls out loudly in Aramaic: '*Eloi, Eloi lema sabachthani*', which the narrator translates for readers as 'My God, my God, why hast thou forsaken me?' These words are also found at the beginning of Psalm 22. Since other passages in this chapter, as will be discussed later, contain allusions to this psalm, we may assume that Jesus' exclamation is taken from it. The psalm does not only speak of persecution and despair but also of deliverance and gratitude. In spite of this Jesus' words here express only the former. They are remarkable enough to be examined more closely, the more so because they contrast sharply in several ways with what has gone before. In Gethsemane Jesus has still addressed God as '*abba*'. Now he uses the more distant '*Eloi*'. The greatest contrast, however, is not found in what Jesus says but in what is present in the story elsewhere but absent from it here. The voice from heaven, calling Jesus 'my dear son', sounds twice in the book: at the beginning (1:11) to install Jesus, and in the middle (9:7) to confirm him in his vocation. Nowhere in the book is there a moment at which Jesus and the reader need to hear that voice more urgently than now when Jesus gives expression to his desolation. It would have made a fine literary conclusion as well. But the narrator has the voice remain silent. Heaven does not speak. There is no answer to Jesus' desperate call. And the literary conclusion? It is effected differently a few lines farther down. What heaven does not say comes after Jesus' death from the mouth of the centurion.

The bystanders who apparently have no Aramaic mistake '*Eloi*' for Elijah and think that Jesus is calling on Elijah to take him down from the cross. Someone then give Jesus a sponge soaked in sour wine, probably to postpone his death so as to enable them to see if Elijah will answer his supposed prayer. Thus, even on the last page of the book, Elijah is still present, if only as a result of a misunderstanding.

When Jesus expires with a loud cry the curtain of the temple is torn in two from top to bottom. It is obviously a sign which refers to the end of the temple ordinance, like the fig tree that is withered from the roots (11:20). It symbolizes the defeat of the temple authorities when they achieve their aim at last.

First Testament Colouring

In this section, just as in the first part of the book, there are several express references to the First Testament. The narrator has Jesus twice connect the event with 'what stands written' (14:21 and 14:27), and on another occasion Jesus interprets what happens as the fulfilment of the scriptures (14:49). In this way the reader's attention is drawn to connections with passages from the First Testament based on choice of words and similarities in structure and content. It is, moreover, remarkable that explicit quotations are exceptional rather than usual.

The only quotation presented as such is to be found in 14:27: 'I will strike the shepherd down and the sheep will be scattered.' The source is not given but Jesus quotes here the ending of Zechariah 13:7, thereby replacing the imperative of the first verb ('strike') with the first person, ('I will strike'), under the influence of Isaiah 52:6. Already in Zechariah the shepherd is a messianic figure, whereas Isaiah 52 and 53 deal with the servant of JHWH, who symbolizes the fall and deliverance of persecuted Israel or of a misunderstood prophet. JHWH permits the tortures, humiliations, and finally even death because his vicarious suffering is beneficial to many. But the servant of JHWH will also be allowed to see the light and be exalted to the heights. It is quite certain that this song of the servant of JHWH – nowadays specified as Isaiah 52:13 – 53:12 – is one of the passages that have coloured this part of Mark. This is most noticeable where Jesus speaks about the sheep that will be scattered (Isaiah 53:6) and the blood that is shed for many (53:4-5; 53:10; 53:12), where he is represented as being silent before his judges (53:7) and innocent (53:9), and where his arrest and execution as a robber (53:12) and his burial in the tomb of a rich man (53:9) are related.

Two other First Testament passages are of special importance in this chapter, the first being Psalm 22, from which words and phrases are borrowed regularly. It is a prayer of someone who was so much harassed by enemies and persecutors that he felt desperate and deserted even by God but was released from his distressful situation and now thanks God. Quite a few elements in the story of Jesus' elimination have been taken from the first part –

a poignant lament – of this psalm. Its opening line, 'My God, my God, why have you deserted me?', is spoken by Jesus on the cross (22:1). But the soldiers who cast lots to divide Jesus' clothes among them (22:18), the passers-by who, wagging their heads jeer at him (22:7), the abuse (22:6), Jesus calling out to God (22:2-3; 22:24), and the fact that no answer is forthcoming (22:2), reflect what is prayed in the psalm as well. Most of the other allusions to passages from psalms are also taken from laments. They are usually small details like 'one who is eating with me' (14:18; see Psalm 41:9), the delivery 'into the hands of the sinners' (14:41; see for example Psalm 71:4), again Jesus' silence (14:61 and 15:5; see Psalms 38:14-16 and 39:9), and the offering of the sour wine (15:36; see Psalm 69:21). Exactly the opposite occurs when Jesus answers the high priest's question about his identity with words derived from a royal psalm (14:62; see Psalm 110:1) and from the triumphant Daniel 13:7.

The other First Testament passage of more than usual importance is Wisdom of Solomon 2:12-20, where the 'godless' are described. For readers who do not have it in their Bible the passage concerned is as follows:

> Let us lie in wait for the virtuous man, since he annoys us
> and opposes our way of life,
> reproaches us for our breaches of the law
> and accuses us of playing false to our upbringing.
> He claims to have knowledge of God,
> and calls himself a son of the Lord.
> Before us he stands, a reproof to our way of thinking,
> the very sight of him weighs our spirits down;
> his way of life is not like other men's,
> the paths he treads are unfamiliar.
> In his opinion we are counterfeit;
> he holds aloof from our doings as though from filth;
> he proclaims the final end of the virtuous as happy
> and boasts of having God for his father.
> Let us see if what he says is true,
> let us observe what kind of end he himself will have.
> If the virtuous man is God's son, God will take his part

and rescue him from the clutches of his enemies.
Let us test him with cruelty and with torture,
and thus explore this gentleness of his
and put his endurance to the proof.
Let us condemn him to a shameful death
since he will be looked after – we have his word for it.

In particular the words that the passers-by and the temple authorities address to Jesus when he is hanging on the cross seem to be based on the last four verses of the above quotation. But the other verses also contain elements that may have contributed to the First Testament colouring of the story in this section.

The passages from the First Testament responsible for this effect, such as Isaiah 52-53, Wisdom 2, and the penitential psalms, are practically all concerned with persecution and oppression, torture and execution. The reader who understands these connections realizes that what is related of Jesus in this chapter is not without precedent in the history of Israel. Jesus is not the first to be tortured and murdered, to call out in the end that God has deserted him. One should, however, immediately realize that there is a difference in stature between Jesus and his predecessors. Jesus' adversaries are not foreign tyrants or their executioners who want to persuade people to despise the Torah or renounce JHWH. On the contrary. They are not only fellow-countrymen of Jesus, but also the officially recognized authorities and God-fearing persons of the nation. In addition the reader realizes that Jesus' liquidation somehow forms part of a great pattern. That God would want or approve of Jesus' death expresses this so inadequately that to speak in this way can only give rise to misunderstandings. But the words which Isaiah 52-53 devote to the servant of God make it impossible for the reader to think that the one who does not speak when Jesus is hanging on the cross is really absent from the event.

Who Exactly is Jesus?

All the names which express different aspects of the person of Jesus have now been mentioned. At the same time the embargo resulting from the silence enjoined on demons and disciples has been lifted. Jesus has in fact confirmed, even in front of the high priest and the high court, that he is the messiah and the son of the Most High, and to this he has added that he is also the son of man who will be seen coming with the clouds of heaven to judge all men on judgement day. The reader understands full well that the inscription on the cross 'the king of the Jews' as well as its translation by the chief priests and scribes 'the king of Israel' is an extremely inadequate reproduction of this status. The centurion is much nearer the truth when he says, 'Truly this man was God's son.' But even this cannot be the whole truth. After all, the good news promised in the title of the book is not that Jesus *was* messiah and son of God, but that he still *is*. Nevertheless, as a distant and late echo of the voice from heaven, these words of the centurion form the only frail human line of communication between Jesus' lifetime and later centuries.

Even so, the reader still has a few questions. How can the kingdom of God draw near and be realized now that Jesus has been murdered? How can Jesus be God's son if he allows him to be killed so that what he has begun is nipped in the bud? Does God really love this son if the moment Jesus calls out to him in despair he remains deaf and does not speak, although his voice has sounded from heaven on two occasions before? Fortunately, the reader knows the book is not yet finished, and recollects that Jesus has said, three times, that he will rise from the dead after three days.

The Secret Disclosed, the Riddle Solved

One of the themes of the book concerns a secret and perhaps even a riddle. It is true that the word 'secret' occurs only in 4:11 in that peculiar phrase that the secret of the kingdom of God has been 'given' to those who are inside. But the fact that the demons, some of the people that are cured and those witnessing a cure, and finally the disciples are repeatedly forbidden to tell who Jesus is or what they have experienced confirms readers in their conviction that there is more to know about Jesus than the disciples apparently do. And gradually the awareness grows that readers also may be able to understand more than they have done so far. This awareness is strongest towards the middle of the book when readers realize while reading 8:14–21 that they understand no more than the disciples what the remainder of the broken loaves refers to.

On the other hand, the veil has been lifted several times for readers in the course of the book. The baskets full of broken pieces left over after the two feedings refer back to their origin: the superabundance of the feedings which contrasts with the small beginning, a few loaves and fishes. But they refer back even further, namely, to the seed of which the major part gets lost but the relatively small remainder yields a disproportionately large amount of wheat again. However, the baskets full of fragments gathered after the feedings with which nothing at all happens refer also to what is still to come. And the fact that the disciples have forgotten to take loaves (8:14) – to the one loaf they have on board I shall return presently – refers perhaps also to their inability to look ahead and anticipate what the future will bring. Another very important fact is that the two parable stories of the seed and the vineyard told by Jesus in Galilee and Jerusalem respectively and reflecting what happens there (4:3–8 and 12:1–9) make it clear to readers that there is no eating without drinking, no bread without wine. With this readers are fully prepared for the disclosure of the secret.

The disclosure takes place in this part of the book. Unfortunately, it is difficult for readers to recognize it when text additions put headings like 'The Institution of the Lord's Supper' (as in some editions of the Authorized Version and in the United Bible Societies Greek New Testament), 'The Lord's Supper Instituted' (as in the New Scofield Reference Bible), or 'The Institution of the Eucharist' (as in the Jerusalem Bible) at the top of 14:22–25. In the case of Mark such subtitles are incorrect. Unlike 1 Corinthians 11:23–24 and Luke 22:15–20 it does not contain a reference to a repetition, let alone a permanent institution, of what Jesus does here with the twelve. If they are not misled by such a subheading, readers will easily recognize the familiar *this is* in Jesus words 'this is my body' and 'this is my blood of the covenant, shed for many', especially if they read the text in Greek (because translations have a habit of varying here). It is a phrase used in Mark to explain an unknown custom (7:2; 15:42), a foreign term (7:34; 15:22; 15:34), or something that needs further clarification (12:24; 15:16). The reader will no doubt remember that the phrase occurs also in the interpretation of the parable of the seed, be it in the plural *these are* (4:15; 4:16; 4:20). In all these places it may be rendered 'that means'. Once the reader understands this, he will suddenly begin to see daylight. The words 'this is my body', which refer to the bread that has been broken and distributed, and 'this is my blood', which refer to the wine that has been poured out and drunk, really offer the clue to the interpretation of an entire network of secondary meanings.

The secret of the kingdom, given to those who are on the inside, consists in the real knowledge of the true identity of Jesus. That true identity is brought up in other ways as well. An example of this is found at the end of the central section where Jesus compares the ideal state of affairs in that kingdom with the conduct of those recognized to be the rulers of the nations. The latter lord it over their subjects, whereas in the kingdom of God people do not rule but serve, 'for even the son of man did not come to be served but to serve, and to surrender his life as a ransom for many' (10:45). But in the case of the disciples and perhaps also of readers, these and suchlike words have been carried off by the wind like seeds that have not fallen into good soil. They have not struck root in the memory and apparently need the visual representation of the broken bread and the poured wine to be remembered.

The code which serves as the key to decipher the network of secondary meanings can be represented as follows:

field			*vineyard*
wheat			*grapes*
bread	BODY	BLOOD	*wine*
take			*take*
break	MURDERED	SHED	*pour out*
give			*give*
eat			*drink*

This key unlocks the secret of Jesus' identity which the disciples were unable to solve. The secret is that the names used to explain who Jesus is cannot give a complete picture of his person and work unless it is clearly stated that this messiah and son of God eventually allowed his body to be broken and his blood to be shed by those who had given the highest priority to his violent death. Conversely, one can also say that anyone watching this bloody murder without realizing that the blood of the messiah and son of God is spilled here does not understand what is happening.

Now we can also solve part of the riddle which is presented by the parable of the seed. When discussing the parable we noticed that the only element left unexplained in the subsequent interpretation is the figure of the sower himself and that this leads one to suspect that the proclaimer of the word and the sower of the seed must somehow or other be connected with the teller of the parable, Jesus. Now that the secret has been revealed we realize that the sower Jesus fares no better than the seed he scatters on the field. His activity is for the most part unprofitable. And just as the seed not picked and eaten by the birds is accepted into the soil to die, so through his death Jesus leaves the scene of the living. But in the last part of the book it will become clear that like the seed the sower will come to new life, and again like the seed abundantly so, for the blood of this one person has been shed for the benefit of many.

There is yet another dark place which receives light from this. It is 8:14 where the narrator observes that despite the two feedings the disciples have forgotten to take loaves, with the result that they have no more than one loaf with them in the boat. After the equation between Jesus' broken body and the broken bread has taken place, it is clear that the one loaf which the disciples have brought along in contrast with the many fragments they have left behind, is none other than one of the persons on board, namely Jesus himself. Of course the disciples do not understand that, as is quite obvious from the story. But now that the narrator has provided the key to unlock the secret, the reader is able to understand afterwards what the disciples could not possibly understand then.

The plot concerned with the incomprehension of the disciples

is still unresolved. It is even an open question whether the book
has brought readers any closer to a solution. After all, the disciples
have completely dropped out of the picture; the one named last on
the list of apostles has delivered Jesus to his enemies, the one
named first has disowned him, and the others have chosen to flee
rather than stay with Jesus and risk their lives. Jesus is dead. It is
true that the curtain of the temple was torn in two when he died,
but the only voice that made itself heard was that of the centurion,
and what he said about Jesus lookd backwards, not forward.

11

DISCLOSURE

15:40 – 16:8

Context and Structure

This section not only forms the end of the book but also presents the second and final climax of the first plot, for it appears that the murdered Jesus has been raised from the dead and will resume his activities. This no doubt causes the greatest possible surprise among Jesus' adversaries and presumably also among his supporters, who, as readers will recall, have not understood his predictions. The narrator, however, does not say anything about their reactions. Nevertheless, from his account of the visit of the women to the grave it is clear how unexpected the climax comes, at least to these supporters of Jesus. Of Jesus' adversaries the only one mentioned again is Pilate. Readers for their part cannot really be surprised by this outcome. That the book ends with Jesus' resurrection is entirely in line with the predictions they have read. The narrator has, however, a surprise or two in store for them. But as someone who has already read to the end I must not run ahead of things.

The division of this section simply coincides with the flow of the story which, as in the previous section, follows the natural course of events. The first surprise is that on the last page the verses 15:40-41 introduce a group of wholly new characters, a great number of women, three of whom are mentioned by name. These three play a very important part in the last two episodes of the book. The first records Jesus' burial, which is attended by two of the three women (15:42-47). In the second and final episode the three women go to the tomb because they intend to finish the

198

anointing of Jesus' body, but they find that the stone which closed
the entrance has been moved away and then receive a message
from a young man telling them Jesus has risen and ordering them
to inform the disciples of this (16:1-8). Each story has its own
structure in which the movements of the characters play an
important part.

Place and Time

The *scene* of the action is Jesus' tomb, to which the reader is taken,
slowly but surely, in the first episode, until actually led into it,
together with the women, in the second. At the end the women
flee from the tomb in terror. But it would be superficial to leave
the story with this general observation, for the nature of the tomb
is changed right in front of the reader's eyes. Like the desert it is
originally a place of death and destruction, the last resting-place
for anyone there. For that reason it is closed with a stone that can
be removed from the outside but not from the inside. This tomb,
however, takes on a different character at the end of the book. The
stone has been rolled back and the tomb opened so that two-way
traffic is possible. With Jesus leaving the tomb the grave turns
from a permanent resting-place into a place of transition, and
owing to his resurrection it turns from a place of death and
destruction into a place where – as in the desert of 1:2-13 – new life
springs up.

A few things can also be said about the different *times* mentioned. At first the hourly timetable of the previous part
continues. After the ninth hour (15:34) the evening follows, and
with it comes the end of preparation-day and the beginning of the
sabbath (15:42). After Jesus' burial on the eve of the sabbath a day
of rest follows, during which the story is likewise suspended. The
narrator proceeds with the events taking place after the sabbath,
on the Saturday evening. That evening, when the day of rest is
over, the women go and buy aromatic oils (16:1). After this a
change occurs which is clearly marked by the indications of time.
A new way of counting is adopted. The first day of the week
becomes important now. And what happens on that day is set at

at the crack of dawn, at sunrise (16:2). The first day of the week, the early hour and the sunrise indicate that a new beginning is made and, perhaps even that the sabbath-ordinance has had its day and is replaced by a new ordinance in which the first day of the week is more important than the seventh. The rising of the sun is – especially after the darkness that two days earlier covered all the land from the sixth to the ninth hour – a portent of new light, new warmth and new life.

The Men

In this part of the book Jesus is conspicuous by his absence. In the first episode there is only his corpse, in the second even less: just an open grave. Whether Jesus' lifeless body is still in it or not, the text does not say. Nor do we hear whether the women went to look at the place where his body had been laid two days before. The narrator does tell us, however, that Jesus himself is not there because he has risen. Jesus is only present as someone spoken about, as the subject of a communication. But that communication is exceptional, because unlike information on the dead in general and the observation of the centurion in particular, it does not relate to the past but is formulated in the present and even the future tense (16:6-7). Yet it concerns the Jesus who is not in the tomb, where the reader is, with the women.

Having betrayed, deserted and rejected their master at his arrest, the male *supporters* of Jesus do not show up even after his death, in contrast to the disciples of John, who after his execution took his body and laid it in a tomb (16:29). Their absence is of a different kind to that of Jesus, and marks, within the book, the completion of their failure. In contrast with this stands the action of Joseph of Arimathea. He is the last in a series of characters who, from Bartimaeus onwards, have come onto the stage in order to play an important supporting role in a short episode. Joseph is not represented as a disciple of Jesus, yet both from a social and religious viewpoint he is depicted favourably: he is a respected councillor, a man awaiting the coming of God's kingdom. It is, moreover, courageous of him to concern himself with the executed Jesus (15:43). After the body has been handed over by Pilate, Joseph buries it with care and in accordance with custom, and then closes the tomb by rolling the stone against the entrance. The relatively detailed way Jesus' burial is related strengthens the reader's impression of correctness and care, and deepens the contrast with the disciples' behaviour.

Pilate and the centurion are also mentioned again, the former because he has to decide about the handing over of the body, the latter as the one who confirms Jesus' death. So in the absence of Peter, James and John, three other men, the centurion with his remarkable pronouncement that the murdered Jesus was God's son, Joseph and Pilate, temporarily form a new group around Jesus for the burial.

The Women

This is the first time that we discuss women as a special group. And with good reason. A number of individual women have appeared in the book before. Some of them belong to the category of those needing healing, especially Simon's mother-in-law, who is the first person to be cured by Jesus (1:29-31), the woman suffering from haemorrhages and the twelve-year-old daughter of Jairus (5:21-43), and finally the daughter of the Syrophoenician woman, who makes such a witty reply that Jesus grants her request (7:24-30). Jesus' mother, on the other hand, is rejected when she announces the arrival of herself and his brothers (3:31-33). Besides these there is the poor widow who not only compares favourably with the other people dropping money into the alms box, but is also obviously contrasted with the scribes of whom Jesus says, among other things, that they eat up the house of the widows (12:38-44). Unfavourable, however, is the part played by two other women – mother and daughter – in John's execution (6:17-29). In another way the same goes for the high priest's maid who gets Peter into trouble during the interrogation of Jesus (14:54-70). Finally we should mention the woman who anoints Jesus at Bethany and who is praised by him with words not used of any man in the book (14:3-9).

The attentive reader will probably have noticed that there are no names in the preceding paragraph. This is not because I want to avoid them but because, with one exception, they are not found in Mark. The only woman mentioned by name is Herodias, Philip's wife, whom Herod married and who of all the women plays the most unfavourable role in the book. So, in contrast with most men, from John the baptist, Simon Peter and Andrew at the beginning, to Simon of Cyrene and Joseph of Arimathea at the end, all the other women appear in the book without their names being mentioned. Besides, they are often described as the wife, concubine, daughter, mother, widow or maid of someone else, and what is significant, none of these women appears on more than one page of the book. So far there has been no reference whatever to any women belonging to the circle of Jesus' followers, let alone that of his helpers, so the reader is under the impression that Jesus has been followed almost exclusively by men.

Accordingly the reader is quite surprised to find that in the closing part of the book, on the very last page in fact, this impression is rectified with one powerful stroke. After Jesus' death, while all male followers are conspicuous by their absence, a great number of women appear to be present at the cross (15:40-41). To the reader their presence is completely unexpected. Admittedly, they stand there as spectators watching from a distance, but they *are* present. Moreover, three of them are mentioned by name. Of these two, Mary of Magdala and Salome, are not in any way connected with men, while the third, Mary the mother of James and Joses (a Greek corruption of Joseph), is connected with men only to distinguish her from the various other Marys in the book. In this brief space these three names are, with a slight variation, mentioned twice (15:40 and 16:1), and two of them even a third time (15:47).

This gives them a distinct identity, but these women are also afforded the very important description that they followed Jesus and waited on him when he was in Galilee. It is therefore not an exaggeration to say that they belonged in every respect to Jesus' supporters, or rather that they still belonged to them, as we can see from their presence at the cross. Apart from the three mentioned by name there are, according to the text, many other women there who have come up to Jerusalem with him. So in addition to the twelve and the larger circle of male disciples, a large group of women have accompanied Jesus on his way to the city and the place of his execution. Against the inner circle of three men, Peter, James and John, there is also one of three women, the two Marys and Salome, against the larger outer circle of men there is also one of women. (It is noteworthy that the narrator, in 15:40-41, in passing, explicitly connects Galilee and Jerusalem and the way between them, which are so important for the structure of the book.) In a way the two groups are mirror images of each other, and the mirror is – if I may mix the metaphor – the murdered Jesus himself. Before the execution only the men who have followed him play a part; after the execution only the women. But they do not reflect each other in every respect, for as the book presents matters the men become less faithful the nearer they come to the place of execution, whereas the women show their faith precisely on Golgotha. And they continue to do so, for when Jesus is buried by Joseph of Arimathaea two of the women are watching where he is laid (15:47). If in this section Jesus and the disciples are characterized by their absence, the women appear to be present at everything that happens.

In another respect the image of the mirror holds true, however, for the faith of the women declines as the story moves away from the execution. Perhaps the fact that only two of the three women watch where Jesus is buried already implies a decline of their faithful presence. The latter is certainly the case – be it in a qualitative sense – when they go to the tomb. Their behaviour shows a most remarkable lack of adaptation to the real situation.

First of all the three women go to the tomb in order to embalm Jesus. For several reasons readers recognize that this is inappropriate. They know that for reasons of hygiene it is not self-evident that one should not go and embalm a dead person until the third day, and if they read John 11:39 as well and remember what Martha says when Jesus has Lazarus' tomb opened on the fourth day, they find their opinion confirmed. Readers also recall that Jesus has already been anointed beforehand for his burial by an anonymous woman (14:8); but above all they wonder if the women ought not to know that Jesus was to rise that third day. On the way to Jerusalem itself, where the women have also followed him, Jesus has repeatedly spoken to his disciples about this, not mysteriously or unintelligibly but quite plainly (8:32). That they now come to the grave to embalm a dead person shows evidence of a fundamental error. They approach Jesus as a dead person on the day he is to rise from the dead. It is also strange that they should worry about the rolling away of the stone (16:3). Not only does it appear afterwards that the stone has already been rolled back, but readers who remember that Joseph rolled it against the entrance by himself can hardly imagine that the three women together would not be able to roll it back again. As a result the information given afterwards, 'although it was very big' (16:4), cannot give a plausible explanation for this concern and continues to intrigue others.

But even more important and inappropriate, without a doubt, is what is related at the very end of the story. After the women have learned from the messenger that Jesus has risen (16:6) and consequently is no longer in the tomb, they are expressly ordered to tell the disciples and Peter that Jesus will go on before them into Galilee and that they will see him there. The way the women react to this message is appalling: they leave the tomb and flee in a panic. And – the narrator adds in a closing sentence – 'they said nothing to anybody, for they were afraid.' To this most disconcerting sentence of the whole book we shall have to return. For the moment the point is that the women also fail in the end. They hold out considerably longer than the male followers of Jesus. None of them betrays or disowns Jesus. But eventually they too take flight. And besides, they do not carry out the perfectly unambiguous order of the heavenly messenger. The narrator pleads in excuse that they get into panic and are afraid. Of what? the reader wonders. Is it still the confusion created by the unexpected figure in the white robe? Or is perhaps the effect of his words? Such questions get no answer. But does it matter? It looks as if it is hardly possible to find an answer that is really a valid excuse for this failure.

The Messenger

Set in opposition to the women is the character of the young man whom they encounter in the tomb (16:5-7). When they see him the tension caused by the sight of the stone rolled away from the entrance is broken. The stone rolled back indicates that someone has entered or left the tomb. The question who this could be has now been answered. Instead of telling them how the young man has got into the tomb, the narrator has readers go with the women to buy spices and accompany them to the grave. Neither do readers learn whether the stone has been rolled away by the young man, although that is the conclusion that forces itself upon them. It is possible, then, that the remark about the size of the stone is meant to prepare readers for a confrontation with a person endowed with superhuman power. Be that as it may, the women see the youth sitting in the tomb on the right-hand side. This is the favourable side and the one which only bodes well. The fact that he wears a white robe marks him out as someone who has to do with the end time. On account of this readers recognize him as a heavenly messenger, the only one besides John in the book.

What the young man says confirms that he is a messenger sent by God. He knows about Jesus' resurrection – which, after all, is not witnessed by anyone in Mark – and knows also what Jesus has said to his disciples. After the reassuring greeting typical of unusual messengers, his words addressed to the women contain three messages. First, he indicates that he knows what has brought the women to the tomb: they are looking for Jesus, the man from Nazareth, who was crucified. Then follows the second communication, which is in fact the first half of his message: 'He has risen.' This means that the Jesus they are looking for is no longer in the tomb. The tomb is no more than the place where they laid him. In this subtle way the messenger gives the women a reprimand: they were not wanted in the tomb and have no business to be there now. But what is more, here rings out for the first time (and the last, because the book is practically finished) the good news, of which the whole book tells the beginning: the Jesus who was murdered has been raised from the dead, thereby turning his grave, and in principle every grave, into a place to pass through, a place of transition. The words the young man uses are quite similar to then existing and already classical confessions of faith like 1 Corinthians 15:3-5, and form the shortest possible summary of them: Jesus was crucified and has risen from the dead.

The third communication sets up the women themselves as messengers of Jesus' resurrection. They are ordered to go and tell the disciples and Peter that Jesus, as he foretold to them – the reader remembers 14:28 – will again go on before them into Galilee and that they will see him there. In Mark this is a decisive step further than the assertion made by the centurion, who in recognizing Jesus as God's son broke from the outside through the disciples' lack of understanding, but only looked back on what was past, not forward to what is still to come, in saying: 'Truly this man was God's son.' The words of the messenger, on the other hand, look forward to the future when once again Jesus goes on before his disciples into Galilee. So the murder of Jesus was not the end. What preceded it was no more than a beginning. With the words of the messenger the narrator places readers in their own time, the time between the resurrection and the coming of the son of man. He makes it clear that the risen Jesus will continue to lead the way. And so readers realize what the narrator wants to impress on them: to know and understand Jesus, and even use the right names for him – like the demons in the book – is only one side of the picture. None of this is of much value if the other side is missing, namely, the actual following of Jesus on the way. But what are readers supposed to make of Galilee? It is most unlikely that the author of the book means to say that it is only possible to follow Jesus' way to Galilee. But what Galilee does in fact represent for readers cannot be said with any certainty. For all the characters concerned, the three women, the disciples, Peter, and also Jesus himself, Galilee is home, a fact which lends probability to the opinion that readers are referred to the place where they live and work.

The last part of the message the women have to deliver concerns seeing: in Galilee they will see Jesus. What sort of seeing is this? Many – and the same holds for the copyist who felt obliged to add 16:9-20 – are of the opinion that the word 'see' can only refer to the seeing of Jesus appearing after his resurrection. But there is nothing in the whole book that makes readers expect that such appearances to anyone and everyone will take place. Yet it would have been easy enough for the narrator to point forward to them, for example by adding a few words to the three predictions of Jesus' execution and resurrection in 8:31, 9:31 and 10:33-34. Besides, the book does speak of a future seeing of Jesus, but in the context of the coming of God's kingdom or the son of man. This is the case in 9:1, 13:26 and 14:62. Does 16:7 perhaps refer to the seeing of Jesus when he is come as son of man? In so far as the message concerns readers it is quite possible, but as a message meant for the disciples and Peter it sounds contradictory. After all, the book was not written until after Peter's death, and without him having been allowed to see Jesus come as son of man. So only a third possibility remains: the seeing of Jesus is the positive counterpart of the disciples' and Peter's blindness, which far from being removed or cured within the book is still indirectly expressed in this ending through their conspicuous absence. From the third section entitled 'Much Wheat from Little Seed', it has been clear that the incomprehension of the disciples forms one of the two plots governing the book. The seeing has got everything to do with this plot. From 8:32-34 the reader may remember that whoever opposes Jesus, as Peter did at Caesarea Philippi, is not in a position to understand him. Jesus' words 'get behind me' are not only meant for Peter but for everyone, as 8:34 shows. Here the same idea reappears in the sequence 'He will go on before you in Galilee' and 'You will see him there'. This is not the seeing of people who are in front of someone, but that of people who follow someone who shows them the way by walking ahead of them.

The Messengers That Fail and the Fate of the Message

As we have already said above, the women in their turn are made into messengers by the heavenly messenger. The message entrusted to them is of vital importance for the further course of events, for if they fail to pass it on, those for whom the message is intended will never – within the bounds set to the world of the book by the narrator – hear what the messenger said. And if they do not impart it to anyone else, the contents of the message will never be known to anyone. Well, that is exactly what readers are told in the last sentence, which in all respects is a shocking ending, not only of this section but of the whole book. Readers are left little less upset than the women. They cannot close the book with an easy mind. The book, which at the start presented itself as history with an open beginning, did seem – since it ends with this story, and does not tell what becomes of the disciples and Peter – to be a book with an equally open ending. But that open ending – the future seeing of the disciples and Peter when they follow Jesus again – is rather drastically undone in the very last line of the book, which concludes with the information that the women do not deliver the message and even fail to speak of it to anybody.

On second thoughts readers recognize that the situation is even more serious than first thought, and wonder if the narrator did not realize that with that last sentence he really destroyed his whole book. For if the women had not said anything to anyone, and no one else had been present when they received the message, how then could the narrator have come by the story? It would rest on nothing and the same would apply to the end of the book. Without the news of Jesus' resurrection the book cannot be read as the history of the beginning of good news. That Jesus was murdered and that his followers too must reckon with the possibility of being persecuted is, after all, far from being good news with which you can please people. But if readers recall the earlier part of the book, they will come to the conclusion that their dismay is unnecessary. The disciples and Peter have already heard Jesus himself say that after his resurrection he will again go before them in Galilee (14:28). So they are not exclusively dependent on the women, which is also clear from the words of the messenger (16:7). But the question therefore becomes all the more intriguing why the book ends like this, and so it is all the more necessary to think again about the effect of this ending upon readers.

What readers realize on considering the matter again is that, although the message has not been passed on to the disciples and to Peter, it has been delivered to themselves as readers, be it not through the women. It is the narrator who, in telling us what the others have not been told, has in the meantime passed his message on to readers. Up to now readers have taken the narrator at his word and put trust in him, even when he talked about events he could not have witnessed or about the motives and feelings of his characters. I even think that the narrator's credit with his readers is so great that when reading 16:7-8 most of them do not so much as ask themselves how the narrator came to know these things. On further consideration the effect of the last few lines may also be that readers realize that the message of the heavenly messenger in Mark is really not meant at all for the disciples and Peter, but for no one but the readers themselves. Also the fact that the narrator conveys the message to them by making use of the voice of the heavenly messenger, the first one to bring the good news, rather than that of the three women, is perhaps quite functional. Thus the narrator reserves for himself, to the exclusion of all others, the part played by the messenger in the story. In this way he sets himself up at the end of the book as evangelist, bringer of the good news.

The book has now regained its open ending. But this does not now refer to future events round the disciples and Peter but to the position of readers of the book. After they have heard there is no other way for them to follow but the way of Jesus, whatever may be the consequences, they cannot just shut the book and go on with the day's affairs.

A Double Climax

Accordingly this ending, which closes the story but at the same time discloses the way of Jesus to the readers, offers a double climax as befits a story with a double plot. The first plot concerns the opposition of Jesus' powerful adversaries who lay hands on him, silence and murder him. As a result his supporters are scattered and there is no sign of any of them anywhere. But powerful as they may seem, the adversaries are not supreme. God does not undo the murder but the effect of that murder. He raises Jesus from the dead, and that is exactly why Jesus can forever lead the way and people can still hear him and see him.

The second plot concerns the failure of the disciples to understand Jesus. At the end of the story it appears that they and their regular spokesman Peter are no more perceptive than at the beginning. In this respect it is not a story with a happy ending. There is only Jesus' promise that they will see, but the book keeps readers completely in the dark as to how, where, when and even if this promise has ever been realized. Meanwhile – and this is partly due to the highly intriguing ending – the readers have become so deeply involved in the story that the message hs become a challenge to them. Within the story the disciples are not cured of their blindness. The readers, on the other hand, if they have read the book well, are no longer blind but see. And more than that. For is they see what the book means, they realize that it is not so important what names they use to describe their understanding of Jesus. What is far more important is to follow Jesus on his way. And so, apart from offering a model how to interpret Jesus the book tells the reader how to model himself or herself on him.

Beginning and End of the Book

However open-ended it may be, the book forms a complete whole, as can be seen from the many thematic connections between beginning and end. One of these has already been mentioned, namely, that the first and last story of the book are set in places of death where new life springs up and the grave turns from a final resting-place into a place of transition, like the desert. I shall go no further into this analogy here but restrict myself to a number of other connections.

It will not have escaped the reader's attention how important it is that the narrator entitled his story 'Beginning of the good news', and that indeed, in the last few lines of the book that good news is actually announced in the words of the messenger (16:6). Also, the mere presence of a heavenly messenger in itself connects beginning and end because John the baptist, Elijah come back, and the nameless young man facing the women in the tomb are the only two heavenly messengers that appear in the whole book. The narrator describes the clothing of both: the hair shirt of Elijah that belongs to the old era, the time of preparation and repentance, on the one hand, and the shining, cheerful white garment of the young man that marks the new era, on the other. Both messengers bring a message about Jesus and both express it in his absence: in the case of the former he is not there yet, and in that of the latter he is there no longer.

Moreover, it strikes the reader that the central theme of the 'way' is mentioned both at the beginning and at the end, be it in a very different manner. The quotation in 1:2-3 is about preparing and straightening the way and the paths for the one to come, who according to the context is Jesus, so the quotation is really about his way. In the book's closing story the theme is implicit in the announcement of the messenger that Jesus will go before his disciples again into Galilee. The way itself is not mentioned but without doubt assumed. The preparing of the way naturally belongs to the beginning, the travelling of the way both to the central part of the story and to the end.

Another important connection is that between the baptism of Jesus and his resurrection. To walk down into a river or baptismal font and be immersed means to die and be buried. And the coming out of the water and the rising from the river or the baptismal font represents rising from the grave and death, as it is said or assumed in several places in the letters of Paul (for example, Romans 6:3-8; Colossians 2:12-13).

And finally, both passages are, without mentioning his name, about God and his decisive action. In the opening story he is present as the one who not only authorizes the voice of the last of the prophets, John the baptist, but also makes his own voice heard from heaven, introduces Jesus to readers, and equips him with the Holy Spirit. In the closing story he is – again without being mentioned – present as the one who has sent the heavenly messenger and particularly as the one who has raised Jesus from the dead.

Finished and Not Yet Finished

So, apart from the epilogue in 16:9-20, both story and book are finished and at the same time not finished. The book is finished because after this page there follows no other. The story is finished because it does not continue. But at the same time it is not finished. We do not come across the words 'the end', and as a closing sentence 16:8 does not come anywhere near to 16:20. On the contrary, with the announcement that Jesus will go before his disciples again in Galilee and that one will see him there, the narrator breaks through the natural limitations of his story. He confronts the reader with the permanent challenge of the son of man who, murdered by man and rehabilitated by God, continues to call on people to follow him. With this also ends, in fact, the task of the commentator or pre- reader, who should withdraw in time to stop himself saying so much about this open ending that it is blocked up again.

12

AN ADDED EPILOGUE
16:9 – 20

Why an Epilogue?

When readers of Mark have (perhaps with some difficulty) got used to the remarkable effect the ending of 16:8 has had on them, they can probably imagine that this explosive and unusual ending soon met with such grave objections from copyists that the book has come down to us with a different one. Someone unaware of the jump from the women and the disciples to the importance of Jesus forever going before the readers themselves is easily inclined to think that this ending is inappropriate.

One is no doubt strengthened in that opinion by the fact that, compared with the other gospels, Mark appears to deviate from the convention that gospels are rounded off with stories about one or more appearances of the risen Jesus to his disciples. The obvious nature of this convention, based on what, according to the consensus of opinion, a book about Jesus ought to contain, has probably had a controlling influence on the tradition of the text. It is equally probable that the conventional idea of a normal and respectable gospel became even more influential when the gospel according to Matthew had gradually become the standard gospel as a result of it being frequently used in the liturgy. Consequently Mark was adapted. That was relatively easy as it only had to be stretched and extended in order to resemble the standard gospel. A respected text is lengthened rather than shortened.

The Nature of the Additional Matter

The addition does not consist of really new matter. On the

contrary, it is largely composed of small fragments consisting of stories in abridged form, taken from the other gospels and Acts, and fitted together into a new whole. This can easily be seen from the following list of the different elements and their respective origin.

16:9-10	appearance to Mary of Magdala	John 20:11-18
16:12-13	appearance to two disciples on their way	Luke 24:13-35
16:14	appearance to the eleven during a meal	Luke 24:36-43
16:15-17	order to proclaim the good news	Matthew 28:19-20
16:17-18	signs connected with believing	Acts 28:3-6
16:19	ascension of Jesus	Acts 1:9-11
16:20	proclamation strengthened by signs	Acts 14:31

Precisely because it is connected with the other gospels and Acts, this added conclusion gives us hardly any information other than what we can read in the other books of the Second Testament, and accordingly there was not really much point in including it in the canon, thereby turning Mark into a book like the others.

The fact that the author (if we may call him that) of this ending has incorporated in his own account various stories from the other gospels in condensed form means that his stories of Jesus' appearances after his resurrection are rather left in the air. In particular, there is no distinct indication of place. Where and how Jesus appears to Mary remains entirely obscure; it may be outside, possibly also at the tomb, as well as inside. It is different with the appearance to the two. They are on their way to the fields and in the open air. The eleven see Jesus while they are at table, but where that table is remains obscure. As a result the reader has some difficulty picturing what is related in this added part.

The Characters

If the reader remains in the dark about where the appearances take place, it is, on the other hand, quite clear who are involved and how. First of all, the risen Jesus himself is continuously represented as acting and speaking. He appears to Mary, then to two disciples, and finally to the eleven. He shows himself, be it under another form (16:12), as a living person, and addresses the eleven before he is taken up into heaven from the place where they are at table. He is completely in control of the situation and is clearly the principal character of this episode. The other characters seem to have been arranged in such a way that the reader is gradually led back to the eleven remaining disciples. In this appended conclusion the reader is not told, however, that the three women, or one of them, informs the disciples of what the messenger has said in the tomb. Of the three, only Mary of Magdala is mentioned by name, and it is noteworthy that she says that Jesus is alive since she saw him on the first day of the week, but does not relate what happened before then. The two men belong to the circle of the disciples, and in their turn tell the others that they have seen Jesus. Finally, Jesus himself also comes and speaks to the eleven.

No More than a Compilation?

Has the copyist, who really acts as an editor, done no more than supply a compilation which, apart from a conclusion that is acceptable to himself, also provides a masterly closing sentence to the whole book (16:19-20)? The reader who thinks so overlooks how well conceived the added conclusion is, precisely in so far as it forms part of the entire text.

For one thing, it is obvious that the compiler has seen to it that this second conclusion also has been written in such a way that what is begun at the beginning of the book is rounded off at the end. Thus he relates in 16:19 the way Jesus, who is installed in the opening scene, leaves the stage and the book again at the end. The same applies to the eleven who have remained after the treason of Judas. Jesus is taken up into heaven and takes his place there at the right hand of God, the eleven set out to proclaim him everywhere. A second element relates to the word 'good news', which dominates the beginning so much. The word is not only used again here but also forms part of a summarizing passage containing Jesus' order to the eleven to go out to the whole world and proclaim the good news to all creation. A third element refers to baptism. In the opening story the baptizing of John and the baptism of Jesus play a very important role; in this closing story Jesus tells the eleven that whoever believes and receives baptism is sure to be saved.

But there are also clear connections with other parts of the book. A case in point is Jesus' announcement that those who believe will cast out demons in his name. This reminds the reader not only of the many demons Jesus himself has cast out in the book, but also of the commission to the twelve to do the same (3:15), the success with which they carry out this order at first (6:13), and the problems they have with the young demoniac later (9:17-29). The way this second ending is interwoven with Mark becomes even more noticeable, perhaps, where 16:18 speaks of the sick that will be cured through the laying on of hands, and does so in words almost completely taken from 6:5.

Finally, the order to go and proclaim the good news everywhere and to everyone (16:15), as well as the carrying out of that order (16:20), repeats in almost identical words what the book has already said about this, particularly in 13:10 and 14:9.

The Same Theme

But the most important aspect of the added conclusion is that it returns several times to the theme which more than any other is characteristic of the book, namely, the unbelief of Jesus' disciples. As to that particular theme the author could partly fall back on data from Luke, where the disciples and the eleven do not believe the women who tell them what they have heard from two messengers (Luke 24:11). Although Luke's story about the two disciple with whom Jesus catches up on the way to Emmaus marks the exact moment of transition to belief, unbelief nevertheless plays an important part in it (Luke 24:13-32). Unbelief is clearly stressed in the second ending of Mark as well. Thus Mary of Magdala is not believed by Jesus' followers when she tells them that Jesus is alive and that she has seen him (16:11) and – in contradistinction to what Luke says about this (Luke 24:33-35) – neither do the two who have seen Jesus find a ready ear, but are on the contrary mistrusted (16:13). And this is underlined by Jesus himself, when eventually he appears to the eleven also and reproaches them for being too incredulous and obstinate to trust those who have seen him risen (16:14). In this way the blindness of the disciples is by no means automatically cured by Jesus' resurrection.

So perhaps this second ending also has, to some extent, an open character, despite the resounding closing sentence. It is after all peculiar that the text, which has the disciples go and proclaim everywhere, does not say, in contrast to Matthew 28:17, that they also give expression to their belief in Jesus by word or gesture.

Another Ending, Another Book

But even if the ending with 16:9-20 is also to some extent open, that does not alter the fact that Mark is an entirely different book when read with this added epilogue. Obviously the last sentence, 16:19-20, functions as the conclusion of the book, just like Matthew 28:16-20, Luke 24:52-53, John 20:30-31 and 22:25 (John too has a double ending!). And since the book and the story are thus as clearly brought to a close as other stories are with the words 'and they lived happily ever after', readers can safely leave the world and time of the book and return to their own world and time. That is just what is impossible for readers who finish the reading of Mark with the story of 16:1-8. Such readers are left nearly as upset and bewildered as the women figuring in it. The story does not leave them in peace. The image of the murdered Jesus whom God has raised from the dead, and who will continue to lead the way to whoever wishes to follow him, is engraved upon their minds.

THE GOSPEL ACCORDING TO MARK[1]

1 **Beginning of the good news of Jesus messiah (son of God).**

2 As it is written in the prophet Isaiah: 'Here is my messenger
3 whom I send before you, and who prepares your way; the voice
of one crying in the desert, "Prepare the way of the Lord; make his
4 paths straight."' And so it was that John the baptist appeared in
the desert proclaiming a baptism in token of repentance, for the
5 forgiveness of sins. All Judaea and all the people of Jerusalem
went out to him, and were baptized by him in the river Jordan,
confessing their sins.

6 John was dressed in a rough coat of camel's hair, with a leather
7 belt round his waist, and he fed on locusts and wild honey. His
proclamation ran: 'After me comes one who is mightier than I. I
8 am not fit to unfasten his shoes. I have baptized you in water; he
will baptize you in holy spirit.'

9 It happened at this time that Jesus came from Nazareth in
10 Galilee and was baptized in the Jordan by John. At the moment
when he came up out of the water, he saw the heavens torn open

---

[1] This translation of Mark follows the New English Bible, with two modifications. Firstly, only words that are names in the strict sense – unlike son of man, sabbath, spirit, or the twelve – are capitalized. Secondly, some words and sentences have been translated more literally in order to bring the reader in closer contact with the original text and the thinking of the author of *Reading Mark*. An example of this is the translation of 4:21. The NEB has: 'He said to them, "Do you bring in the lamp to put it under the meal-tub, or under the bed? Surely it is brought to be set on the lampstand?" . . .' The reader cannot possibly understand why the writer speaks (p. 80) of a personification of the lamp that can be seen as an image of Jesus unless this passage is translated literally.

and the spirit, like a dove, descending upon him. And a voice   11
spoke from heaven: 'You are my dear son; I am pleased with you.'
Thereupon the spirit drove him out into the desert, and there he   12,13
remained for forty days tempted by Satan. He was among the
wild beasts; and the messengers looked after him.

In Galilee: success and opposition

After John had been delivered up, Jesus came into Galilee   14
proclaiming the good news of God: 'The time has come; God's   15
kingdom is close at hand; repent, and believe the good news.'
Jesus was walking by the Sea of Galilee when he saw Simon and   16
his brother Andrew on the lake at work with a casting-net; for
they were fishermen. Jesus said to them, 'Come with me, and I   17
will make you fishers of men.' And at once they left their nets and   18
followed him.
When he had gone a little further he saw James son of Zebedee   19
and his brother John, who were in the boat overhauling their nets.
He called them; and, leaving their father Zebedee in the boat with   20
the hired men, they went off to follow him.
They came to Capernaum, and on the sabbath he went to   21
synagogue and began to teach. The people were astounded at his   22
teaching, for, unlike the doctors of the law, he taught with a note
of authority. Now there was a man in the synagogue possessed by   23
an unclean spirit. He shrieked: 'What do you want with us, Jesus   24
of Nazareth? Have you come to destroy us? I know who you are –
the Holy One of God.' Jesus rebuked him: 'Be silent,' he said,   25
'and come out of him.' And the unclean spirit threw the man into   26
convulsions and with a loud cry left him. They were all   27
dumbfounded and began to ask one another, 'What is this? A new
kind of teaching! He speaks with authority. When he gives
orders, even the unclean spirits submit.' The news spread rapidly,   28
and he was soon spoken of all over the district of Galilee.
On leaving the synagogue they went straight to the house of   29
Simon and Andrew; and James and John went with them.
Simon's mother-in-law was ill in bed with fever. They told him   30,31
about her at once. He came forward, took her by the hand, and

helped her to her feet. The fever left her and she waited upon them.

32   That evening after sunset they brought to him all who were ill
33   or possessed. And the whole town was there, gathered at the
34   door. He healed many who suffered from various diseases. He drove out many demons. He would not let the demons speak, because they knew who he was.

35   Very early next morning he got up and went out. He went
36   away to a lonely spot and remained there in prayer. But Simon
37   and his companions searched him out, found him, and said, 'They
38   are all looking for you.' He answered, 'Let us move on to the country towns in the neighbourhood; I have to proclaim my
39   message there also; that is what I came out to do.' So all through Galilee he went, proclaiming his message in the synagogues and casting out the demons.

40   Once he was approached by a leper, who knelt before him
41   begging his help. 'If only you will,' said the man, 'you can cleanse me.' In warm indignation Jesus stretched out his hand, touched
42   him, and said, 'Indeed I will; be clean again.' The leprosy left him
43   immediately, and he was clean. Then he dismissed him with this
44   stern warning: 'Be sure you say nothing to anybody. Go and show yourself to the priest, and make the offering laid down by
45   Moses for your cleansing; that will certify the cure.' But the man went out and made the whole story public; he spread it far and wide, until Jesus could no longer show himself in any town, but stayed outside in the open country. Even so, people kept coming to him from all quarters.

2   When after some days he returned to Capernaum, the news
2   went round that he was at home; and such a crowd collected that the space in front of the door was not big enough to hold them. And while he was proclaiming the message to them, a man was
3   brought who was paralyzed. Four men were carrying him, but
4   because of the crowd they could not get him near. So they opened up the roof over the place where Jesus was, and when they had broken through they lowered the stretcher on which the
5   paralyzed man was lying. When Jesus saw their faith, he said to the paralyzed man, 'My friend, your sins are forgiven.'
6   Now there were some lawyers sitting there, and they thought

to themselves, 'Why does the fellow talk like that? He is 7
blaspheming! Who but God alone can forgive sins?' Jesus knew in 8
his own mind that this was what they were thinking, and said to
them: 'Why do you harbour thoughts like these? Is it easier to say 9
to this paralyzed man, "Your sins are forgiven", or to say, "Stand
up, take your bed, and walk"? But to convince you that the son of 10
man has the right on earth to forgive sins – he turned to the
paralyzed man – 'I say to you, stand up, take your bed, and go 11
home.' And he got up, and at once took his stretcher and went out 12
in full view of them all, so that they were astounded and praised
God. 'Never before,' they said, 'have we seen the like.'

Once more he went away to the lake-side. All the crowd came 13
to him, and he taught them there. As he went along, he saw Levi 14
son of Alphaeus at his seat in the custom-house, and said to him,
'Follow me'; and Levi rose and followed him.

When Jesus was at table in his house, many bad characters – 15
tax-gatherers and others – were seated with him and his disciples;
for there were many who followed him. The pharisee scribes 16
noticed him eating in bad company, and said to his disciples, 'He
eats with tax-gatherers and sinners!' Jesus heard it and said to
them, 'It is not the healthy that need a doctor, but the sick; I did 17
not come to invite virtuous people, but sinners.'

Once, when John's disciples and the pharisees were keeping a 18
fast, some people came to him and said, 'Why is it that John's
disciples and the disciples of the pharisees are fasting, but yours
are not?' Jesus said to them, 'Can you expect the bridegroom's 19
friends to fast while the bridegroom is with them? As long as they
have the bridegroom with them, there can be no fasting. But the 20
time will come when the bridegroom will be taken away from
them, and on that day they will fast.

'No one sews a patch of unshrunk cloth on to an old coat; if he 21
does, the patch tears away from it, the new from the old, and
leaves a bigger hole. No one puts new wine into old wine-skins; if 22
he does, the wine will burst the skins, and then the wine and skins
are both lost. Fresh skins for new wine!'

One sabbath he was going through the cornfields; and his 23
disciples, as they went, began to pluck ears of corn. The pharisees 24
said to him, 'Look, why are they doing what is forbidden on the

25   sabbath?' He answered, 'Have you never read what David did
26   when he and his men were hungry and had nothing to eat? He
      went into the House of God, in the time of Abiathar the High
      Priest, and ate the sacred bread, though no one but a priest is
      allowed to eat it, and even gave it to his men.'
27   He also said to them, 'The sabbath was made for the sake of
28   man and not man for the sabbath: therefore the son of man is
      sovereign even over the sabbath.'
3   On another occasion when he went to synagogue, there was a
2   man in the congregation who had a withered arm; and they were
      watching to see whether Jesus would cure him on the sabbath, so
3   that they could bring a charge against him. He said to the man
4   with the withered arm: 'Come and stand out here.' Then he
      turned to them: 'Is it permitted to do good or to do evil on the
      sabbath, to save life or to destroy life?' They had nothing to say;
5   and, looking round at them with anger and sorrow at their
      obstinate stupidity, he said to the man, 'Stretch out your arm.' He
6   stretched it out and his arm was restored. But the pharisees, on
      leaving the synagogue, began plotting against him with the
      partisans of Herod to see how they could do away with him.

7 8   Jesus went away to the lake-side with his disciples. Great numbers
      from Galilee, Judaea and Jerusalem, Idumaea and Transjordan,
      and the neighbourhood of Tyre and Sidon, heard what he was
9   doing and came to see him. So he told his disciples to have a boat
10   ready for him, to save him from being crushed by the crowd. For
11   he cured so many that sick people of all kinds came crowding in
      upon him to touch him. The unclean spirits too, when they saw
      him, would fall at his feet and cry aloud, 'You are the Son of God';
12   but he insisted that they should not make him known.
13   He then went up into the hill-country and called the men he
14   wanted; and they went and joined him. He appointed twelve as
15   his companions, whom he would send out to preach, with a
16   commission to drive out demons. So he appointed the twelve: to
17   Simon he gave the name Peter; then came the sons of Zebedee,
      James and his brother John, to whom he gave the name
18   Boanerges, Sons of Thunder; then Andrew and Philip and
      Bartholomew and Matthew and Thomas and James the son of

Alphaeus and Thaddaeus and Simon the zealot, and Judas   19
Iscariot, the man who betrayed him.

He entered a house; and once more such a crowd collected   20
round them that they had no chance to eat. When his family heard   21
of this, they set out to take charge of him; for people were saying
that he was out of his mind.

The scribes who had come down from Jerusalem said, 'He is   22
possessed by Beelzebub', and, 'He drives out demons by the
prince of demons.' So he called them to come forward, and spoke   23
to them in parables: 'How can Satan drive out Satan? If a   24
kingdom is divided against itself, that house will never stand; and   25
if Satan is in rebellion against himself, he is divided and cannot   26
stand; and that is the end of him.

'On the other hand, no one can break into a strong man's house   27
and make away with his goods unless he has first tied the strong
man up; then he can ransack the house.

'I tell you this: no sin, no slander, is beyond forgiveness for   28 29
men; but whoever slanders the holy spirit can never be forgiven;
he is guilty of eternal sin.' He said this because they had declared   30
that he was possessed by an unclean spirit.

Then his mother and his brothers arrived, and remaining   31
outside sent someone to call him. A crowd was sitting round and   32
word was brought to him: 'Your mother and your brothers are
outside asking for you.' He replied, 'Who is my mother? Who are   33
my brothers?' And looking round at those who were sitting in the   34
circle about him he said, 'Here are my mother and my brothers.
Whoever does the will of God is my brother, my sister, my   35
mother.'

On another occasion he began to teach by the lake-side. The   4
crowd that gathered round him was so large that he had to get into
a boat on the lake, and there he sat, with the whole crowd on the
beach right down to the water's edge. And he taught them many   2
things by parables.

As he taught he said:

'Listen! A sower went out to sow. And it happened that as he   3 4
sowed, some seed fell along the footpath; and the birds came and
ate it up. Some seed fell on rocky ground, where it had little soil,   5

6 and it sprouted quickly because it had no depth of earth; but when the sun rose the young corn was scorched, and as it had no root it
7 withered away. Some seed fell among thistles, and the thistles
8 shot up and choked the corn, and it yielded no crop. And some of the seed fell into good soil, where it came up and grew, and bore fruit; and the yield was thirtyfold, sixtyfold, even a hundredfold.'
9 He added, 'If you have ears to hear, then hear.'
10 When he was alone, the twelve and others who were round him
11 questioned him about the parable. He replied, 'To you the secret of the kingdom of God has been given; but to the outsiders
12 everything comes in riddles; so that they may look and look, but see nothing; hear and hear, but understand nothing; otherwise they might turn to God and be forgiven.'
13 So he said, 'Do you not understand this parable? How then are
14 you to understand all the parables? The sower sows the word.
15 Those along the footpath are people in whom the word is sown, but no sooner have they heard it than Satan comes and carries off
16 the word which has been sown in them. It is the same with those who receive the seed on rocky ground; as soon as they hear the
17 word, they accept it with joy, but it strikes no root in them; they have no staying-power; then, when there is trouble or persecution on account of the word, they fall away at once.
18 Others again receive the seed among thistles; they hear the word,
19 but worldly cares and the false glamour of wealth and all kinds of
20 evil desire come in and choke the word, and it proves barren. And there are those who receive the seed in good soil; they hear the word and welcome it; and they bear fruit thirtyfold, sixtyfold, or a hundredfold.'
21 He said to them, 'Does the lamp come in to be put under the bushel or under the bed? Does it not come in to be put on the
22 lamp-stand? For nothing is hidden unless it is to be disclosed, and
23 nothing put under cover unless it is to come into the open. If you have ears to hear, then hear.'
24 He also said, 'Take note of what you hear; the measure you give
25 is the measure you will receive, with something more beside. For the man who has will be given more, and the man who has not will forfeit even what he has.'
26 He said, 'The kingdom of God is like this. A man scatters seed

on the land; he goes to bed at night and gets up in the morning,   27
and the seed sprouts and grows – how, he does not know.   The   28
ground produces a crop by itself, first the blade, then the ear, then   29
full-grown corn in the ear; but as soon as the crop is ripe, he plies
the sickle, because harvest-time has come.'
He said also, 'How shall we picture the kingdom of God, or by   30
what parable shall we describe it? It is like the mustard-seed,   31
which is smaller than any seed in the ground at its sowing. But   32
once sown, it springs up and grows taller than any other plant,
and forms branches so large that the birds can settle in its shade.'
With many such parables he would give them his message, so   33
far as they were able to receive it. He never spoke to them except   34
in parables; but privately to his disciples he explained everything.

Miracles of Christ

That day, in the evening, he said to them, 'Let us cross over to the   35
other side of the lake.' So they left the crowd and took him with   36
them in the boat where he had been sitting; and there were other
boats accompanying him. A heavy squall came on and the waves   37
broke over the boat until it was all but swamped. Now he was in   38
the stern asleep on a cushion; they roused him and said, 'Master,   39
do you not care we perish?' He awoke, rebuked the wind, and said
to the sea, 'Hush! Be still!' The wind dropped and there was a dead
calm. He said to them, 'Why are you such cowards? Have you no   40
faith even now?' They were awestruck and said to one another,   41
'Who can this be whom even the wind and the sea obey?'
So they came to the other side of the lake, into the country of   5
the Gerasenes. As he stepped ashore, a man possessed by an   2
unclean spirit came up to him from among the tombs where he
had his dwelling. He could no longer be controlled; even his   3
chains were useless; he had often been fettered and chained up, but   4
he had snapped his chains and broken the fetters. No one was
strong enough to master him. And so, unceasingly, night and   5
day, he would cry aloud among the tombs and on the hill-sides
and cut himself with stones. When he saw Jesus in the distance, he   6
ran and flung himself down before him, shouting loudly, 'What   7

8   do you want with me, Jesus, son of the Most High God? In God's
     name do not torment me.' (For Jesus was already saying to him,
9   'Out, unclean spirit, come out of this man!') Jesus asked him,
     'What is your name?' 'My name is Legion,' he said, 'there are so
10   many of us.' And he begged hard that Jesus would not send them
     out of the country.
11   Now there happened to be a large herd of pigs feeding on the
12   hill-side, and the spirits begged him, 'Send us among the pigs and
13   let us go into them.' He gave them leave; and the unclean spirits
     came out and went into the pigs; and the herd, of about two
     thousand, rushed over the edge into the lake and were drowned.
14   The men in charge of them took to their heels and carried the
     news to the town and country-side; and the people came out to see
15   what had happened. They came to Jesus and saw the madman
     who had been possessed by the legion of demons, sitting there
16   clothed and in his right mind; and they were afraid. The
     spectators told them how the madman had been cured and what
17   had happened to the pigs. Then they begged Jesus to leave the
     district.
18   As he was stepping into the boat, the man who had been
     possessed begged to go with him. Jesus would not allow it, but
19   said to him, 'Go home to your own folk and tell them what the
20   Lord in his mercy has done for you.' The man went off and spread
     the news in the Ten Towns [Greek Decapolis] of all that Jesus had
     done for him; and they were all amazed.
21   As soon as Jesus had returned by boat to the other shore, a great
22   crowd once more gathered round him. While he was by the
     lake-side, the president of one of the synagogues came up, Jairus
     by name, and, when he saw him, threw himself down at his feet
23   and pleaded with him. 'My little daughter', he said, 'is at death's
     door. I beg you to come and lay your hands on her to cure her and
24   save her life.' So Jesus went with him, accompanied by a great
     crowd which pressed upon him.
25   Among them was a woman who had suffered from
26   haemorrhages for twelve years; and in spite of long treatment by
     many doctors, on which she had spent all she had, there had been
27   no improvement; on the contrary, she had grown worse. She had
     heard what people were saying about Jesus, so she came up from

behind in the crowd and touched his cloak; for she said to herself,   28
'If I touch even his clothes, I shall be cured.' And there and then   29
the source of her haemorrhages dried up and she knew in herself
that she was cured of her trouble. At the same time Jesus, aware   30
that power had gone out of him, turned round in the crowd and
asked, 'Who touched my clothes?' His disciples said to him, 'You   31
see the crowd pressing upon you and yet you ask, "Who touched
me?"' Meanwhile he was looking round to see who had done it.   32
And the woman, trembling with fear when she grasped what had   33
happened to her, came and fell at his feet and told him the whole
truth. He said to her, 'My daughter, your faith has cured you. Go   34
in peace, free for ever from this trouble.'

    While he was still speaking, a message came from the presi-   35
dent's house, 'Your daughter is dead; why trouble the rabbi
further?' But Jesus, overhearing the message as it was delivered,   36
said to the president of the synagogue, 'Do not be afraid; only
have faith.' After this he allowed no one to accompany him except   37
Peter and James and James's brother John. They came to the   38
president's house, where he found a great commotion, with loud
crying and wailing. So he went in and said to them, 'Why this   39
crying and commotion? The child is not dead: she is asleep'; and   40
they only laughed at him. But after turning all the others out, he
took the child's father and mother and his own companions and
went in where the child was lying. Then, taking hold of her hand,   41
he said to her, 'Talitha cum', which means, 'Get up, my child.'
Immediately the girl got up and walked about, for she was twelve   42
years old. At that they were beside themselves with amazement.
He gave them strict orders to let no one hear about it, and told   43
them to give her something to eat.

    He left that place and went to his home town accompanied by   6
his disciples. When the sabbath came he began to teach in the   2
synagogue; and the large congregation who heard him were
amazed and said, 'Where does he get it from?', and 'What wisdom
is this that has been given him?', and, 'How does he work such   3
miracles? Is not this the carpenter, the son of Mary, the brother of
James and Joseph and Judas and Simon? And are not his sisters
here with us?' So they fell foul of him. Jesus said to them, 'A   4
prophet will always be held in honour except in his home town,

5 and among his kinsmen and family.' He could work no miracle
6 there, except that he put his hands on a few sick people and healed
them; and he was taken aback by their want of faith.

7 On one of his teaching journeys round the villages he summoned
the twelve and sent them out in pairs on a mission. He gave them
8 authority over unclean spirits, and instructed them to take
nothing for the journey beyond a stick: no bread, no pack, no
9 money in their belts. They might wear sandals, but not a second
10 coat. 'When you are admitted to a house', he added, 'stay there
11 until you leave those parts. At any place where they will not
receive or listen to you, shake the dust off your feet as you leave,
12 as a warning to them.' So they set out and called publicly for
13 repentance. They drove out many demons, and many sick people
they anointed with oil and cured.

14 Now King Herod heard of it, for the fame of Jesus had spread;
and people were saying, 'John the baptist has been raised to life,
and that is why these miraculous powers are at work in him.'
15 Others said, 'It is Elijah.' Others again, 'He is a prophet like one of
16 the old prophets.' But Herod, when he heard of it, said, 'This is
John, whom I beheaded, raised from the dead.'

17 For this same Herod had sent and arrested John and chained
him in prison at the instance of his brother Philip's wife,
18 Herodias, whom he had married. John had told Herod, 'You have
19 no right to your brother's wife.' Thus Herodias nursed a grudge
against him and would willingly have killed him, but she could
20 not; for Herod went in awe of John, knowing him to be a good
and holy man; so he kept him in custody. He liked to listen to
him, although the listening left him greatly perplexed.

21 Herodias found her opportunity when Herod on his birthday
gave a banquet to his chief officials and commanders and the
22 leading men of Galilee. Her daughter came in and danced, and so
delighted Herod and his guests that the king said to the girl, 'Ask
23 what you like and I will give it to you.' And he swore an oath to
her: 'Whatever you ask I will give you, up to half my kingdom.'
24 She went out and said to her mother, 'What shall I ask for?' She
25 replied, 'The head of John the baptist.' The girl hastened back at
once to the king with her request: 'I want you to give me here and

now, on a dish, the head of John the baptist.' The king was greatly   26
distressed, but out of regard for his oath and for his guests he
could not bring himself to refuse her. So the king sent a soldier of   27
the guard with orders to bring John's head. The soldier went off   28
and beheaded him in the prison, brought the head on a dish, and
gave it to the girl; and she gave it to her mother.

When John's disciples heard the news, they came and took his   29
body away and laid it in a tomb.

The apostles now rejoined Jesus and reported to him all that   30
they had done and taught. He said to them, 'Come with me, by   31
yourselves, to some lonely place where you can rest quietly.' (For
they had no leisure even to eat, so many were coming and going.)
Accordingly, they set off privately by boat for a lonely place. But   32 33
many saw them leave and recognized them, and came round by
land, hurrying from all the towns towards the place, and arrived
there first. When he came ashore, he saw a great crowd; and his   34
heart went out to them, because they were like sheep without a
shepherd; and he had much to teach them. As the day wore on, his   35
disciples came up to him and said, 'This is a lonely place and it is   36
getting very late; send the people off to the farms and villages
round about, to buy themselves something to eat.' 'Give them   37
something to eat yourselves', he answered. They replied, 'Are we
to go and spend twenty pounds [literally 200 denarii] on bread to
give them a meal?' 'How many loaves have you?' he asked; 'go
and see.' They found out and told him, 'Five, and two fishes also.'   38
He ordered them to make the people sit down in groups on the   39
green grass, and they sat down in rows, a hundred rows of fifty   40
each. Then, taking the five loaves and the two fishes, he looked up   41
to heaven, said the blessing, broke the loaves, and gave them to
the disciples to distribute. He also divided the two fishes among
them. They all ate to their hearts' content; and twelve great   42 43
basketfuls of scraps were picked up, with what was left of the fish.
Those who ate the loaves numbered five thousand men.   44

As soon as it was over he made his disciples embark and cross to   45
Bethsaida ahead of him, while he himself sent the people away.
After taking leave of them, he went up the hill-side to pray. It   46 47
grew late and the boat was already well out on the water, while he
was alone on the land. Somewhere between three and six in the   48

morning, seeing them labouring at the oars against a head-wind, he came towards them, walking on the lake. He was going to pass
49 them by; but when they saw him walking on the lake, they thought it was a ghost and cried out; for they all saw him and were
50 terrified. But at once he spoke to them: 'Take heart! It is I; do not
51 be afraid.' Then he climbed into the boat beside them, and the
52 wind dropped. At this they were completely dumbfounded, for they had not understood the incident of the loaves; their minds were closed.
53   So they finished the crossing and came to land at Gennesaret,
54 55 where they made fast. When they came ashore, he was immediately recognized; and the people scoured that whole country-side and brought the sick on stretchers to any place
56 where he was reported to be. Wherever he went, to farmsteads, villages, or towns, they laid out the sick in the market-places and begged him to let them simply touch the edge of his cloak; and all who touched him were cured.

Growing tension

7 A group of pharisees, with some doctors of the law who had
2 come from Jerusalem, met him and noticed that some of his disciples were eating their food with 'defiled' hands – in other
3 words, without washing them. (For the pharisees and the Jews in
4 general never eat without washing the hands, in obedience to an old-established tradition; and on coming from the market-place they never eat without first washing. And there are many other points on which they have a traditional rule to maintain, for
5 example, washing of cups and jugs and copper bowls.) Accordingly, these pharisees and lawyers asked him, 'Why do your disciples not conform to the ancient tradition, but eat their food
6 with defiled hands?' He answered, 'Isaiah was right when he
7 prophesied about you hypocrites in these words: "This people pays me lip-service, but their heart is far from me: their worship of me is vain, for they teach as doctrines the commandments of
8 men." You neglect the commandment of God, in order to maintain the tradition of men.'

He also said to them, 'How well you set aside the command- 9
ment of God in order to maintain your tradition! Moses said, 10
"Honour your father and your mother", and "The man who
curses his father or mother must suffer death." But you hold that 11
if a man says to his father or mother, "Anything of mine which
might have been used for your benefit is Corban" ' (meaning, set
apart for God), 'he is no longer required to do anything for his 12
father or mother. Thus by your own tradition, handed down 13
among you, you make God's word null and void. And many
other things that you do are just like that.'

On another occasion he called the people and said to them, 14
'Listen to me, all of you, and understand this: nothing that goes 15
into a man from outside can defile him; no, it is the things that
come out of him that defile a man.'

When he had left the people and gone indoors, his disciples 17
questioned him about the parable. He said to them, 'Are you as 18
dull as the rest? Do you not see that nothing that goes from
outside into a man can defile him, because it does not enter into his 19
heart but into his stomach, and so passes out into the drain?' Thus 20
he declared all foods clean. He went on, 'It is what comes out of a 21
man that defiles him. For from inside, out of a man's heart, come 22
evil thoughts, acts of fornication, of theft, murder, adultery,
ruthless greed, and malice; fraud, indecency, envy, slander,
arrogance, and folly; these evil things all come from inside, and 23
they defile a man.'

Then he left that place and went away into the territory of Tyre. 24
He found a house to stay in and he would have liked to remain
unrecognized, but this was impossible. Almost at once a woman 25
whose young daughter was possessed by an unclean spirit heard
of him, came in, and fell at his feet. She was a hellenist, a 26
Syrophoenician by birth. She begged him to drive the spirit out of
her daughter. He said to her, 'Let the children be satisfied first; it is 27
not fair to take the children's bread and throw it to the dogs.' 'Sir,' 28
she answered, 'even the dogs under the table eat the children's
scraps.' He said to her, 'For saying that, you may go home 29
content; the unclean spirit has gone out of your daughter.' And 30
when she returned home, she found the child lying in bed; the
spirit had left her.

31   On his return journey from Tyrian territory he went by way of
Sidon to the Sea of Galilee through the territory of the Ten
32   Towns. They brought to him a man who was deaf and had an
impediment in his speech, with the request that he would lay his
33   hand on him. He took the man aside, away from the crowd, put
34   his fingers into his ears, spat, and touched his tongue. Then,
looking up to heaven, he sighed, and said to him, '*Ephphatha*',
35   which means 'Be opened'. With that his ears were opened, and at
the same time the impediment was removed and he spoke plainly.
36   Jesus forbade them to tell anyone; but the more he forbade them,
the more they published it. Their astonishment knew no bounds:
37   'All that he does, he does well,' they said; 'he even makes the deaf
hear and the dumb speak.'

8   There was another occasion about this time when a huge crowd
had collected, and, as they had no food, Jesus called his disciples
2   and said to them, 'I feel sorry for all these people; they have been
3   with me now for three days and have nothing to eat. If I send them
home unfed, they will turn faint on the way; some of them have
4   come from afar.' The disciples answered, 'How can anyone
5   provide all these people with bread in this lonely place?' 'How
6   many loaves have you?' he asked; and they answered, 'Seven.' So
he ordered the people to sit down on the ground; then he took the
seven loaves, and, after giving thanks to God, he broke the bread
and gave it to his disciples to distribute; and they served it out to
7   the people. They had also a few small fishes, which he blessed and
8   ordered them to distribute. They all ate to their hearts' content,
9   and seven baskets were filled with scraps that were left. The
10   people numbered about four thousand. Then he dismissed them;
and, without delay, got into the boat with his disciples and went
to the district of Dalmanutha.
11   Then the pharisees came out and engaged him in discussion. To
12   test him they asked him for a sign from heaven. He sighed deeply
to himself and said, 'Why does this generation ask for a sign? I tell
13   you this; no sign shall be given to this generation.' With that he
left them, re-embarked, and went off to the other side of the lake.
14   Now they had forgotten to take bread with them; they had no
15   more than one loaf in the boat. He began to warn them: 'Beware,'

he said, 'be on your guard against the leaven of the pharisees and
the leaven of Herod.' They said among themselves, 'It is because   16
we have no bread.' Knowing what was in their mind, he asked   17
them, 'Why do you talk about having no bread? Have you no
inkling yet? Do you still not understand? Are you minds closed?
You have eyes: can you not see? You have ears: can you not hear?   18
Have you forgotten? When I broke the five loaves among five   19
thousand, how many basketfuls of scraps did you pick up?,
'Twelve', they said. 'And how many when I broke the seven   20
loaves among four thousand?' They answered, 'Seven.' He said,   21
'Do you still not understand?'

They arrived at Bethsaida. There the people brought a blind   22
man to Jesus and begged him to touch him. He took the blind man   23
by the hand and led him away out of the village. Then he spat on
his eyes, laid his hands upon him, and asked whether he could see
anything. The man's sight began to come back, and he said, 'I see   24
men; they look like trees, but they are walking about.' Jesus laid 25
his hands on his eyes again; he looked hard, and now he was cured
so that he saw everything clearly. Then Jesus sent him home,   26
saying, 'Do not tell anyone in the village.'

Jesus and his disciples set out for the villages of Caesarea Philippi. 27
On the way he asked his disciples, 'Who do men say I am?' They   28
answered, 'Some say John the baptist, others Elijah, others one of
the prophets.' 'And you,' he asked, 'who do you say I am?' Peter   29
replied, 'You are the messiah.' Then he gave them strict orders   30
not to tell anyone about him; and he began to teach them that the   31
son of man must undergo great sufferings, be rejected by the
elders, chief priests, and scribes, and be put to death, and rise   32
again after three days. He spoke about it plainly. At this Peter
took him by the arm and began to rebuke him. But Jesus turned   33
round, and, looking at his disciples, rebuked Peter. 'Get behind
me, satan,' he said; 'you think as men think, not as God
thinks.'

Then he called the people to him, as well as his disciples, and   34
said to them, 'Anyone who wishes to be a follower of mine must
leave self behind; he must take up his cross, and come with me.
Whoever cares for his own safety is lost; but if a man will let   35

himself be lost for my sake and for the good news, that man is
36   safe. What does a man gain by winning the whole world at the
37 38 cost of his true self? What can he give to buy that self back? If
anyone is ashamed of me and my words in this wicked and
godless age, the son of man will be ashamed of him, when he
comes in the glory of his father and of the holy angels.'

9   He also said, 'I tell you this: there are some of those standing
here who will not taste death before they have seen the kingdom
of God already come in power.'

2   Six days later Jesus took Peter, James, and John with him and
led them up a high mountain where they were alone; and in their
3   presence he was transfigured; his clothes became dazzling white,
4   with a whiteness no bleacher on earth could equal. They saw
5   Elijah appear, and Moses with him, and there they were,
conversing with Jesus. Then Peter spoke; 'Rabbi,' he said, 'how
6   good it is that we are here! Shall we make three shelters, one for
you, one for Moses, and one for Elijah?' (For he did not know
7   what to say, they were so terrified.) Then a cloud appeared,
casting its shadow over them, and out of the cloud came a voice:
8   'This is my dear son, listen to him.' And now suddenly, when
they looked around, there was nobody to be seen but Jesus alone
with themselves.

9   On their way down the mountain, he enjoined them not to tell
anyone what they had seen until the son of man had risen from the .
10   dead. They seized upon those words, and discussed among
themselves what this 'rising from the dead' could mean. And they
11   put a question to him: 'Why do our teachers say that Elijah must
12   come first?' He replied, 'Yes, Elijah does come first to set
everything right. Yet how is it that the scriptures say of the son of
man that he is to endure great sufferings and to be treated with
13   contempt? However, I tell you, Elijah has already come and they
have worked their will upon him, as the scriptures say of him.'

14   When they came back to the disciples they saw a large crowd
15   surrounding them and scribes arguing with them. As soon as they
saw Jesus the whole crowd were overcome with awe, and they
16   ran forward to welcome him. He asked them, 'What is this
17   argument about?' A man in the crowd spoke up: 'Master, I
brought my son to you. He is possessed by a spirit which makes

him speechless. Whenever it attacks him, it dashes him to the   18
ground, and he foams at the mouth, grinds his teeth, and goes
rigid. I asked your disciples to cast it out, but they failed.' Jesus   19
answered: 'What an unbelieving and perverse generation! How
long shall I be with you? How long must I endure you? Bring him
to me.' So they brought the boy to him; and as soon as the spirit   20
saw him it threw the boy into convulsions, and he fell on the
ground and rolled about foaming at the mouth. Jesus asked his   21
father, 'How long has he been like this?' 'From childhood,' he
replied; 'often it has tried to make an end of him by throwing him   22
into the fire or into water. But if it is at all possible for you, take
pity upon us and help us.' 'If it is possible!' said Jesus. 'Everything   23
is possible to one who has faith.' 'I have faith,' cried the boy's   24
father; 'help me where faith falls short.' Jesus saw then that the   25
crowd was closing in upon them, so he rebuked the unclean spirit.
'Deaf and dumb spirit,' he said, 'I command you, come out of
him and never go back!' After crying aloud and racking him   26
fiercely, it came out; and the boy looked like a corpse; in fact,
many said, 'He is dead.' But Jesus took his hand and raised him to   27
his feet, and he stood up.

Then Jesus went indoors, and his disciples asked him privately,   28
'Why could not we cast it out?' He said, 'There is no means of   29
casting out this sort but prayer.'

They now left that district and made a journey through Galilee.   30
Jesus wished it to be kept secret; for he was teaching his disciples,   31
and telling them, 'The son of man will be delivered into the hands
of men who will kill him, but three days after being killed, he will
rise again.' But they did not understand what he said, and were   32
afraid to ask.

So they came to Capernaum; and when he was indoors, he   33
asked them, 'What were you arguing about on the way?' They
were silent, because on the way they had been discussing who was   34
the greatest. He sat down, called the twelve, and said to them, 'If   35
anyone wants to be first, he must make himself last of all and
servant of all.' Then he took a child, set him in front of them, and   36
put his arm round him. 'Whoever receives one of these children in   37
my name,' he said, 'receives me; and whoever receives me,
receives not me but the one who sent me.'

38   John said to him, 'Master, we saw a man driving out demons in
      your name, and as he was not one of us, we tried to stop him.'
39   Jesus said, 'Do not stop him; no one who does a work of divine
      power in my name will be able the next moment to speak evil of
40 41 me. For he who is not against us is on our side. I tell you this: if
      anyone gives you a cup of water because you are followers of the
      messiah, that man assuredly will not go unrewarded.
42   'As for the man who is a cause of stumbling to these little ones
      who have faith, it would be better for him to be thrown into the
43   sea with a millstone round his neck. If your hand is your undoing,
      cut it off; it is better for you to enter into life maimed than to keep
45   both hands and go to hell and the unquenchable fire. And if your
      foot is your undoing, cut it off; it is better to enter into life a
      cripple than to keep both your feet and be thrown into hell. And if
47   it is your eye, tear it out; it is better to enter into the kingdom of
      God with one eye than to keep both eyes and be thrown into hell,
48   where the devouring worm never dies and the fire is not quenched.
49   'For everyone will be salted with fire.
50   'Salt is a good thing; but if the salt loses its saltness, what will
      you season it with?
      'Have salt in yourselves; and be at peace with one another.'

10   On leaving those parts he came into the region of Judaea and
      Transjordan; and when a crowd gathered round him once again,
2   he followed his usual practice and taught them. The question was
3   put to him; 'Is it lawful for a man to divorce his wife?' This was to
4   test him. He asked in return, 'What did Moses command you?'
      They answered, ' Moses permitted a man to divorce his wife by
5   note of dismissal.' Jesus said to them, 'It was because your minds
6   were closed that he made this rule for you; but in the beginning, at
7   the creation, God made them male and female. For this reason a
      man shall leave his father and mother, and be made one with his
8   wife; and the two shall become one flesh. It follows that they are
9   no longer two individuals: they are one flesh. What God has
      joined together, man must not separate.'
10   When they were indoors again the disciples questioned him
11   about this matter; he said to them, 'Whoever divorces his wife and
12   marries another commits adultery against her: so too, if she

divorce her husband and marries another, she commits adultery.'
They brought children for him to touch. The disciples rebuked   13
them, but when Jesus saw this he was indignant, and said to them,   14
'Let the children come to me; do not try to stop them; for the
kingdom of God belongs to such as these. I tell you, whoever   15
does not accept the kingdom of God like a child will never enter
it.' And he put his arms round them, laid his hands upon them,   16
and blessed them.

As he was starting out on a journey, a stranger ran up, and,   17
kneeling before him, asked, 'Good Master, what must I do to win
eternal life?' Jesus said to him, 'Why do you call me good? No one   18
is good except God alone. You know the commandments: "Do   19
not murder; do not commit adultery; do not steal; do not give
false evidence; do not defraud; honour your father and mother." '
'But, Master,' he replied, 'I have kept all these since I was a boy.'   20
Jesus looked straight at him; his heart warmed to him, and he said,   21
'One thing you lack: go, sell everything you have, and give to the
poor, and you will have riches in heaven; and come, follow me.'
At these words his face fell and he went away with a heavy heart;   22
for he was a man of great wealth.

Jesus looked round at his disciples and said to them, 'How hard   23
it will be for the wealthy to enter into the kingdom of God!' They   24
were amazed that he should say this, but Jesus insisted, 'Children,
how hard it is to enter the kingdom of God! It is easier for a camel   25
to pass through the eye of a needle than for a rich man to enter the
kingdom of God.' They were more astonished than ever, and said   26
to one another, 'Then who can be saved?' Jesus looked at them
and said, 'For men it is impossible, but not for God; everything is   27
possible for God.'

At this Peter spoke. 'We here,' he said, 'have left everything to   28
become your followers.' Jesus said, 'I tell you this: there is no one   29
who has given up home, brothers or sister, mother, father or
children, or land, for my sake and for the sake of the good news,
who will not receive in this age a hundred times as much – houses,   30
brothers and sisters, mothers, and children, and land – and
persecutions beside; and in the age to come eternal life. But many   31
who are first will be last and the last first.'

Challenge to Jerusalem

32 They were on the road, going up to Jerusalem, Jesus leading the
way; and the disciples were filled with awe, while those who
followed behind were afraid. He took the twelve aside and began
33 to tell them what was to happen to him. 'We are now going to
Jerusalem,' he said, 'and the son of man will be delivered up to the
chief priests and the scribes; they will condemn him to death and
34 hand him over to the Gentiles. He will be mocked and spat upon,
flogged and killed; and three days afterwards, he will rise
again.'
35   James and John, the sons of Zebedee, approached him and said,
36 'Master, we should like you to do us a favour.' 'What is it you
37 want me to do?' he asked. They answered, 'Grant us the right to
sit in state with you, one at your right and the other at your left.'
38 Jesus said to them, 'You do not understand what you are asking.
Can you drink the cup that I drink, or be baptized with the
39 baptism I am baptized with?' 'We can,' they answered. Jesus said,
'The cup that I drink you shall drink, and the baptism I am
40 baptized with shall be your baptism; but to sit at my right or left is
not for me to grant; it is for those to whom it has already been
assigned.'
41   When the other ten heard this, they were indignant with James
42 and John. Jesus called them to him and said, 'You know that in the
world the recognized rulers lord it over their subjects, and their
43 great men make them feel the weight of authority. That is not the
44 way with you; among you, whoever wants to be great must be
your servant, and whoever wants to be first must be the willing
45 slave of all. For even the son of man did not come to be served but
to serve, and to give up his life as a ransom for many.'
46   They came to Jericho; and as he was leaving the town, with his
disciples and a large crowd, Bartimaeus son of Timaeus, a blind
47 beggar, was seated at the roadside. Hearing that it was Jesus of
48 Nazareth, he began to shout, 'Son of David, Jesus, have pity on
me!' Many of the people told him to hold his tongue; but he shouted
49 all the more, 'Son of David, have pity on me.' Jesus stopped and
50 said, 'Call him' so they called the blind man and said, 'Take heart;
stand up; he is calling you.' At that he threw off his cloak, sprang up,

and came to Jesus. Jesus said to him, 'What do you want me to do for   51
you?' 'Master,' the blind man answered, 'I want my sight back.'
Jesus said to him, 'Go; your faith has cured you.' And at once he   52
recovered his sight and followed him on the way.

They were now approaching Jerusalem, and when they reached   11
Bethphage and Bethany, at the Mount of Olives, he sent two of
his disciples with these instructions: 'Go to the village opposite,   2
and, just as you enter, you will find tethered there a colt which no
one has yet ridden. Untie it and bring it here. If anyone asks,   3
"Why are you doing that?", say, "Our Master needs it, and will
send it back here without delay."' So they went off, and found the   4
colt tethered at a door outside in the street. They were untying it
when some bystanders asked, 'What are you doing, untying that   5
colt?' They answered as Jesus had told them, and were then   6
allowed to take it. So they brought the colt to Jesus and spread   7
their cloaks on it, and he mounted. And people carpeted the road   8
with their cloaks, while others spread brushwood which they had   9
cut in the fields; and those who went ahead and the others who
came behind shouted, 'Hosanna! Blessings on him who comes in   10
the name of the Lord! Blessings on the coming kingdom of our
father David! Hosanna in the heavens!'

He entered Jerusalem and went into the temple, where he   11
looked at the whole scene; but, as it was now late, he went out to
Bethany with the twelve.

On the following day, after they had left Bethany, he felt   12 13
hungry, and, noticing in the distance a fig-tree in leaf, he went to
see if he could find anything on it. But when he came there he
found nothing but leaves; for it was not the season for figs. He   14
said to the tree, 'May no one ever again eat fruit from you!' And
his disciples were listening.

So they came to Jerusalem, and he went into the temple and   15
began driving out those who bought and sold in the temple. He
upset the tables of the money- changers and the seats of the dealers
in pigeons; and he would not allow anyone to use the temple court   16
as a thoroughfare for carrying goods. The he began to teach them,
and said, 'Does not scripture say, "My house shall be called a   17
house of prayer for all the nations"? But you have made it a

18 robbers' cave.' The chief priests and the doctors of the law heard of this and sought some means of doing away with him; for they were afraid of him, because the whole crowd was spellbound by
19 his teaching. And when evening came he went out of the city.
20 Early next morning, as they passed by, they saw that the fig-tree had withered from the roots up; and Peter, recalling what
21 had happened, said to him, 'Rabbi, look, the fig-tree which you
22 cursed has withered.' Jesus answered him, 'Have faith in God. I
23 tell you this: if anyone says to this mountain, "Be lifted from your place and hurled into the sea", and has no inward doubts, but
24 believes that what he says is happening, it will be done for him. I tell you, then, whatever you ask for in prayer, believe that you have received it and it will be yours.
25 'And when you stand praying, if you have a grievance against anyone, forgive him, so that your father in heaven may forgive you the wrongs you have done.'

27 They came once more to Jerusalem. And as he was walking in
28 the temple court the chief priests, lawyers, and elders came to him and said, 'By what authority are you acting like this? Who gave
29 you authority to act in this way?' Jesus said to them, 'I have a question to ask you too; and if you give me the answer, I will tell
30 you by what authority I act. The baptism of John: was it from
31 God, or from men? Answer me.' This set them arguing among themselves: 'What shall we say? If we say, "from God", he will say,
32 "Then why did you not believe him?" Shall we say, "from men"?' – but they were afraid of the people, for all held that John was in fact a
33 prophet. So they answered, 'We do not know.' And Jesus said to them, 'Then neither will I tell you by what authority I act.'
12 He went on to speak to them in parables: 'A man planted a vineyard and put a wall round it, hewed out a winepress, and built a watch-tower; then he let it out to vine-growers and went
2 abroad. When the season came, he sent a servant to the tenants to collect from them his share of the produce. But they took him,
3 4 thrashed him, and sent him away empty-handed. Again, he sent them another servant, whom they beat about the head and treated outrageously. So he sent another, and that one they killed; and
5 many more beside, of whom they beat some, and killed others.

He had now only one left to send, his own dear son. In the end he 6
sent him. "They will respect my son", he said. But the tenants
said to one another, "This is the heir; come on, let us kill him, and 7
the property will be ours." So they seized him and killed him, and 8
flung his body out of the vineyard. What will the owner of the 9
vineyard do? He will come and put the tenants to death and give
the vineyard to others.

'Can it be that you have never read this text: "The stone which 10
the builders rejected has become the main corner-stone. This the 11
Lord's doing, and it is wonderful in our eyes"?'

Then they began to look for a way to arrest him, for they saw 12
that the parable was aimed at them; but they were afraid of the
people, so they left him alone and went away.

A number of pharisees and men of Herod's party were sent to trap 13
him with a question. They came and said, 'Master, you are an 14
honest man, we know, and truckle to no one, whoever he may be;
you teach in all honesty the way of life that God requires. Are we
or are we not permitted to pay taxes to the Roman Emperor? Shall 15
we pay or not?' He saw how crafty their question was, and said,
'Why are you trying to catch me out? Fetch me a silver piece, and 16
let me look at it.' They brought one, and he said to them, 'Whose
head is this, and whose inscription?' 'Caesar's', they replied. Then 17
Jesus said, 'Pay Caesar what is due to Caesar, and pay God what is
due to God.' And they heard him with astonishment.

Next Sadducees came to him. (It is they who say that there is no 18
resurrection.) Their question was this: 'Master, Moses laid it 19
down for us that if there are brothers and one dies leaving a wife
but no child, then the next should marry the widow and carry on 20
his brother's family. Now there were seven brothers. The first 21
took a wife and died without issue. Then the second married her,
and he too died without issue. So did the third. Eventually the 22
seven of them died, all without issue. Finally the woman died. At 23
the resurrection, when they come back to life, whose wife will she
be, since all seven had married her?' Jesus said to them, 'You are 24
mistaken, and surely this is the reason: you do not know either the
scriptures or the power of God. When they rise from the dead, 25
men and women do not marry; they are like angels in heaven.

26 'But about the resurrection of the dead, have you never read in
the Book of Moses, in the story of the burning bush, how God
spoke to him and said, "I am the God of Abraham, the God of
27 Isaac, and the God of Jacob"? God is not the God of the dead but of
the living. You are greatly mistaken.'
28 Then one of the scribes, who had been listening to these
discussions and had noted how well he answered, came forward
29 and asked him, 'Which commandment is first of all?' Jesus
answered, 'The first is, "Hear, O Israel: the Lord our God is the
30 only Lord; love the Lord your God with all your heart, with all
31 your soul, with all your mind, and with all your strength." The
second is this: "Love your neighbour as yourself." There is no
32 other commandment greater than these.' The scribe said to him,
'Well said, Master. You are right in saying that God is one and
33 beside him there is no other. And to love him with all your heart,
all your understanding, and all your strength, and to love your
neighbour as yourself – that is far more than any burnt offerings
34 or sacrifices.' When Jesus saw how sensibly he answered, he said
to him, 'You are not far from the kingdom of God.'
35 After that nobody ventured to put any more questions to him;
and Jesus went on to say, as he taught in the temple, 'How can the
teachers of the law maintain that the messiah is the son of David?
36 David himself said, when inspired by the holy spirit, "The Lord
said to my lord, 'Sit at my right hand until I make your enemies
37 your footstool.' " David himself calls him "Lord"; how can he
also be David's son?'
38 There was a great crowd and they listened eagerly. He said as he
taught them, 'Beware of the scribes, who love to walk up and
down in long robes, receiving respectful greetings in the street;
39 and to have the chief seats in synagogues, and places of honour at
40 feasts. These are the men who eat up the property of widows,
while they say long prayers for appearance' sake, and they will
receive the severest sentence.'
41 Once he was standing opposite the temple treasury, watching
as people dropped their money into the chest. Many rich people
42 were giving large sums. Presently there came a poor widow who
dropped in two tiny coins, together worth a farthing. He called
43 his disciples to him. 'I tell you this,' he said, 'this poor widow has

given more than any of the others; for those others who have   44
given had more than enough, but she, with less than enough, has
given all that she had to live on.'

As he was leaving the temple, one of his disciples exclaimed,   **13**
'Look, Master, what huge stones! What fine buildings!' Jesus said 2
to him, 'You see these great buildings? Not one stone will be left
upon another; all will be thrown down.'

When he was sitting on the Mount of Olives facing the temple   3
he was questioned privately by Peter, James, John, and Andrew.
'Tell us', they said, 'when will this happen? What will be the sign 4
when the fulfilment of all this is at hand?'

Jesus began: 'Take care that no one misleads you. Many will   5 6
come claiming my name, and saying, "I am he"; and many will be
misled by them.

'When you hear the noise of battle near at hand and news of   7
battles far away, do not be alarmed. Such things are bound to
happen; but the end is still to come. For nation will make war   8
upon nation, kingdom upon kingdom; there will be earthquakes
in many places; there will be famine. With these things the birth-
pangs of the new age begin.

'As for you, be on your guard. You will be handed over to the   9
courts. You will be flogged in the synagogues. You will be
summoned to appear before governors and kings on my account
to testify in their presence. But before the end the good news must 10
be proclaimed to all nations. So when you are arrested and taken   11
away, do not worry beforehand about what you will say, but
when the time comes say whatever is given you to say; for it will
not be you that will be speaking, but the holy spirit. Brother will 12
betray brother to death, and the father his child; children will turn
against their parents and send them to their death. All will hate   13
you for your allegiance to me; but the man who holds out to the
end will be saved.

'But when you see "the disastrous abomination" where it   14
ought not to be (let the reader understand), then those who are in
Judaea must take to the hills. If a man is on the roof, he must not 15
come down into the house to fetch anything out; if in the field, he 16
must not turn back for his coat. Alas for women with child in   17

18   those days, and for those who have children at the breast! Pray
19   that it may not come in winter. For those days will bring distress
      such as never has been until now since the beginning of the world
20   which God created – and will never be again. If the Lord had not
      cut short that time of troubles, no living thing could survive.
      However, for the sake of his own, whom he has chosen, he has
      cut short the time.
21   'Then, if anyone says to you, "Look here is the messiah", or,
22   "Look, there he is", do not believe it. Impostors will come
      claiming to be messiahs or prophets, and they will produce signs
      and wonders to mislead God's chosen, if such a thing were
23   possible. But be on your guard; I have forewarned you of it all.
24   'But in those days, after that distress, the sun will be darkened,
25   the moon will not give her light; the stars will come falling
26   from the sky, the celestial power will be shaken. Then they will
      see the son of man coming in the clouds with great power and
27   glory, and he will send out the angels and gather his chosen from
      the four winds, from the farthest bounds of earth and the farthest
      bounds of heaven.
28   'Learn a lesson from the fig-tree. When its tender shoots appear
29   and are breaking into leaf, you know that summer is near. In the
      same way, when you see all this happening, you may know that
30   the end is near, at the very door. I tell you this: the present
31   generation will live to see it all. Heaven and earth will pass away;
      my words will never pass away.
32   'But about that day or that hour no one knows, not even the
      angels in heaven, not even the son; only the father.
33   'Be alert, be wakeful. You do not know when the moment
34   comes. It is like a man away from home: he has left his house and
      put his servants in charge, each with his own work to do, and he
35   has ordered the door-keeper to stay awake. Keep awake, for you
      do not know when the master of the house is coming. Evening or
      midnight, cock-crow or early dawn – if he comes suddenly, he
36 37 must not find you asleep. And what I say to you, I say to
      everyone: Keep awake.'

The final conflict

Now the festival of passover and unleavened bread was only two **14**
days off; and the chief priests and the doctors of law were trying to
devise some cunning plan to seize him and put him to death. 'It **2**
must not be during the festival,' they said, 'or we should have
rioting among the people.'

Jesus was at Bethany, in the house of Simon the leper. As he sat **3**
at table, a woman came in carrying a small bottle of very costly
perfume, pure oil of nard. She broke it open and poured the oil **4**
over his head. Some of those present said to one another angrily,
'Why this waste? The perfume might have been sold for thirty **5**
pounds (literally 300 denarii) and the money given to the poor;
and they turned upon her with fury. But Jesus said: Let her alone. **6**
Why must you make trouble for her? It is a fine thing she has done
for me. You have the poor among you always, and you can help **7**
them whenever you like; but you will not always have me. She **8**
has done what lay in her power; she is beforehand with anointing
my body for burial. I tell you this: wherever in all the world the **9**
good news is proclaimed, what she has done will be told as her
memorial.'

Then Jesus Iscariot, one of the twelve, went to the chief priests **10**
to deliver up Jesus to them. When they heard what he had come **11**
for they were greatly pleased, and promised him money; and he
began to look for a good opportunity to betray him.

Now on the first day of unleavened bread, when the passover **12**
lambs were being slaughtered, his disciples said to him, 'Where
would you like us to go and prepare your passover supper?' So he **13**
sent two of his disciples with these instructions: 'Go into the city,
and a man will meet you carrying a jar of water. Follow him, and **14**
when he enters a house give this message to the householder:
"The Master says, 'Where is the room reserved for me to eat the
passover with my disciples?' " He will show you a large room **15**
upstairs, set out in readiness. Make the preparations for us there.'
Then the disciples went off, and when they came into the city they **16**
found everything just as he had told them. So they prepared for
the passover.

17 18   In the evening he came to the house with the twelve. As they sat
         at supper Jesus said, 'I tell you this: one of you will betray me –
19   one who is eating with me.' At this they were dismayed; one by
20   one they said to him, 'Not I, surely?' 'It is one of the twelve', he
21   said, 'who is dipping into the same bowl with me. The son of man
         is going the way appointed for him in the scriptures; but alas for
         that man by whom the son of man is betrayed! It would be better
         for that man if he had never been born.'

22   During supper he took bread, and having said the blessing he
         broke it and gave it to them, with the words, 'Take this; this is my
23   body.' Then he took a cup, and having offered thanks to God he
24   gave it to them; and they all drank from it. And he said, 'This is
25   my blood, the blood of the covenant, shed for many. I tell you
         this: never again shall I drink from the fruit of the vine until that
         day when I drink it new in the kingdom of God.'

26   After singing the passover hymn, they went out to the Mount
27   of Olives. And Jesus said, 'You will all fall from your faith; for it
         stands written, "I will strike the shepherd down and the sheep will
28   be scattered." Nevertheless, after I am raised again I will go on
29   before you into Galilee.' Peter answered, 'Everyone else may fall
30   away, but I will not.' Jesus said, 'I tell you this: today, this very
         night, before the cock crows twice, you yourself will disown me
31   three times.' But he insisted and repeated, 'Even if I must die with
         you, I will never disown you.' And they all said the same.

32   When they reached a place called Gethsemane, he said to his
33   disciples, 'Sit here while I pray.' And he took Peter and James and
         John with him. Horror and dismay came over him, and he said to
34   them, 'My heart is ready to break with grief; stop here, and stay
35   awake.' Then he went forward a little, threw himself on the
         ground, and prayed that, if it were possible, this hour might pass
36   him by. 'Abba-, Father-,' he said, 'all things are possible for you;
         take this cup away from me. Yet not what I want matters, but
         what you want.'

37   He came back and found them asleep; and he said to Peter,
38   'Asleep, Simon? Were you not able to stay awake for one hour?
         Stay awake, all of you; and pray that you may be spared the test.
39   The spirit is willing, but the flesh is weak.' Once more he went

away and prayed. On his return he found them asleep again, for   40
their eyes were heavy; and they did not know how to answer
him.

The third time he came and said to them, 'Still sleeping? Still   41
taking your ease? Enough! The hour has come. Now the son of
man is to be betrayed and to fall into the hands of sinners. Up, let   42
us go forward! My betrayer is upon us.'

Suddenly, while he was still speaking, Judas, one of the twelve,   43
appeared, and with him was a crowd armed with swords and
cudgels, sent by the chief priests, lawyers, and elders. Now the   44
traitor had agreed with them upon a signal: 'The one I kiss is your
man; seize him and get him safely away.' When he reached the   45
spot, he stepped forward at once and said to Jesus, 'Rabbi', and
kissed him. Then they seized him and held him fast.   46

One of the party drew his sword, and struck at the high priest's   47
servant, cutting off his ear. Then Jesus spoke: 'Do you take me for   48
a bandit, that you have come with swords and cudgels to arrest
me? Day after day I was within your reach as I taught in the   49
temple, and you did not seize me. But let the scriptures be   50
fulfilled.' Then the disciples all deserted him and ran away.

Among those following was a young man with nothing on but   51
a linen cloth. They tried to seize him; but he slipped out of the   52
linen cloth and ran away naked.

Then they led Jesus away to the high priest's house, where the   53
chief priests, elders, and doctors of the law were all assembling.
Peter followed him at a distance right into the high priest's   54
courtyard; and there he remained, sitting among the attendants,
warming himself at the fire.

The chief priests and the whole council tried to find some   55
evidence against Jesus to warrant a death-sentence, but failed to
find any. Many gave false evidence against him, but their   56
statements did not tally. Some stood up and gave false evidence to   57
this effect: 'We heard him say, "I will pull down this temple, made   58
with human hands, and in three days I will build another, not
made with hands." But even on this point their evidence did not   59
agree.

Then the high priest stood up in his place and questioned Jesus: 60

61   'Have you no answer to the charges that these witnesses bring against you?' But he kept silence; he made no reply.

Again the high priest questioned him: 'Are you the messiah, the
62   son of the Blessed One?' Jesus said, 'I am; and you will see the son of man seated at the right hand of God and coming with the
63   clouds of heaven.' Then the high priest tore his robes and said,
64   'Need we call further witnesses? You have heard the blasphemy. What is your opinion?' Their judgement was unanimous: that he was guilty and should be put to death.

65   Some began to spit on him, blindfolded him, and struck him with their fists, crying out, 'Prophesy!' And the high priest's men set upon him with blows.

66   Meanwhile Peter was still below in the courtyard. One of the high priest's serving-maids came by and saw him there warming
67   himself. She looked into his face and said, 'You were there too,
68   with this man from Nazareth, this Jesus.' But he denied it: 'I know nothing,' he said; 'I do not understand what you mean.' Then he went outside into the porch; and the maid saw him there
69   again and began to say to the bystanders, 'He is one of them'; and
70   again he denied it.

Again, a little later, the bystanders said to Peter, 'Surely you are
71   one of them. You must be; you are a Galilean.' At this he broke into curses, and with an oath he said, 'I do not know this man you
72   speak of.' Then the cock crew a second time; and Peter remembered how Jesus had said to him, 'Before the cock crows twice you will have disowned me three times.' And he burst into tears.

15   When morning came, the chief priests, having made their plan with the elders and scribes and all the council, put Jesus in chains;
2   then they led him away and delivered him up to Pilate. Pilate asked him, 'Are you the king of the Jews?' He replied, 'The words
3   are yours.' And the chief priests brought many charges against
4   him. Pilate questioned him again: 'Have you nothing to say in your defence? You see how many charges they are bringing
5   against you.' But to Pilate's astonishment, Jesus made no further reply.

6   At the festival season he used to release one prisoner at the
7   people's request. As it happened, the man known as Barabbas was

then in custody with the rebels who had committed murder in the rising. When the crowd appeared asking for the usual favour, 8 Pilate replied, 'Do you wish me to release for you the king of the 9 Jews?' For he knew it was out of malice that they had brought 10 Jesus before him. But the chief priests incited the crowd to ask 11 him to release Barabbas rather than Jesus. Pilate spoke to them 12 again: 'Then what shall I do with the man you call king of the Jews?' They shouted back, 'Crucify him!' 'Why, what harm has 13 14 he done?' Pilate asked; but they shouted all the louder, 'Crucify him!' So Pilate, in his desire to satisfy the mob, released Barabbas 15 to them; and he had Jesus flogged and handed him over to be crucified.

Then the soldiers took him inside the building to the so-called 16 praetorium, where they called together the whole company. They dressed him in purple, and plaiting a crown of thorns, 17 placed it on his head. Then they began to salute him with, 'Hail, 18 king of the Jews!' They beat him about the head and spat upon 19 him, and then knelt and paid mock homage to him. When they 20 had finished their mockery, they stripped him of the purple and dressed him in his own clothes.

Then they took him out to crucify him. A man called Simon, 21 from Cyrene, the father of Alexander and Rufus, was passing by on his way in from the country, and they pressed him into service to carry his cross.

They brought him to the place called Golgotha, which means 22 'Place of a skull'. He was offered drugged wine, but he would not 23 take it. Then they fastened him to the cross. They divided his 24 clothes among them, casting lots to decide what each should have.

It was the third hour when they crucified him. And the inscrip- 25 26 tion giving the charge against him read, 'The king of the Jews'. 27 Two bandits were crucified with him, one on his right and the other on his left.

The passers-by hurled abuse at him: 'Aha!' they cried, wagging 29 their heads, 'you would pull the temple down, would you, and build it in three days? Come down from the cross and save 30 31 yourself!' So too the chief priests and the scribes jested with one

another: 'He saved others,' they said, 'but he cannot save himself.
32   Let the messiah, the king of Israel, come down now from the
cross. If we see that, we shall believe.' Even those who were
crucified with him taunted him.
33   At the sixth hour darkness fell over the whole land, which
34   lasted until the ninth hour. At the ninth hour Jesus cried aloud,
35   *Eloi, Eloi, lema sabachthani?*', which means, 'My God, my God,
why have you deserted me?' Some of the bystanders heard this,
36   and said, 'Hark, he is calling Elijah.' A man ran and soaked a
37   sponge in sour wine and held it to his lips on the end of a cane. 'Let
us see,' he said, 'if Elijah will come and take him down.' Then
38   Jesus gave a loud cry and breathed his last. And the curtain of the
39   temple was torn in two from top to bottom. And when the
centurion who was at his post opposite him saw that he had given
up the ghost in this way, he said, 'Truly this man was God's son.'
40   A number of women were also present, watching from a
distance. Among them were Mary of Magdala, Mary the mother
41   of James the younger and of Joseph, and Salome, who had all
followed him and waited on him when he was in Galilee, and
there were several others who had come up to Jerusalem with
him.
42   By this time evening had come; and as it was preparation-day
43   (that is, the day before the sabbath), Joseph of Arimathaea, a
respected member of the council, a man who looked forward to
44   the kingdom of God, bravely went to Pilate and asked for the
body of Jesus. Pilate was surprised to hear that he was already
dead; so he sent for the centurion and asked him whether it was
45   long since he died. And when he heard the centurion's report, he
46   gave Joseph leave to take the dead body. So Joseph bought a linen
sheet, took him down from the cross, and wrapped him in the
sheet. Then he laid him in a tomb cut out of the rock, and rolled a
47   stone against the entrance. And Mary of Magdala and Mary the
mother of Joseph were watching and saw where he was laid.
16   When the sabbath was over, Mary of Magdala, Mary the
mother of James, and Salome bought aromatic oils intending to
2   go and anoint him; and very early on the first day of the festival, at
3   sunrise, they went to the tomb. They were wondering among
themselves who would roll away the stone for them from the

entrance to the tomb. But when they looked up they saw that the   4
stone had been rolled back already; although it was very big.
They went into the tomb, where they saw a youth sitting on the   5
right-hand side, wearing a white robe; and they were dumbfounded. But he said to them, 'Fear nothing; you are looking for   6
Jesus of Nazareth, who was crucified. He has been raised again; he
is not here; look, there is the place where they laid him. But go
and give this message to his disciples and Peter: "He is going on   7
before you into Galilee; there you will see him, as he told you."'
Then they went out and ran away from the tomb, beside them-   8
selves with terror. They said nothing to anybody, for they were
afraid.

And they delivered all these instructions briefly to Peter and his
companions. Afterwards Jesus himself sent out by them from east
to west the sacred and imperishable message of eternal salvation.

[*When he had risen from the dead early in the morning on the first day*   9
of the week, he appeared first to Mary of Magdala, from whom he had ·
formerly cast out seven demons. She went and carried the news to his   10
mourning and sorrowful followers, but when they were told that he was   11
alive and that she had seen him they did not believe it.

Later he appeared in a different guise to two of them as they were   12
walking, on their way into the country. These also went and took the   13
news to the others, but again no one believed them.

Afterwards, while the eleven were at table he appeared to them and   14
reproached them for their incredulity and dullness, because they had not
believed those who had seen him after he was raised from the dead. Then   15
he said to them: 'Go forth to every part of the world, and proclaim the
good news to the whole creation. Those who believe it and receive   16
baptism will find salvation; those who do not believe will be condemned.
Their faith will be attended by the following signs: in my name they will   17
cast out demons and speak new tongues; if they handle snakes or drink any   18
deadly poison, they will come to no harm; and the sick on whom they lay
their hands will recover.'

So after talking with them the Lord Jesus was taken up into heaven,   19
and he took his seat at the right hand of God; but they went out to make   20
their proclamation everywhere, and the Lord worked with them and
confirmed the message by the signs that accompanied it.]

INDEX OF REFERENCES